ao

Northern Myanmar
Pages 178–185

tkyina

D0963381

ashio

EASTERN
MYANMAR • Kengtung

Eastern Myanmar
Pages 162–177

Bago Region
Pages 88–99

• Hpa-an

Mawlamyine (Moulmein)

• Thanbyuzayat

• Dawei

SOUTHEASTERN
MYANMAR

• Myeik
(Mergui)

**Southeastern
Myanmar**
Pages 186–195

• Kawthaung

EYEWITNESS TRAVEL

MYANMAR (BURMA)

EYEWITNESS TRAVEL

MYANMAR (BURMA)

Author **David Abram**

LONDON, NEW YORK,
MELBOURNE, MUNICH AND DELHI
www.dk.com

Produced by Bigmetalfish Design Services
Project Manager and Designer Sunita Gahir
Project Editor Ankita Awasthi Tröger

Author David Abram
Photographer James Tye
Illustrators Peter Bull Art Studio, Arun Pottirayil

For Dorling Kindersley Ltd
Publishing Director Georgina Dee
Publisher Vivien Antwi
List Manager Kate Berens
Executive Editor Michelle Crane
Senior Cartographic Editor Casper Morris
Cartography Manager Suresh Kumar
Senior Cartographer Subhashree Bharti
Cartographer Reetu Pandey
Senior DTP Designer Jason Little
Senior Picture Researcher Ellen Root
Production Controller Charlotte Cade

Printed and bound by Vivar Printing Sdn Bhd

First American Edition, 2014
14 15 16 17 10 9 8 7 6 5 4 3 2 1

Published in the United States by Dorling Kindersley Publishing, Inc.,
345 Hudson Street, New York 10014

Copyright © 2014 Dorling Kindersley Limited, London
A Penguin Random House Company

Published in Great Britain by Dorling Kindersley Limited.

A catalog record for this book
is available from the Library of Congress.

ISSN 1542 1554

ISBN 978 1 46541 711 4

Floors are referred to throughout in accordance with
American usage; ie the "first floor" is at ground level.

MIX
Paper from
responsible sources
FSC™ C018179
www.fsc.org

**The information in this
DK Eyewitness Travel Guide is checked regularly.**
Every effort has been made to ensure that this book is as up-to-date as possible
at the time of going to press. Some details, however, such as telephone numbers,
opening hours, prices, gallery hanging arrangements and travel information are
liable to change. The publishers cannot accept responsibility for any consequences
arising from the use of this book, nor for any material on third party websites, and
cannot guarantee that any website address in this book will be a suitable source of
travel information. We value the views and suggestions of our readers very highly.
Please write to: Publisher, DK Eyewitness Travel Guides, Dorling Kindersley,
80 Strand, London, WC2R 0RL, UK, or email: travelguides@dk.com.

Front cover main image: Pagodas of Old Bagan in front of the great Thatbyinnyu Temple

◀ Distinctive leg-rowing Intha fishermen of Inle Lake, Eastern Myanmar

Contents

The colossal standing Buddha of Bodhi
Tataung, near Mandalay

Introducing
Myanmar

A traditional Burmese dance performance
at Yangon's Karaweik Palace

Monks in a long-tailed boat being rowed past the Nga Phe Kyaung monastery on Inle lake, Eastern Myanmar

The clear turquoise waters of the pristine Ngapali beach, Western Myanmar

Mandalay's Mahamuni Buddha, one of Myanmar's most venerated Buddha statues

The magnificent Ananda Temple in the Bagan Archeological Zone

HOW TO USE THIS GUIDE

This Dorling Kindersley Travel Guide helps you to get the most from your visit to Myanmar. It provides detailed practical information and expert recommendations. *Introducing Myanmar* maps the country and its areas, sets them in their historical and cultural context, and describes events through the entire year. *Myanmar Area by*

Area is the main sightseeing section, which covers all the important sights, with photographs, maps, and illustrations. Information on hotels, restaurants, shopping, entertainment, and outdoor activities is found in *Travelers' Needs*. The *Survival Guide* has advice on everything from travel and medical services to banks and communications.

Myanmar Area by Area

The country has been divided into eight areas, each with a separate chapter. The most interesting places to visit have been numbered on a *Regional Map* at the beginning of each chapter.

1 Introduction

The landscape, history, and character of each area is described here, showing how the region has developed over the centuries and what it offers to the visitor today.

2 Regional Map

This shows the road network and gives an overview of the entire region. All the sights are numbered here and there are also useful tips on getting around the area.

Sights at a Glance lists all the chapter's sights, following the numbering on the *Regional Map*.

A suggested route for a walk is shown with a dotted red line.

Stars indicate the sights that no visitor should miss.

3 Street by Street Map

This gives a bird's-eye view of a key area covered in the chapter. The numbering of the sights matches the fuller descriptions on the pages that follow.

4 Detailed information

All the important towns and other places to visit are described individually. They are listed in order, following the numbering on the *Regional Map*.

Each area of Myanmar can be quickly identified by its color coding, shown on the inside front cover.

A feature offers in-depth information on a topic related to the sight or the region.

5 Town Map

Major towns have a map showing the main sights, each of which is described in detail. The map also shows the town's transport hubs.

Story boxes highlight a special feature or interesting story about the town or sight.

6 Myanmar's Top Sights

These are given two or more full pages. Historic buildings are dissected to show their interiors; other places of interest are shown in a bird's-eye view, with specific sights picked out and described.

Numbered circles point out major features of the sight listed in the key.

The Visitors' Checklist provides all the practical information needed to plan your visit.

7 Practical Information

The Travelers' Needs and Survival Guide sections offer advice and information on the practical aspects of your trip, including getting around, responsible travel, health, money, and hotels and restaurants.

Directories contain contact details for all organisations or companies mentioned in the text.

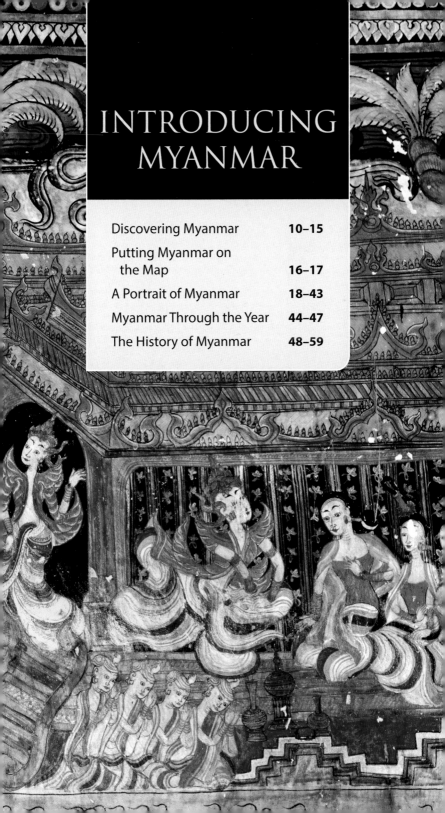

INTRODUCING MYANMAR

DISCOVERING MYANMAR

The following tours have been designed to cover as many of Myanmar's highlights as possible in the relatively short time available to most visitors to the country. First come a pair of two-day routes around the principal cities, Yangon (Rangoon) and Mandalay. Next is a two-week itinerary taking in the must-see sights of the whole country – from the two big cities to magical Inle Lake in the east and the chimeric ruins of medieval Bagan in the west – with suggestions for extending the trip to three or four weeks. The generally poor state of Myanmar's roads means that to complete the itinerary in a fortnight requires travelers to take domestic flights between key points. In the case of the extension to the town of Kengtung in the far east of the country, flying is the only permitted means of travel for foreign visitors, while Sittwe in Rakhine State can also be accessed by ferry.

Two Weeks in Myanmar

- Wonder at the scale and splendor of Yangon's gilded **Shwedagon Pagoda**, Myanmar's most revered and visited Buddhist monument.

- Wander through the bustling streets of **Yangon's Colonial Quarter**, where decrepit Raj-era buildings form a charismatic backdrop.

- Gaze at the massive reclining Buddhas of **Bago**, a day trip away from Yangon.

- Visit the otherworldly **Kyaiktiyo Golden Rock Pagoda**, whose eponymous rock seems about to topple into the void.

- Experience the unique atmosphere of **Inle Lake**, famed for its one-legged rowing, stilt villages, and floating gardens.

- Explore the evocative remains of one of the country's erstwhile capitals at **Inwa (Ava)**, which include a monastery covered in stucco and another made entirely of teak.

- Explore **Mandalay's** markets after a tour of the palace and nearby monuments, survivors from Burma's golden age in the 19th century.

- Gaze over the sublime Ayeyarwady River flowing past Bodawpaya's unfinished stupa at **Mingun**, Myanmar's own colossal pyramid.

- Follow winding, stepped paths past glass-mosaic temples and golden stupas to the top of **Sagaing Hill** for views over the Ayeyarwady.

- Soak up the magical mood of sunrise over the lake at **Amarapura**, near Mandalay, as commuters, monks, and gardeners file across the famous teak U Bein's Bridge.

- Marvel at the forest of glowing red temple towers, elegantly tapering spires, and medieval monasteries rising from the parched plains of **Bagan**, one of Southeast Asia's most exotic spectacles.

Key

— Two weeks in Myanmar
— Optional extensions
=: Flight transfers

CHIN

Mrauk U

Sittwe Airport ✈ ● Sittwe

RAKHIN

Chin villages
The Chin villages along the Lemro River make a worthwhile side trip for visitors to the ancient city of Mrauk U. Displaced by an insurgency from their home near the Bangladesh border, the villagers now derive an income from fishing and farming. A visit offers a brief insight into their way of life.

◀ A 17th-century fresco in Bagan's Ananda Temple depicting a Burmese court scene

Sagaing

Literally hundreds of gilded stupas, temples, and whitewashed monasteries soar above the west bank of the Ayeyarwady River at Sagaing Hill, near Mandalay. A network of stepped paths connect the shrines, which afford expansive views over the spiritual heartland of Upper Burma.

Inle Lake

Resting on stilts, the villages, temples, monasteries, and gardens of Inle Lake's Intha people rise serenely from the water. This unique aquatic way of life is said to have evolved when, in the 18th century, a local king refused permission for the Intha to build on dry land.

The rooftops of Yangon city with the soaring Shwedagon Pagoda in the background

Two Days in Yangon

Yangon's vibrant street life, busy riverfront, and photogenic colonial architecture make it an exhilarating point of arrival. The former capital is also home to the country's most revered religious monument, the Shwedagon Pagoda.

- **Arriving** Located on the northern limits of the city, Yangon's Mingaladon Airport is roughly an hour's drive from downtown.

- **Moving on** Mingaladon Airport serves domestic as well as international flights. Yangon's Central Train Station is in the city center, two blocks north of the Sule Pagoda.

Day 1
Morning Start the day in quintessential Burmese style with a *mohinga* (noodle soup) breakfast at one of the stalls on Mahabandula Road. Then head east to the **Sule Pagoda** *(see p70)*, the gleaming centerpiece of downtown Yangon, to take a walk through the **colonial quarter** *(see pp68–9)*, with its faded Raj-era buildings and packed streets. After tea at the **Strand Hotel** *(see p71)*, a short walk along the riverfront leads to one of Myanmar's most important religious sites, the **Botataung Pagoda** *(see p71)*.

From there, take a cab across town to the **National Museum** *(see p72)*, whose prize exhibit is the Konbaungs' Lion Throne.

Afternoon Mingle with the worshippers kneeling before the giant reclining Buddha at the **Kyauk Htat Gyi Pagoda** *(see p78)*, then cross the road to visit the serene-faced **Nga Htat Gyi** *(see p78)*, a huge Buddha statue with a sumptuously carved wooden backdrop. A 20-minute taxi ride south takes you to **Bahadur Shah Zafar's Dargah** *(see pp72–3)*, the atmospheric tomb of India's last Mughal emperor. Finally, as dusk falls, explore the superb **Shwedagon Pagoda** *(see pp74–7)*.

Day 2
Morning Just after dawn, return to the Shwedagon Pagoda to experience the stupa in the ethereal light of early morning, then head uptown to the **Kaba Aye Pagoda** and the adjacent **Mahapasana Guha** *(see pp80–81)*, modern shrines on the shores of Inya Lake. Nearby, the **Lawka Chantha Abhaya Labha Muni** *(see p81)*, a huge Buddha carved from a single block of white marble, is another contemporary wonder that draws large crowds on weekends.

Afternoon It takes around an hour by taxi to reach **Thanlyin** *(see p82)* and **Kyauktan** *(see p83)*, on the far side of the Yangon River, where a gilded hilltop pagoda and an island temple provide welcome escapes from the city traffic. Later, experience Yangon's café culture along the shores of **Kandawgyi Lake** *(see p79)* as the floodlit Shwedagon Pagoda is reflected in its waters.

Public gardens around Kandawgyi Lake near the Shwedagon Pagoda

For practical information on traveling around Myanmar, see pp238–41

Three Days in Mandalay

From the gilded hilltop stupas of Sagaing to the whitewashed temples looted by the British in 1885, Mandalay spans nearly six centuries of royal history. Its streets today display a typically Burmese blend of tradition and modernity.

- **Arriving** Domestic flights land at Mandalay's vast airport, a long 28-mile (45-km) drive southeast of downtown.

- **Moving on** Ayeyarwady ferries and pleasure boats depart from the jetties at the end of 35th Street, due west of the city center.

Horse carts traveling along a tree-lined road in Inwa (Ava), near Mandalay

Day 1

Morning The buildings inside the forbidding walls of the **Mandalay Palace** *(see pp144–5)* are mostly modern reconstructions, but they still give a sense of how extraordinary the complex must have looked in the 19th century. From there, head across town for some typically Burmese sights and smells at **Zegyo Market** *(see p143)*, followed by a retreat to the relative calm of the golden **Eindawya Pagoda** *(see p143)*.

Afternoon After the heat of midday has subsided, stroll through the area below **Mandalay Hill** *(see pp146–9)*, winding through the temples and pagodas of the old northeast quarter of the city en route to the summit in time for the legendary sunset view.

White stupas surrounding the Sandamuni Pagoda in the Mandalay Hill area

Day 2

Morning Shortly after dawn, join the ranks of monks and market gardeners filing across Amarapura's **U Bein's Bridge** *(see p152)*, one of Myanmar's most photographed landmarks, to reach the beautiful white and gold **Kyauktawgyi Pagoda** *(see p152)* on the far side of the lake. The huge **Pahtodawgyi Pagoda** *(see p152)*, visible to the northwest, is the next stop – a forgotten gem and an evocative remnant of a lost royal city. Take a 20-minute drive back into town to the **Mahamuni Temple** *(see p142)*, full of worshippers from daybreak to late evening and an altogether more intense site. After a glimpse of its famous gold-encrusted Buddha, explore the marble carving and metalware workshops of the surrounding streets, followed by a quick tour of the **Jade Market** *(see p142)*. Then stroll down to the **Shwe In Bin Kyaung** *(see p142)*. An enclave of serenity in the bustle of Mandalay, the richly carved teak monastery is a rare survivor of the 19th-century capital, and one that sees amazingly few visitors.

Afternoon Head across town to see gold leaf being made in the traditional way in the gold pounders' district *(see p142)*, before a spot of **souvenir shopping** *(see p217)* in the city's mega malls along 78th and 79th Streets. In the evening, enjoy a music and dance recital, marionette performance, or *a-nyeint* act *(see pp220–21)* at one of the several cultural shows staged across Mandalay.

Day 3

Morning Catch the 9am boat up the Ayeyarwady to **Mingun** *(see pp156–7)* to see the massive unfinished stupa and its adjacent monuments. Rather than return via the river, take a taxi along the pretty west bank to the township of **Sagaing** *(see p153)*, where hundreds of temples, stupas, and monasteries crown a ridge of tree-covered hills.

Afternoon From the Mandalay side of the river, hop on the ferry to **Inwa (Ava)** *(see pp154–5)* for a leisurely tour of the ancient ruins by horse cart. Scattered across paddy fields and banana groves, the monuments of this former royal capital include spectacular stucco and teak monasteries, the latter still in use as a school for novices, along with dozens of impressive brick and gilded stupas.

Two Weeks in Myanmar

- **Airports** Arrive and depart from Yangon's Mingaladon International Airport.

- **Transport** At least four domestic flights would be required to cover the following itinerary in a fortnight, as well as the use of a hired car and driver for three full days.

- **Booking ahead** Advance booking is not necessary for any of the monuments or sites featured on this itinerary, although flights tend to be in very short supply during peak season (December to February). A reputable local travel agent will be a great help in reserving tickets at this time.

Bago's giant reclining Shwetalyaung Buddha, dating from the 10th century

Days 1 and 2: Yangon
Follow the two-day Yangon visit described on page 12.

Day 3: Bago
An early start is recommended for the 90-minute trip to **Bago** *(see pp92–5)*, where the remains of medieval Pegu, former capital of the Mons, include the huge Shwetalyaung Buddha.

Day 4: Kyaiktiyo
Travel by car for three hours from Bago to Kinpun, which is the springboard for the exquisite **Kyaiktiyo Golden Rock Pagoda** *(see pp190–91)*. Stay in one of the upscale hotels near the summit to be in situ for twilight, when the gilded balancing boulder is gently illuminated by candles, and dawn, when the rising sun makes it an ethereal sight.

The famous floating gardens of the Intha people of Inle Lake, Eastern Myanmar

Day 5: Yangon to Nyaungshwe
Catch the early bus back to Yangon to connect with an onward flight to Heho Airport, gateway to Inle Lake. Spend the rest of the day exploring the back streets, monasteries, and photogenic pagodas of **Nyaungshwe** *(see p169)*.

Day 6: Inle Lake
Long-tailed boat tours of **Inle Lake** *(see pp166–8)*, home of the Intha people, tend to begin before dawn. The first port of call should be one of the five-day markets for a glimpse of the local ethnic minority people in traditional dress. Other must-sees include the Intha's floating gardens, the stilt village of Nampan, the revered Phaung Daw U Pagoda at Ywama, and Inthein for its ancient Shan stupas. Along the way, stops at small cheroot factories, silversmiths, and lotus silk weaving workshops offer visitors some authentic local shopping opportunities.

Day 7: Pindaya/Mandalay
Leave Inle in the morning, taking a taxi to get to the Shwe Umin Cave at **Pindaya** *(see pp174–5)*, where thousands of Buddhas and stupas cram the interior of a limestone cavern. After lunch by the lakeside at Pindaya village, in one of the breezy restaurants overlooking the water, get to Heho Airport in time to catch an onward flight to Mandalay.

Days 8, 9, and 10: Mandalay
Follow the recommended three-day itinerary for Mandalay detailed on page 13.

To extend your trip...
Two possible two-day side trips from Mandalay are worth considering. The first is to the former British hill capital of **Pyin U Lwin** *(see p160)*, famed for its mild climate and beautiful botanical gardens. Continue northeast by rail to cross the spectacular **Gokteik Bridge** *(see p160)*, a trestle bridge spanning a jungle-draped canyon. The second is to the town of **Monywa** *(see p158)*, which serves as a springboard for visits to the extravagantly decorated **Thanboddhay Pagoda** *(see p158)*, modern hilltop colossi at **Bodhi Tataung** *(see p158)*, and ancient **Pho Win Taung Caves** *(see p159)*.

The colorful structures of the unique Thanboddhay Pagoda

Day 11: Mandalay to Bagan

There is no better way to travel to the ruins of the former Bamar capital at **Bagan** *(see pp116–37)* than via the Ayeyarwady River. Dedicated tourist boats take around 11 hours to cover the distance, leaving plenty of time to relax and watch rural life on the riverbank slip by.

Day 12: Bagan

An early start is required to reach the **Shwesandaw Pagoda** *(see p134)* in time for sunrise – well worth the effort for the extraordinary spectacle of its surrounding temples taking shape in the orange-tinted half-light. Visit the nearby **Dhammayangyi Temple** *(see p135)* before having a well-earned noodle breakfast in **Old Bagan** *(see pp122–3)* and exploring the area's highlights. Once the heat of midday has abated, around 3–4pm, work your way through the remaining sites of the northern group, including **Upali Thein** *(see p126)* with its wonderful murals and the elegant **Htilominlo** *(see p127)* nearby, and ending at Anawrahta's golden **Shwezigon Pagoda** *(see p128)* on the outskirts of Nyaung U village.

Decorative stuccowork on the exterior of the graceful Htilominlo temple, Bagan

Day 13: Bagan

Devote the morning to the temples around the villages of **Myinkaba** *(see pp132–3)* and **New Bagan** *(see p132)*, browsing the lacquerware showrooms and puppet-making workshops en route. Admire the beautiful green-glazed tiles encrusting the base of the beautifully proportioned **Mingalazedi** *(see*

The south-facing Kassapa Buddha in Bagan's Ananda Temple

p134), the last great stupa built at Bagan, and the fine UNESCO-restored murals at the nearby **Gubyaukgyi Temple** *(see p133)*. After lunch, venture to the **Southern Plain** *(see p129)* on the fringes of the archeological zone around the village of Minnanthu. The interiors of its isolated shrines swirl with exquisite, Tantric-influenced murals, including Nandamannya Temple's famous *Temptation of Mara*, depicting the futile seduction of the Buddha.

Day 14: Bagan to Yangon

Celebrate the final day of sightseeing with an unforgettable **balloon ride** *(see p129)* over the atmospheric ruins of Bagan at daybreak, followed by a champagne breakfast. The onward flight to Yangon should get you there in time for a spot of last-minute souvenir shopping and a concluding visit to the dazzling Shwedagon Pagoda.

To extend your trip…

If you have another week to spare, take a trip to **Sittwe** *(see p107)* in Rakhine State to visit the magical ruins of **Mrauk U** *(see pp110–14)*, whose weed-choked stupas and ordination halls rise from a spellbinding landscape of scrub-covered hills. The best way to reach this isolated site is by boat up the Kaladan River from Sittwe, a slow but memorable approach. En route back to Yangon, pause at **Ngapali** beach *(see p106)* to laze in the soft white sand and turquoise water. A second destination easily added on is **Kengtung** *(see p177)*, capital of Myanmar's Golden Triangle region. The town is inhabited by ethnic Tai tribes, and the surrounding hills hold minority villages that are inspirational targets for day treks.

Mist threading through the evocative medieval ruins of Mrauk U

Putting Myanmar on the Map

Bordered by Bangladesh and India in the west, China in the north, Laos in the east, and Thailand in the east and south, Myanmar (Burma) juts into the Andaman Sea and Bay of Bengal. Covering 262,227 sq miles (676,578 sq km), it has a population of around 60 million, the majority of whom live in the fertile Delta region in the south, and in the semi-arid plains of the interior, flanking the Ayeyarwady River and its major tributary, the Chindwin. Enfolding the central river valleys are forested mountains, which grow higher and wilder as they approach the frontiers with India and China. In the far north, the eastern arm of the Himalayas forms the border with China, with peaks rising to 12,300 ft (5,900 m). The eastern third of the country consists of the Shan Plateau, a vast tract of largely denuded mountains and valleys.

Key

— Highway
— Main road
— Other road
— International border
△ Peak

Southeast Asia

A PORTRAIT OF MYANMAR

Towering, gilded pagodas, spectacular archeological sites, beautiful beaches and stunning mountains, and a fascinating traditional culture that is at the forefront of local life are among the reasons why record-breaking numbers of visitors have been beguiled by Myanmar since the easing of the tourism boycott in 2010. With Aung San Suu Kyi released from house arrest and a program of sweeping political reforms now underway, the future finally looks bright for a country blighted for decades by civil war and economic stagnation.

Stretching 1,275 miles (2,050 km) from the eastern arm of the Himalayas to the palm-fringed coast of the Andaman Sea, Myanmar encompasses an astonishing array of landscapes. The country's heartland, enfolded by a giant horseshoe of jungle-covered mountains, is a vast, semi-arid plain formed by the flat-bottomed valleys of the Ayeyarwady (Irrawaddy), Sittaung, Chindwin, and Thanlwin Rivers, which flow south into the Bay of Bengal and Gulf of Mottama (Martaban). Fed by a maze of streams, rivulets, irrigation canals, and ditches, the low-lying deltas where these mighty rivers debouche into the ocean form sprawling patchworks of paddy fields – the country's rice bowl.

To the north and east, the denuded hills and steep-sided river gorges of the limestone Shan Plateau ripple all the way to the border of Yunnan Province in China, and the opium-growing belt of the so-called Golden Triangle region where the frontiers of Laos and Thailand intersect with those of Myanmar. In the west, meanwhile, a band of narrower, loftier mountains track the border with India and Bangladesh, culminating in the far north at the Hkakabo Razi massif, Myanmar's – and Southeast Asia's – highest peak at 19,294 ft (5,881m).

At the opposite, far southern end of the country, the land tapers to a narrow belt along the pristine Tenasserim coast, where the myriad coral-fringed islets and islands of the unspoiled Myeik (Mergui) Archipelago comprise one of Southeast Asia's last true marine wilderness regions, the final stronghold of the nomadic Moken sea gypsies.

Workers farming fields in the countryside around Kalaw and Nyaungshwe in Eastern Myanmar

◄ The temples and fields of the Bagan Archeological Zone in the dawn light

A member of the Padaung ethnic minority, whose women are well known for wearing brass neck rings

The People

Myanmar's physical diversity is mirrored by its ethnic make up. The Burmese-speaking Bamars, descended from Indo-Tibetan nomads who conquered the central plains in the 9th and 10th centuries AD, comprise around 68 percent of the 60-million-strong population, and dominate the country's government, civil, and military service. The outlying regions, however, host a complex jigsaw of minority peoples,

Gilded teak Buddha statue, crafted in late Konbaung style

such as the Rakhines (Arakanese), Mon, Karen, Kachin, Chin, and Shan, all of whom have at one time or another fought – or are still fighting – insurgencies against the Burmese state.

The hill areas of the border zones and Shan Plateau are home to smaller, more fragmented groups such as the Pa-O, Padaung, Danu, and Akha, distinguished by their elaborate traditional costumes. The Burmese melting pot is further enhanced by the presence of large numbers of Indians, descendants of workers who came to Burma during the British era, and Chinese immigrants, who today dominate the economy of Mandalay and form the majority in several large towns in the northeast.

Religion and Culture

The hierarchical, feudal nature of traditional Burmese society, established by the rulers of medieval Bagan from the 11th century and cemented by their successors, largely disintegrated after the British annexation of the late 19th century, and was replaced by a radical form of autocratic, military-backed socialism during the post-Independence period. One constant, however, has spanned the country's long and troubled history. A pervasive influence on Burmese culture for more than two millennia, Buddhism is believed to have taken root in the region during the lifetime of its founder, Gautama Buddha (c. 563–483 BC), and the faith is today followed by 89 percent of Myanmar's inhabitants. In a largely low-rise country, the huge golden *zedis* (stupas), erected, enlarged, and embellished by generations of local rulers, are striking manifestations of the enduring popularity of the religion.

Support for the *sangha*, or monkhood, is another constant. Around half a million young Burmese men are members of a monastic order, and 75,000 women are nuns – a higher share of the population than in any other country in the world. A greater proportion of income is also donated to religious orders in Myanmar than anywhere else, while nearly every Buddhist boy spends at least a few weeks living as a monk in a monastery from the age of seven.

Among the defining sights of the country are long lines of monks in wine-colored robes, filing around the streets of towns and cities as local residents spoon hot rice into their alms bowls – a striking example of Burmese "merit making," through which people improve their chances of better future lives by doing good deeds in the present one.

The school of Buddhism that is followed in Myanmar is Theravada, which was first brought to the region by the Pyus around the 5th century AD, flourished under patronage from the Mon kings in the early medieval period, and was later adopted as the state religion by the rulers of Bagan. Regarded by its adherents as a purer form of Buddhism, truer in spirit to the original teachings of the Buddha, the Theravada tradition emphasizes the role of Vipassana meditation as a path to enlightenment.

The great importance placed by Burmese families on Buddhist philosophy and morality accounts in no small part for the overwhelmingly considerate,

non-confrontational, and honest way people conduct their lives in Myanmar. Travelers better accustomed to more hard-edged Asian countries are often struck by the well-mannered way in which tourists are generally treated: it is relatively rare to be shortchanged in a restaurant, quoted an inflated fare by a taxi driver, or sold fake goods.

That said, the Buddhist teachings of non-violence have not prevented young monks from forming the vanguard of protests against Myanmar's military government. Monks literally stood in the firing line during the mass revolt of 2007, which came to be known as the Saffron Revolution after the color of their robes.

More controversially, Burmese monks have also been at the forefront of violence directed against the country's Muslim minority in recent years. Around 5 percent of the population follow Islam. Descended from traders, soldiers, prisoners of war, and refugees from India, as well as royal advisors from Persia and merchants from China, the country's Muslims live in widely separated communities, the largest of which remains in Yangon – a legacy of the British era, when millions of Indian

Young monk receiving morning alms from a woman, Bagan

Muslims traveled to Lower Burma and the Ayeyarwady Delta in search of work.

Communal conflict between Buddhists and Muslims has erupted sporadically throughout the country since Independence, but has intensified in recent years, particularly in the northwestern state of Rakhine (Arakan), where tens of thousands of Muslims of the Rohingya minority group have been displaced by outbreaks of violence.

Government and Politics

The proliferation of armed insurgencies mounted by ethnic minority groups was, in the late 1950s, the catalyst for the creation of a military government in Burma. Since then, several coups have meant that the army has stayed in tight control of the country. Demonstrations, popular uprisings, and campaigns for greater democracy and freedom of expression have been ruthlessly suppressed by the ruling junta, leading to the implementation of sanctions and a tourism boycott by Western countries.

Myanmar has, however, seen major changes to its political system in recent years: parliament now includes members of the formerly outlawed National League for Democracy (NLD), among them the party's iconic leader, Aung San Suu Kyi, whose image is now freely displayed on posters and T-shirts across the country. The press enjoys much more independence than it has since British times, and several regional armies have signed landmark ceasefire agreements with the Tatmadaw (Burmese military), bringing long-running civil wars to an end.

The reforms, however, amount to far less of a revolution than the pro-democracy movement and international community had hoped for. Neither the media nor the judiciary is truly free, and little of the wealth generated by state-controlled businesses (such as the oil and gas industries) reach the country's poor. While spending on the armed forces remains in excess of 20 percent of total government outlay, the budget for health provision languishes at 4 percent. Nor, pending the creation of a new constitution, has parliamentary reform changed the overall complexion of the system, which remains in the firm grip of the generals.

Even so, there exists in Myanmar today a great sense of optimism. People openly discuss the country's politics in a way that they haven't dared to for a generation, and feel the day is fast approaching when the opinions of ordinary citizens will be listened to by the ruling elite. A recent example was the suspension of building work on a massive dam across a tributary of the Ayeyarwady River after Burmese environmentalists garnered opposition to the scheme. It was part of a hydroelectricity project set to provide power to its Chinese backers, and hefty payouts for local officials.

Economy and Development

The primary driver for political change in Myanmar over recent years has been the moribund state of the country's economy. While its neighbors have been living through a period of unprecedented prosperity, Myanmar has remained the

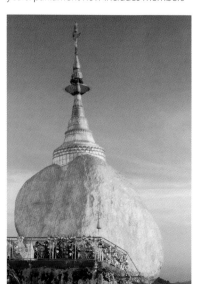
Kyaiktiyo's Golden Rock Pagoda, a revered Burmese pilgrimage site

poorest state in Southeast Asia. One third of its population is estimated to live below the poverty line.

Chronic mismanagement of the economy by the country's military junta is widely held to be the root cause of this. Vast sums have been earned by the government through foreign exports of gas, tropical timber, and gemstones, but the rewards have largely accrued to a crony elite of around 20 families who founded their fortunes on the back of favors from the military junta.

The same clique looks set to benefit most from the current upsurge in foreign investment, as promises to liberalize the country's economy attract potential backers from abroad, in particular the global oil and gas industries, lured by Myanmar's vast, untapped reserves.

Meanwhile, as export-oriented industries struggle to gather momentum, the country remains heavily reliant on agriculture to meet the needs of its poor. Farming currently provides employment for around 70 percent of the population, and since the collapse of rice production during the period of military rule, most of what is grown is consumed domestically.

Tourism

The other great hope for Myanmar's economic future is tourism. Stagnant for decades due to the NLD-led boycott, visitor numbers have soared since 2010, with a million arrivals in 2012, and about 1.5 million the following year. This sudden spike has led to all manner of challenges, principally a shortage of accommodations. Hotel tariffs have, as a consequence, rocketed to levels comparable with those in Europe and North America. Shortages of water and electricity have also occurred in popular destinations as the authorities struggle to meet the demand.

On lifting the tourism boycott, NLD leader Aung San Suu Kyi expressed concern that the rewards from mass tourism in her country should not merely benefit the government and junta-backed elite

The Mekong flowing through Myanmar's Golden Triangle area

who run the major domestic airlines and hotel chains, but also ordinary Burmese. To that end, she asked that foreign visitors opt for "small-scale tourism," avoiding large operators in favor of traveling independently and spending their money with locally owned businesses. Current trends, however, suggest that the overwhelming majority of visitors enter on pre-arranged tours and stay in luxury hotels owned by associates of the government.

Aside from Myanmar's unique culture and visitor attractions, the great asset for Burmese tourism is the essential character of the Burmese themselves. Despite the country's lack of adequate infrastructure and training opportunities for its people, the locals are unfailingly courteous and helpful, and clearly delighted to be able to share their way of life with a wider world from which they have been cut off for so long. It may be a cliché to say so, but the warmth and genuineness of Burmese hospitality linger in the memory every bit as long as impressions of the country's exquisite monuments and landscapes.

Landscape and Wildlife

Extending for 1,275 miles (2,050 km) from north to south, Myanmar encompasses diverse climatic zones and landscapes, and new species are being discovered each year as the country slowly opens up to foreign researchers. Its spectacular coastal jungles and central rain forests are lush year round, while the sun-baked plain at the heart of the country and the paddy fields of the Ayeyarwady Delta remain parched for seven or eight months.

Clear turquoise waters and white sands of Ngapali beach on Myanmar's west coast

The Delta

Alluvial deposits swept annually from the interior by the Ayeyarwady have created a vast, low-lying delta on the Bay of Bengal, Myanmar's most fertile and densely populated region.

The olive-backed sunbird (*Cinnyris jugularis*) builds flask-shaped nests that are often seen hanging from the porches of houses across the Delta region.

Olive ridley sea turtles (*Lepidochelys olivacea*), among the world's most endangered marine species, travel thousands of miles each winter to lay their eggs on the remote sandy beaches of the Delta.

Irrawaddy dolphins (*Orcaella brevirostris*), distinguished by their prominent forehead, have suffered from the introduction of dragnet fishing and gill netting, and now survive in perilously small numbers in the Ayeyarwady River.

The Dry Zone

Sheltered by the Rakhine-Yoma Hills, the central river plains receive less rainfall than the rest of the country. Bleached, cracked soil and sun-scorched scrub predominate in the winter.

The grey-headed parakeet (*Psittacula finschii*) adds splashes of exotic green and coral-red color to skylines across central Myanmar as it screeches between the tree-tops and stone monuments where it usually roosts.

The Kitti's hog-nosed bat (*Craseonycteris thonglongyai*) makes its home in the domes and archways of Bagan's deserted temples, although it is more commonly spotted amid the karst limestone country of the southeast.

The Burmese star tortoise (*Geochelone platynota*), with its exquisitely patterned carapace, is critically endangered and has become a rare sight amid the shady scrub it prefers.

Deforestation in Myanmar

Myanmar's forests are disappearing at an alarming speed. Between 1990 and 2005, the country lost around 18 percent of its woodland, and the rate has grown exponentially over the past decade. In spite of international embargoes, teak, in particular, continues to be exported in huge quantities, earning vast revenues for Myanmar's military. Government corruption and the readiness of the country's neighbors to turn a blind eye in return for short-term financial gain have left great swaths of land bare and unproductive.

Domesticated elephant picking up a log of timber

The Hills

Renowned for their reserves of teak, the hills around Myanmar's central river plains have long been a biodiversity hotspot. However, logging has taken a drastic toll on the region's wildlife.

Pangolins (*Manis pentadactyla*) are becoming rare, and not only due to habitat loss. Despite an international ban on the trade, demand for their meat across the border in China has led to intensified poaching.

Red pandas (*Ailurus fulgens*), rare and fugitive mammals native to the high-altitude forests of the far north, are also victims of deforestation.

Tigers (*Panthera tigris corbetti*) are fast falling victim to poaching to supply demand from Chinese medicine. Myanmar's northern hill tracts now support less than 100 big cats, despite containing the world's largest tiger reserve.

The Coast

Parts of Myanmar's 1,200 miles (1,930 km) of uninterrupted coastline are still backed by tropical forest and mangroves. Offshore, the waters of the Andaman are rich in marine life.

Tropical fish abound in the transluscent bays of the Myeik (Mergui) Archipelago, regarded as one of the world's most pristine marine ecosystems. Diving in the region is strictly limited.

The dugong (*Dugong dugon*) survives in the broad, shallow bays of remote Rakhine and in Myeik, where it grazes on seagrasses. A shy and solitary creature, it lives a nomadic existence and, unlike in many countries, is not hunted in Myanmar.

Manta rays (*Manta birostris/Manta alfredi*) are the giants of the oceans, growing to 23 ft (7 m) in width and weighing up to 3,000 lb (1,350 kg).

The Ayeyarwady River

From its headwaters in the eastern Himalayas, the Ayeyarwady River drains for around 1,250 miles (2,000 km) to its delta on the Bay of Bengal. Since ancient times, this artery has formed a strategic link between China and the ocean. Numerous civilizations have sprung up on its banks. Invaders, missionaries, and merchants from across the globe have battled its currents to reach the capitals for which the river was a lifeline. The writer Rudyard Kipling immortalized it as "the road to Mandalay." Even today, millions remain dependent on its life-giving waters to nourish their crops. Whether in the dry season when water levels are low or during the fast, silty flows of the monsoon, to journey along the river is to experience the timeless essence of the country's core, little altered in centuries.

Mingun
King Bodawpaya lived on an island in the river to supervise the building of his giant stupa at Mingun, eventually left unfinished and now the most striking monument on the Ayeyarwady.

Sagaing
Perfectly placed to dominate trade along the river in medieval times, Sagaing became the country's royal capital in the early 1300s, after the fall of Bagan.

Bagan
Strategically located on a bend in the river, the capital of the Bagan Dynasty was the greatest of all the ancient cities founded along the banks of the Ayeyarwady.

Ayeyarwady Delta

0 kilometers 150
0 miles 150

Myit Sone
The confluence of the Maikha and Malikha Rivers at Myit Sone marks the official start of the Ayeyarwady, although the river's headwaters extend north into the Himalayan glaciers. A controversial hydroelectricity project to dam the river at this point was suspended in 2011.

Putao

Kumon Taung

Malikha *Maikha*

KACHIN

Myit Sone
Myitkyina

First Defile

Bhamo
Presiding over the northernmost stretch of the river that is navigable year round by steamer, Bhamo is where travelers catching government ferries south begin the slow four-day journey to Yangon.

Bhamo

Shweli

Yao

Lashio

Thanlwin (Salween)

SHAN

Second Defile
Forested limestone cliffs surge out of the river downstream from Bhamo. On this picturesque stretch, the Ayeyarwady narrows to 330 ft (100 m) as it flows through the canyon of the Second Defile.

Taunggyi

Nam Pawn

Mekong

KAYAH

Blessings to the People

Irrawaddy, as the writers Rudyard Kipling and George Orwell called the river, was a corruption of the Burmese name Ayeyarwady Myit, literally "Blessings for the People," a testament to the way its silt-laden waters replenish the country's fish stocks and fertile soil each monsoon.

Fishermen on the river at Mandalay

Thanlwin (Salween)

aton

KAYIN

Ayeyarwady Delta
The mighty river finally debouches into the Bay of Bengal through a vast delta – a low, cyclone-prone region that serves as the country's rice bowl.

MON

Cruising the Ayeyarwady

Two millennia after its waters nourished Burma's first planned cities, the Ayeyarwady continues to serve as an essential artery for the millions who live and work in the settlements clustered along its banks. For visitors, the fleet of ferries and cruisers that ply the river offer a unique perspective on the country. Whether in the luxury of a teak-lined, five-star vessel, roughing it third class on a government double-decker to distant Bhamo, or chugging gently upstream from Mandalay to Mingun, journeying on the silty blue-brown waterway is among the defining travel experiences of the country.

Teak-paneled room on a luxury cruiser, with a balcony offering views of Mingun

Luxury Cruises

Taking their cue from the old Irrawaddy Flotilla Company steamers, luxury cruisers sail the more scenic and interesting stretches of the river. Excursions on dry land punctuate the longer cruises, taking in lesser known locations as well as highlights such as Bagan. Bullock carts are sometimes used to transfer passengers to the shore.

Guests on luxury cruisers are treated to onboard swimming pools, air-conditioned cabins, and gourmet meals, as well as dreamy views over the water.

Other Modes of Travel

Government ferries provide a quintessentially Burmese way to explore the river for the cost-conscious long-distance traveler. Numerous day trips are also offered from major tourist centers.

Double- and triple-decker government ferries run year round between Mandalay and Bhamo. Although they are slow, they provide a great way to interact with locals. Covered motorboats are a faster, but less comfortable option.

A day trip to Mingun, an hour upriver from Mandalay, is Myanmar's most popular tourist boat excursion, particularly for the view of the stupa. From September to April, visitors may also travel the river between Mandalay and Bagan.

The express ferry to Bhamo, on the Upper Ayeyarwady, stopping at Kyaukmyaung to collect passengers and cargo

Traveling the Upper Ayeyarwady

The stretch of the river between Bhamo and Mandalay – the Upper Ayeyarwady – is the home of the iconic, green-and-white Inland Water Transport "slow boat." The journey, which includes stops at Shwegu, Katha, and Kyaukmyaung, can last from 24 hours to three nights, depending on the direction of travel. Long waits while crews lever the boats off sandbanks are frequent in April, when water levels are low and the ferries most overloaded.

Hawkers on the Ayeyarwady

Local vendors crowd around the ferries as soon as they dock, some wading into the river to reach the boat, others clambering aboard, creating a cacophony of calls as they move around deck – an essential part of the river's distinctive soundscape. They sell everything from fried samosas, noodles, fruit, fish on sticks, and corn on the cob to soft drinks, beer, cigarettes, and flowers, all carefully arranged in flat, round baskets and trays.

Boats of various sizes berth at Mandalay's harbor, terminus of most river traffic plying the Ayeyarwady River. Since the creation of the expressway and the proliferation of buses, the onward stretch to Yangon has fallen out of use.

Hawkers selling food to ferry passengers

Burmese Buddhism

Around 90 percent of Burmese are Buddhists, and the faith permeates every aspect of life in the country. Originally brought to Myanmar in the 3rd century BC by monks from India, the Buddha's teachings – known as the Pali Canon or *Tipitaka* – intermingled with the worship of *nats*, or local animist spirits. This gave rise to a distinctive form of Theravada Buddhism that bears close similarities to forms of worship practiced by the Thais, but which is in many respects unique. The Burmese believe that Buddhism underpins the strength of the individual, family, and nation, and that right action accrues merit for this life and lives to come.

Shin Arahan, "The Great Reformer," is credited with converting Anawrahta of Bagan in 1056

Theravada Buddhism

The oldest surviving branch of Buddhism, Theravada emerged after the third Buddhist Council of 250 BC. Missionary monks first introduced it to the Mon and Pyu kingdoms of ancient Burma, before Shin Arahan evangelized the Bagan Empire in the 11th century.

The Three Jewels

The *triratna* or Three Jewels of Buddhism – the Buddha (the Great Teacher), the *dhamma* (his teachings or the law), and the *sangha* (the monkhood and those who follow the teachings) – are the cornerstones of the faith.

The Pali Canon

The core Theravada scriptures are a group of texts known as the Pali Canon, or *Tipitaka* (literally "three baskets"). Along with rules for monks and works on metaphysics, these also include accounts of the Buddha's teachings and disclosures.

The Four Noble Truths

A conceptual framework for all Buddhist thought, these teachings delineate the nature of suffering. The fourth truth describes the path leading to the cessation of suffering and is considered to be the essence of Buddhist practice.

Practices and Rituals

Buddhism is, in essence, an esoteric philosophy and ethical system whose goal is to liberate human beings from suffering, and thereby from the cycle of rebirth. Theravada in Myanmar emphasizes core practices that help an individual on this spiritual path. Rituals mark key moments in a person's day, year, or life, and provide chances to gain merit or to petition higher powers for intercession.

Applying gold leaf
Gold leaf is among the favorite donations of Burmese Buddhists. In some famous shrines, it is applied directly by pilgrims. However, only men are allowed to do this.

Vipassana
Literally "seeing through the veil of ignorance," Vipassana is a form of meditation aimed at promoting insight and concentration. It had a great revival in Burma in the early 20th century.

Monks and nuns
Myanmar has around half a million monks and 75,000 nuns, divided between nine legally recognized monastic orders. Monks wear wine-colored robes, while nuns wear pink.

Merit making
Merit (*punya* in Sanskrit) derives from all good thoughts and actions, and contributes towards a person's spiritual liberation. It has three bases: giving, virtue, and mental development. The giving of alms to monks and donations to stupas are common forms of merit making in Myanmar, and laypeople can often be seen pouring uncooked rice into monks' bowls and bags.

The Burmese Pagoda

Known in Burmese as *zedis* or *payas*, pagodas form the focal point of worship in Buddhist shrines in Myanmar. No one knows exactly how many there are, but the country is generally accepted to have more stupas than any other. Whether gilded, whitewashed, or made of crumbling brick, they have dominated skylines in this part of the world for over two millennia, when the relics of the historical Buddha and his followers started being interred inside monumental structures. The elegantly tapering shape of the Burmese *zedi*, inspired by that of the Buddha's own staff and begging bowl, therefore has a symbolic resonance, connecting worshippers directly to the very origins of their faith.

Vane
Immediately below the diamond bud is a flag-shaped vane which shifts with the wind direction.

Inverted alms bowl

Turban band

Bell

Shan stupas
The Shan people of the eastern hill tracts evolved their own distinctive form of the *zedi*, with more elongated, tapering spires. Two of the largest collections, both renovated in recent years, are those at Inthein on Inle Lake and Kakku *(above)* near Taunggyi.

Receding terraces, usually square but sometimes octagonal, symbolize the earth.

Evolution of the Burmese Stupa

Between the oldest surviving stupas of the Pyu civilization (1st century BC–9th century AD) and the resplendent 17th-century pagodas, the design evolved in spectacular fashion, while retaining the essential symbolic elements set down by the Buddha.

Payagyi, Sri Ksetra, is Myanmar's oldest stupa, dating from the 4th century AD when Indian influence was still strong.

Bawbawgyi, Sri Ksetra, dates from a century later than Payagyi, and is cylindrical in form set on a low base.

Bupaya, Bagan (9th century), has a Pyu-style, elongated cylindrical dome, but more gracefully curved sides.

Lawkananda, Bagan (11th century), has a Pyu-style dome, but a more striking, terraced plinth.

Diamond bud (jeweled orb)

Vane

Hti (finial or umbrella)

Banana bud

Lotus petals

Hti (finial or umbrella)
Ceremonially installed when a pagoda is built or renovated, the *hti* is made of tiers of finely wrought, ornately decorated metal that tinkle in the breeze.

Bo bo gyi (planetary posts)
Set in the cardinal directions around the stupa's base, starting from the northeast, are shrines to the Sun (Sunday), Moon (Monday), Mars (Tuesday), Mercury (Wednesday morning), Rahu (Wednesday afternoon), Jupiter (Thursday), Venus (Friday), and Saturn (Saturday). Each day is also associated with its own animal *(see p76)*.

Myanmar's Biggest Stupa

The largest stupa in the country is the one upriver from Mandalay at Mingun *(see pp156–7)*, which was commissioned by Bodawpaya in 1790 but never finished. Had work been completed, the massive brick pile would have reached 490 ft (150 m), even loftier than the great pyramids of Giza. Steps lead up its cracked sides to an upper terrace, but after earthquake damage in 2012, the ascent is currently closed.

Bodawpaya's unfinished stupa at Mingun

Shwezigon, Bagan (1102), introduced the bell shape and octagonal and circular terraces, a pattern used thereafter.

Dhammayazika, Bagan (1196), places the bell-shaped stupa on a five-sided base, an innovation that never caught on.

Mingalazedi, Bagan (13th century), the last great Bagan Dynasty stupa, was conceived on a grander scale than earlier pagodas.

Pahtodawgyi, Amarapura, reflects in its soaring height the grandeur of the Konbaung era at its 19th-century zenith.

Shwedagon, Yangon, fuses the elegant lines of Mon design with the proportions and extravagance of the Konbaung kings.

Buddhas

In Theravada Buddhism, the image of the historical Buddha, Gautama, is of primary significance. Such depictions are objects of veneration and role models, showing the Buddha both as a divine figure and an actual human being, the very incarnation of the virtues and attributes his teachings promote. As such, these likenesses serve as repositories of cosmic power that are capable of fulfilling wishes, and as potent reminders of the "way of truth" and "right action." For Burmese Buddhists, creating, donating, or buying a Buddha image confers great merit, particularly if it is a large one, which explains why so many are seen across Myanmar.

Mandalay's Mahamuni, one of Myanmar's most revered Buddhas

The *Bhumisparsha* Buddha

Just before his enlightenment, the Buddha sat meditating with his hands in the bhumisparsha mudra *(symbolic gesture), left palm upturned in his lap and right hand touching the ground, to call upon the Earth to witness his worthiness to become a Buddha.*

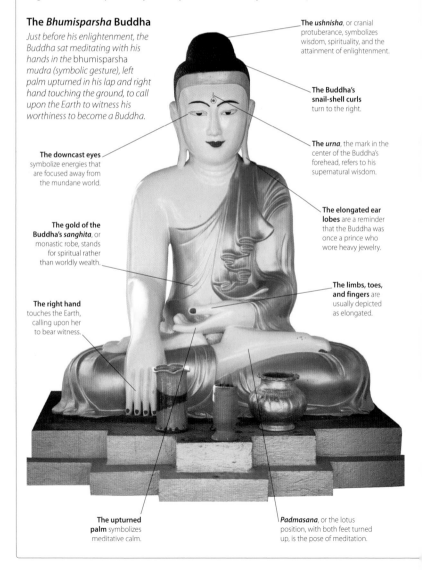

The *ushnisha*, or cranial protuberance, symbolizes wisdom, spirituality, and the attainment of enlightenment.

The Buddha's **snail-shell curls** turn to the right.

The downcast eyes symbolize energies that are focused away from the mundane world.

The *urna*, the mark in the center of the Buddha's forehead, refers to his supernatural wisdom.

The elongated ear lobes are a reminder that the Buddha was once a prince who wore heavy jewelry.

The gold of the Buddha's *sanghita*, or monastic robe, stands for spiritual rather than worldly wealth.

The limbs, toes, and fingers are usually depicted as elongated.

The right hand touches the Earth, calling upon her to bear witness.

The upturned palm symbolizes meditative calm.

Padmasana, or the lotus position, with both feet turned up, is the pose of meditation.

Mudras

Mudras are symbolic or ritual gestures, usually performed with the hands and fingers. Derived from ancient Indian iconography, they are designed to convey deeper meanings to those who use and view them. Apart from religious imagery, they are used in art, classical dance, yoga, and meditation. While several mudras exist, five are most commonly seen in depictions of the Buddha.

Bhumisparsha:
Earth witness mudra

Dhyana:
meditation mudra

Dharmachakra:
teaching mudra

Varada:
compassion mudra

Abhaya:
fearlessness mudra

The Asanas and *Lakshanas*

The Buddha is always shown in a stylized pose, or asana, which may be reclining, sitting, standing, or walking. His body must always show the 32 lakshanas, physical attributes seen as outer manifestations of inner spiritual power. Drawn from the ancient Indian concept of the Mahapurusha, *or Cosmic Being, these include a wide chest and smooth golden skin (legend says the Buddha was born with limbs that shone like the sun).*

Sitting Buddhas, Umin Thounzeh, Sagaing

Buddhapada, or the footprints of the Buddha, symbolize "grounding the transcendent" and display 108 auspicious symbols arrayed around a Wheel of the Law, or *dharmachakra.*

Reclining Buddha, Kyauk Htat Gyi Pagoda, Yangon

Abhaya mudra

Standing Buddha,
Ananda Temple, Bagan

Making Buddhas

One of the largest centers for making Buddha images is the district surrounding Mandalay's Mahamuni Temple, which itself houses the most revered Buddha statue in the country. Lining the tangle of sandy lanes around the shrine are dozens of workshops where images of Gautama Buddha are fashioned in all sizes from white marble, bronze, or brass. The figures produced here are destined for homes, temples, and shrines across the country.

Marble carvers at work near Mandalay's Mahamuni Temple

Theater, Music, and Dance

For centuries, the traditional context for classical Burmese music and dance was the royal court. After the 14th-century conquest of Siam (Thailand), captured Siamese dancers and musicians brought their highly refined and stylized forms to Inwa (Ava) and Amarapura. These intermingled with local forms, originally developed in medieval Bagan from much older, Indian-influenced styles, giving rise to a unique and distinctive cultural legacy that still survives today. Folk idioms also continue to thrive, from *yok thei pwe* marionette theater to *nat pwe* dances.

Konbaung-era illustration showing royalty watching musicians and dancers

Classical Dance

The Burmese classical repertoire (see p220) includes several styles, among which is the popular Kinnara dance. Inspired by the half-bird, half-human creature of Buddhist mythology, it is typified by poses indicating flying. The dancers' costumes imitate 19th-century Konbaung court dress.

Kinnara wings are tied to the hands of the performers.

Stylized movements of the head and eyes follow the music.

Wings are made of brocaded and sequinned stiffened cloth or card.

Performances are accompanied by *kyi waing* gong circles, which are a part of the *hsaing waing*, a traditional musical ensemble.

The footwork resembles the "flat-foot" style of many Indian idioms.

Crouching or kneeling positions are often used.

Classical Music

Nearly all the melodies and songs used in the Burmese classical tradition today draw on the *Maha Gita*, a body of music originally refined in the royal courts. This repertoire now provides the basis for concerts, *yok thei pwe*, and, occasionally, film scores. Classical music is traditionally accompanied by *hsaing waing* ensembles, consisting of instruments unique to Myanmar. Thought to have originated in 17th-century royal courts following the Burmese invasion of Ayutthaya (in Siam), the form is characterized by lively shifts in both melody and rhythm.

A *pattala* (xylophone) being played, Burma, c. 19th century

Folk Traditions

While royal patronage developed the classical arts at court, in the towns and villages less refined folk idioms held sway. Mythological narratives provided the subject matter for all-night puppet shows. Still popular today are a-nyeint pwe and less restrained nat pwe, raunchy spirit possession dances performed by strikingly costumed transvestite oracles accompanied by intense live music (see p42).

Yok thei pwe puppetry, developed into a high art form by the Konbaungs, became widely popular during the 19th century. Historical and religious narratives are recounted and moral messages conveyed by 28 characters *(see p220)*.

Stupa-shaped crowns closely resemble those seen in Buddhist murals from ancient India.

Heavy make up is used by both female and male performers.

A-nyeint pwe is a traditional form of entertainment combining satire, comedy, theater, and dance. The Moustache Brothers *(see p220)* are among the well-known performers of this genre of *pwe*.

Hand gestures are derived from symbolically charged Buddhist mudras.

Kabyalut or ***gabyar-lut***, consisting of 22 basic shape sequences, forms the basis of dance in modern Myanmar.

The *saung gauk* or Burmese harp is the only surviving harp in Asia, and has become Myanmar's best-loved instrument and a national symbol.

Ornate resonator body with 13 to 16 strings

Hne (oboe)

Pat waing (drum circle)

Traditional Dress

One of the most striking aspects of modern Myanmar is the prevalence of traditional dress, which continues to be worn by both men and women, even in trendy Yangon. The cornerstone of the Burmese wardrobe is the *longyi* (or women's *htamein*), a length of patterned cloth which superseded the similar but more voluminous *pahso* in the British era when it became, at least among the upper classes, a statement of support for the Independence movement. *Longyis* (with Shan jackets) and *htameins* are now worn by everyone on formal occasions such as weddings and political functions.

Burmese couple in fine fabrics and jewels, worn originally by courtiers and later by the wealthy

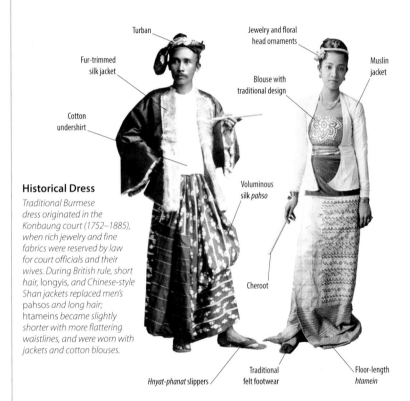

Turban

Jewelry and floral head ornaments

Fur-trimmed silk jacket

Muslin jacket

Blouse with traditional design

Cotton undershirt

Historical Dress

Traditional Burmese dress originated in the Konbaung court (1752–1885), when rich jewelry and fine fabrics were reserved by law for court officials and their wives. During British rule, short hair, longyis, and Chinese-style Shan jackets replaced men's pahsos and long hair; htameins became slightly shorter with more flattering waistlines, and were worn with jackets and cotton blouses.

Voluminous silk *pahso*

Cheroot

Hnyat-phanat slippers

Traditional felt footwear

Floor-length *htamein*

Burmese rubies, prized for their deep red color

Burmese Rubies

Mined in the Mogok Valley, 125 miles (200 km) northeast of the city of Mandalay, Burmese rubies have always formed an integral part of traditional jewelry in Myanmar. They were used to particularly spectacular effect in the sumptuous royal ornaments and costumes of the glittering court of the Konbaungs. Today, these rubies are the most expensive gems per carat in the world, prized for their clarity and deep "pigeon's-blood" color.

Modern *Longyis* and *Htameins*

Longyis replaced *pahsos* as everyday wear only during the British era, with the arrival of immigrants from India wearing their traditional lightweight cotton *lungis*. *Longyis* are usually made in sober plaid patterns, while *htameins* tend to have vivid hues and designs. *Longyis* and *htameins* are versatile and well suited to the climate, with elaborate, embellished varieties for formal attire, or simple, thin cotton ones for daily or work wear.

Longyis and *htameins* worn in daily life

Regional Traditional Dress

Myanmar's many ethnic minorities retain their own styles of dress, in most cases completely distinct from those favored by the Burmese majority. In Chinese-influenced Shan, Mandarin-style jackets are common, while in the remote hill tracts of the far north, east, and west, even everyday costumes may involve elaborate headgear of striking, handwoven cotton turbans and heavy pieces of jewelry.

Chinese-style triangular reed and bamboo hats are commonly worn by both men and women across Shan State and Mandalay Region.

The Pa-O, from the Inle Lake area, traditionally wear dark blue baggy suits with red, yellow, green, or orange plaid turbans, and carry woven Shan bags.

Akha women wear elaborately decorated headdresses, and jackets and skirts of heavily beaded and embroidered dark cloth.

Shan women today often wear the Burmese *htamein*, while men can be seen in baggy trousers and Mandarin-style jackets.

The Nagas still wear their unique traditional costumes for festivals, including huge, colorful bead and feather headdresses.

Traditional Sports

Although relatively unknown in the West, *chinlone*, Myanmar's national game, enjoys a mass following in its homeland. Fittingly for this Buddhist country, the game is essentially non-competitive: participants strive to pass a small cane ball to each other using only their legs. Teams are graded according to how beautifully they play: the complexity and athleticism of their moves, the quickness of their reactions, and the elegance of their posture. The same emphasis on looking good applies to Myanmar's other favorite sport, *lethwei* (Burmese boxing), only here the desired outcome is a knockout blow. Together the two games represent the underlying duality of Burmese culture: cooperative passivity and steely aggression.

Tapandaing, a solo style of *chinlone* played only by women

Chinlone

One of Myanmar's defining eccentricities, chinlone is played with great passion across the country. The main aim is to keep the ball in the air for as long as possible, but play is also rated by the difficulty and execution of named, stylized moves.

Wein kat or team play
In its competitive form, *chinlone* is played by teams of six, who revolve around a central player, as seen in this match between the Myanmar and Cambodia women's teams.

Chinlone moves
There are around 200 ways of kicking the ball, many of them inspired by martial arts and dance. The most highly rated are performed behind the back, without being able to see the ball.

The ball
Chinlone balls are woven from rattan and are fairly small, measuring about 5 in (13 cm) in diameter. They are light and springy, but not too bouncy, and therefore perfect for passing and trick moves.

Street *chinlone*
Chinlone is most often played for pure enjoyment wherever there is sufficient space, including streets, beaches, and riverbanks, such as this game by the side of the Ayeyarwady.

Lethwei

Kick boxing, or lethwei, is a martial art that has been practiced across Southeast Asia for centuries. Its modern form, in which a point system is used, arose in the 1950s. Before then, boxers would continue until one of them was knocked out.

Jumping elbow strike, using the opponent's knee to gain height

Rules of *lethwei*
In this full-contact sport, fighters may use their elbows, hands, knees, legs, feet, and even foreheads. Moves range from jabs to roundhouse kicks that exploit the body's rotational movement to create greater impact.

Back kick, delivering a blow to the side of the head with the foot

Lethwei moves
Burmese boxers learn set moves designed to breach their adversary's defenses, using different parts of the body, including elbow strikes, knee strikes, and elbow punches, the latter one of the most effective means of delivering a knockout.

Knee strike, while forcing the opponent's head downwards

Lethwei in history
Burmese boxing has been popular for centuries, with most villages staging their own matches. An image dated around 1892–6 shows *lethwei* fighters in an open-air sand pit, wearing only loincloths and a wrap of gauze on the hands, surrounded by a ring of spectators.

Festivals of Myanmar

Myanmar's innumerable festivals are nearly all linked to the Buddhist calendar. They range from somber acts of individual worship in local shrines to the mass hysteria of Thingyan, the "water festival" marking the Burmese New Year, when the entire country grinds to a halt and its population gets soaked to the skin. As well as religious events celebrated nationally, each region also holds its own festivals, in which traditional costume is proudly worn for dances. Other excuses to celebrate are the annual *nat pwes*, held in animist shrines, where transvestite oracles perform spirit possession rituals to a backdrop of music and an air of general overindulgence.

The Shwedagon Pagoda Festival (March) is marked by the lighting of thousands of candles around the base of the great stupa *(see pp74–7).*

Nat pwes **(various through the year)**
At gatherings such as the Brother Lords Festival in Taungbyon, music, dance, inebriation, and gambling are part of the day's events as the 37 *nat* spirits are invoked, worshipped, and petitioned *(see pp136–7).*

Golden Bird Festival (September/October)
During Inle Lake's most important religious festival, four of the Phaung Daw U Pagoda's five amorphous, gold-encrusted Buddhas are paddled around the villages in a ceremonial *hamsa* bird barge, pulled by teams of leg rowers in matching costumes *(see pp166–8).*

Taunggyi Balloon Festival (November)
Balloons of all shapes and sizes are exhibited and flown during the day, while ear-splitting explosions rent the night sky over Taunggyi when elaborately decorated giant paper balloons packed with fireworks are let loose over the heads of cheering crowds *(see p172).*

Manau Festival (January)
Echoes of a pre-Christian past resound through the vibrant processional displays of the Kachin, focused on tall, decorated totem poles called *manautaing*, under which thousands gather in traditional dress to celebrate their main festival *(see p182)*.

Ananda Temple Festival (December/January)
Bagan's stately Ananda Temple *(see pp124–5)* is one of the most revered in Myanmar, and its annual festival draws thousands of worshippers, many of whom travel there in bullock carts. Its highlight is a nonstop, 72-hour recitation of Buddhist scriptures by 1,000 monks.

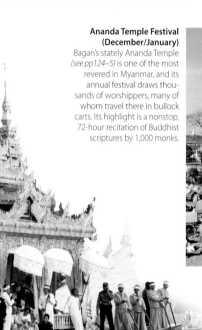

Thingyan (April)
Leading up to New Year, at the height of the hot season, a carnival mood is in the air as crowds gather to splash each other with water. Teams of girls in matching outfits at *pandals* (decorated stalls) attract the most attention.

MYANMAR THROUGH THE YEAR

Myanmar's year is divided into three distinct periods: cool from November to February; hot from March to May; and wet from late May to October. Many festivals mark the transition from one to another, coinciding with phases in the rice-growing calendar. Fields are plowed at the height of the hot season, and paddy planted in the floods after the onset of the annual monsoons. The cool period, beginning in November when the harvest is finished, is the main tourist season and is also when the majority of temple festivals are held. Whether Buddhist or based around the indigenous traditions of *nat* (nature spirit) worship, they are nearly all determined by the lunar calendar. Marking the start of the Buddhist New Year in April, the most widely celebrated is the Water Festival of Thingyan, for which the country grinds to a standstill for a week or more.

Cool Season

Although the period from November to February has the coolest weather compared to the rest of the year, average highs in the central river valleys and coastal areas of the country still hover around 30° C (86° F). With the end of the rains, the skies are reliably blue and at their clearest. This is also the best season for visiting the beaches, where the water is a radiant turquoise under cloudless skies. Up in the mountains around Inle Lake, though, travelers can expect chilly nights.

November

Balloon Festival *(Oct/Nov)*, Taunggyi. Thousands gather on the outskirts of town to watch huge paper balloons – extravagantly decorated and filled with fireworks – being lit and released. Great cheers accompany the ensuing explosions, and prizes are given to the most impressive creations.

Shwezigon Festival *(Oct/Nov)*, Bagan. Candles and fireworks are carried in procession around the famous pagoda on the 14th waxing day of the moon. Alms are offered to Buddhist monks on the full moon, and a fairground springs up with colorful market stalls.

Shwesandaw Festival *(Nov)*, Pyay. On the full moon day of Tazaungmon month, pilgrims attend the town's large pagoda festival, when a venerated tooth relic is shown to the public.

December

Akha New Year *(late Dec)*, Kengtung. The Akha have two New Year celebrations – the Men's New Year (December) and the Swing Festival or Women's

Kachin people performing a traditional dance to celebrate Manau

New Year (August). Offerings are made to ancestor spirits, women wear traditional dress and ornaments, and Akha songs and dances are performed.

January

Manau *(early Jan)*, Myitkyina. Recalling a pre-Christian past, the year's main Kachin festival sees thousands don traditional dress and celebrate beneath *manautaing* (decorated poles).

Naga New Year *(mid-Jan)*, Leshi. Nagas gather in Leshi village dressed in traditional finery to celebrate the Naga New Year.

Ananda Temple Festival *(Jan)*, Bagan. In the Buddhist month of Pyatho, pilgrims travel for days to camp around the temple for its annual festival. Monks conduct a three-day nonstop recitation of the scriptures, and on the morning of the full moon, they are offered bowls of flowers, fruit, incense, and money by laypeople.

Akha people dressed in traditional costumes during Akha New Year celebrations

Average monthly temperature

Temperature Chart
The ideal time to visit is between November and February, when temperatures rarely rise above 32° C (89.6° F). From March, temperatures of 40° C (104° F) and up are the norm for the central valleys, with Yangon only a few degrees below that. The Shan Plateau is the coolest region.

February

Htamane *(Feb)*, nationwide. On the full moon day of Tabodwe month, special sweets are prepared across the country to mark the annual harvest festival.

Mahamuni Temple Festival *(Feb/Mar)*, Mandalay. Offerings of incense and sticky rice delicacies are made at the temple around the Tabodwe full moon, while music and dance recitals take place within its precincts.

Moe-Byae Festival *(Feb)*, Moe-Byae, Shan State. Shan State's principal pagoda festival, held on the Tabodwe full moon day, features traditional crossbow contests as well as a large fair.

Hot Season

Daytime temperatures build from February onwards and by the end of March they regularly exceed 40° C (104° F) in Bagan and Mandalay. By mid-May, humidity levels also rise and outdoor activity can be uncomfortable until the southwest monsoon brings relief in May–June. Exploring archeological sites, such as Bagan and Mrauk U, where shade is in very short supply, can be challenging at this time, when the hottest part of the day is best spent indoors.

March

Shin Pyu **Ceremonies**, nationwide. Throughout the Buddhist months of Tabodwe and Tabaung, families take their sons, dressed as princes, in colorful *shinlaung hlè pwe* processions to local monasteries to begin their *shin pyu*, when they will live and study with monks for a few weeks, or longer.

Offerings of flowers and incense at the Shwedagon Pagoda Festival

Shwe Myintzu Pagoda Festival *(Feb/Mar)*, Indawgyi Lake. Pilgrims travel to this remote shrine in the middle of the lake, reaching the temple by walking across a narrow causeway that mysteriously appears at this time each year.

Festival of 9,000 Lamps *(Mar)*, Kyaiktiyo. The Golden Rock Pagoda hosts its annual festival in March, when thousands of candles are lit around the hilltop shrine in thanksgiving for the teachings of the Buddha.

Kakku Pagoda Festival *(Mar)*, Kakku. Performances of traditional Pa-O song and dance are held alongside a large fair to celebrate this Buddhist site's festival. Candles are lit below the stupas on the final day – one of Shan State's great sights.

Pindaya Pagoda Festival *(Mar)*, Pindaya. Minority people from the surrounding hills flock to the cave temple to worship, cooking and camping inside circles of ox carts – one of the region's most fascinating sights.

Shwedagon Pagoda Festival *(Mar)*, Yangon. Flowers, incense, and water are offered to hundreds of Buddha statues on the pagoda's terrace, and candles are lit around the *zedi*'s base.

Shwemawdaw Pagoda Festival *(Mar/Apr)*, Bago. Performances of traditional Mon theater form the centerpiece of Bago's main pagoda festival.

April

Thingyan *(mid-Apr)*, nationwide. A carnival atmosphere prevails for a week at the height of the hot season, when crowds of youngsters douse each other with water at specially erected *pandals*, or pavilions. In liberated Yangon, scanty dress has become the norm.

Average daily hours of sunshine

Hours

10
8
6
4
2
0

Jan Feb Mar Apr May Jun Jul Aug Sep Oct Nov Dec

Hours

10
8
6
4
2
0

Sunshine Chart
In Myanmar the tropical sun blazes year round – even during the monsoons, it is unusual to have days without any sunshine. Sun protection is essential at any time of the year, and plenty of drinking water should be carried at all times.

Myanmar New Year *(mid-Apr)*, nationwide. At the end of Thingyan, Buddhists perform meritorious deeds such as feeding monks, releasing birds from cages, and paying homage to their elders.

Sittaung Temple Festival *(Apr/May)*, Mrauk U. The ruined city is the venue for a major temple festival involving canal boat races and wrestling contests.

Kason *(Apr/May)*, nationwide. The Buddha's birthday is marked by the carrying of scented water pots, chanting of Pali scripts, and pouring of water at the foot of bodhi trees, symbolizing the Great Teacher's enlightenment and attainment of nirvana.

May

Pa-O Rocket Festival *(May)*, Taunggyi. Locally made rockets stuffed with gunpowder are launched, an event originally staged to predict the weather before the coming monsoon.

Wat Jong Kham Festival *(late May)*, Kengtung. Youngsters from the region's ethnic minorities hurl roasted lablab beans at each other as love tokens.

Popa *Nat Pwe* *(May/Jun)*, Popa Taung Kalat. Pilgrims pay their respects at Popa's *nat* shrines by climbing the 777 steps to the summit of the famous hilltop near Bagan. Strikingly dressed transvestite oracles perform ribald spirit possession dances.

June

Kaba Aye Recitation *(mid-Jun)*, Yangon. Thousands of monks gather at Kaba Aye Pagoda to intone verses from the *Nikaya* scriptures, part of the *Tipitaka* canon; similar events are staged throughout the country.

Statues of the 37 *Mahagiri Nats* at the Shrine of the Mother Spirit of Popa

Pakokku Thiho Shin Pagoda Festival *(mid-Jun)*, Pakokku. This is an important religious event and country fair for residents of the Ayeyarwady's west bank, where the country's best *thanaka* trees are grown.

Devotees pouring water on a bodhi tree during Kason celebrations in Yangon

Average monthly rainfall

Rainfall Chart
Myanmar's rainfall is not evenly distributed. Mandalay gets about 36 in (915 mm) of rain, Taungoo gets 93 in (2,370 mm), while Ye, in Mon State, is deluged with 183 in (4,641 mm). In most places, torrential rain falls daily during the monsoon period.

Wet Season

The incidence of showers increases through May, but by June it is time to prepare for the huge monsoon storms that sweep into the country from the southwest. Beach resorts close and travel throughout Myanmar can be difficult from July through September. October sees a second, shorter intensification of rainfall with the northwest monsoon. At times of heavy downpours, roads are frequently blocked by flooding, and by landslides in the hills; flights are also often diverted, causing long delays.

Women weaving robes for Tazaungdaing, Shwedagon Pagoda, Yangon

July

Dhammasetkya *(mid-Jul)*, nationwide. Coinciding with the onset of the heaviest monsoons, the three-month period of Buddhist Lent starts with the full moon of Waso. Laypeople travel to local monasteries to offer new robes, alms, and other essentials to monks.

Waso *Chinlone* Festival *(Jul/Aug)*, Mandalay. Myanmar's most accomplished *chinlone* players come to the Mahamuni Temple for the country's top tournament. More than 1,000 teams take part, as traditional *hsaing waing* orchestras provide musical accompaniment.

August

Brother Lords Festival *(Jul/Aug)*, Taungbyon, near Mandalay. In the most raunchy and lively of Myanmar's numerous *nat* festivals, two gilded wooden deities are processed around the village, watched by over 10,000 worshippers. *Hsaing*

music, gambling, singing, and drunken spirit possession rituals by transvestite oracles are also among the day's events.

September

Manuha Temple Festival *(mid–late Sep)*, Myinkaba, Bagan. Larger than life papier-mâché figures of heroes, celestial creatures, and *nats* (nature spirits) are paraded around the village shrine. Dances and plays are staged through the night.

Golden Bird Festival *(Sep/Oct)*, Inle Lake. Enshrined inside huge *hamsa* bird boats, four of the Phaung Daw U Pagoda's five Buddha statues are ceremonially paddled around the lake by leg rowers. Fairs and boat races are also held during the event.

October

Thadingyut Festival of Lights *(Sep/Oct)*, nationwide. The Buddha's return from heaven to Earth at the end of the Buddhist Lent is celebrated by all manner of colorful illuminations, with homes brightly lit by candles and lanterns.

Dancing Elephants Festival *(mid-Oct)*, Kyaukse, near Mandalay. Life-sized elephants made of colorful cloth and bamboo, and animated by

pairs of men inside, compete in dance competitions.

Tazaungdaing Weaving Festival *(late Oct/early Nov)*, nationwide. Under the full moon, unmarried women work all night to weave new robes on traditional looms. These are presented to the local temple early the next morning.

Public Holidays

Independence Day (4 Jan)

Union Day (12 Feb)

Full Moon Day of Tabaung (Feb/Mar)

Peasants' Day (2 Mar)

Armed Forces Day (27 Mar)

Myanmar New Year (13–17 Apr)

Full Moon Day of Kason (Apr/May)

Workers' Day (1 May)

Full Moon Day of Waso (Jun/Jul)

Martyrs' Day (19 Jul)

Full Moon Day of Thadingyut (Sep/Oct)

Full Moon Day of Tazaungmon (Oct/Nov)

National Day (10th day after full moon of Tazaungmon)

Christmas Day (25 Dec)

THE HISTORY OF MYANMAR

In common with its neighbors, the roots of Myanmar's contemporary culture – and of its ongoing ethnic strife – can be traced back many centuries. Forming a crossroads between India, China, and Thailand, the region attracted invaders who followed, and subsequently settled in, the great river valleys stretching across the country to the sea. The result is a complex cultural checkerboard whose fault lines continue to generate friction, despite the overarching presence of Buddhism. The religion first traveled here from India along ancient trade routes over two millennia ago to become the region's unifying faith, and continues to define the character of both Myanmar's people and its government.

The earliest traces of *Homo sapiens* in the territory now known as Myanmar/Burma span a period from 11,000 to 5,000 BC – the Anyathian Era – when the first roughly polished stone tools were produced along the banks of the Ayeyarwady River and the western edge of the Shan Plateau. Artifacts and paintings found in the remote Padah-Lin Caves, discovered in the 1930s in the hills north of Pindaya near Inle Lake *(see pp166–8)*, include red-ocher images of human hands and hunting scenes.

Knowledge of smelting and copper casting appears to have spread around the region from 1500–1000 BC, along with rice cultivation, which fueled rapid growth in population. By 200 BC, however, the Pyu, Tibeto-Burman-speaking invaders from China's Yunnan region, had begun to move into the area, establishing settlements along the Ayeyarwady Valley. Over time, these coalesced into well-planned city-states governed from walled capitals dotted on the dry plains flanking the rivers

of Upper Burma, where large-scale irrigation networks were established to fuel intensive agriculture. The first and largest of these urban centers was Hanlin, near Shwebo on the Ayeyarwady's west bank, whose economy was dominated by salt production and control of commerce along the river, by now a thriving trade artery connecting China with the Bay of Bengal. At some point in the 7th century AD, however, Sri Ksetra *(see pp98–9)* super-seded Hanlin as the region's principal hub.

Heavily influenced through contact with India's Andhra kingdom, the Pyus' religious beliefs, architecture, and art reveal a unique blend of Mahayana Buddhism, Tantricism, Hinduism, and local animist *nat* worship, although by the 5th century BC, Theravada Buddhism had gained dominance. In many respects, Pyu culture provided the blueprint for the Bagan Empire that would supersede it. Some Pyu hallmarks, such as the Burmese script, astrological calendar, and pagoda design, have survived into the present era.

11000–5000 BC Anyathian Era

1500–1000 BC Rice cultivation and metalwork begin

Stone bracelet, Taungthaman (Amarapura), c. 500 BC

3rd–2nd centuries BC Arrival of Buddhism in Burma

Sri Ksetra Pyu coin with a Bhadrapitha drum symbol, c. AD 630–830

2nd century BC–1st century AD The Pyu create the first walled cities in the Ayeyarwady Valley

5th century AD City of Sri Ksetra founded; first tall, cylindrical stupas built

AD 97 Roman embassy to China passes through Burma

AD 638 The Vikramas, a Pyu dynasty, launch the first Burmese calendar

11000 BC	5000	1500	1000	300	200	AD 100	600

◀ Detail from a 6th-century stonework relief in the Nyaung Ohak complex, Inthein, Inle Lake

The Rakhine and Mon

Two other groups colonized different parts of the country at around the same time as the Pyu. In the northwest, the Rakhine people lived in similar city-states, with an economy based on rice farming and trade with India. At Wethali and Dhanyawadi, near the medieval city of Mrauk U *(see pp110–14)*, remnants of their ancient walled towns attest to an Indian-influenced Buddhist tradition dating as far back as the 4th century AD.

In the southwest, the Mons, originally from western China, are thought to have colonized the flat coastal land around the Gulf of Mottama (Martaban) in the 9th century, founding a capital at Thaton, the largest regional port of its day. Although they were later defeated by the Bamars and absorbed into the Bagan Empire, the Mons developed a highly sophisticated culture that would greatly influence that of their subsequent overlords.

The Bagan Dynasty

By the early 9th century, a new force from the northeast was beginning to make itself felt all along the Ayeyarwady Valley. An off-shoot of the Nanzhao kingdom of Yunnan, the Mranma people, or Myamars, launched repeated raids on Pyu cities using hordes of mounted archers, eventually destroying Hanlin in 832 and carrying off 3,000 of its inhabitants into slavery. Sri Ksetra was attacked soon after.

Having subjugated the Pyus, the Mranmas, henceforth known in the Burmese Chronicles as Bamars or Burmans, built a fortified settlement – Bagan – on a bend in

Golden spire of the Shwezigon Pagoda, begun in Anawrahta's reign

the Ayeyarwady River, close to its con-fluence with its main tributary, the Chin-dwin. From here, the dynasty carved out a domain extending 200 miles (322 km) from north to south and 80 miles (129 km) across. Gradually, over the next 200 years, the Burmese language became the lingua franca and the separate city-states of the region evolved into a centralized kingdom.

The First Burmese Empire

The Bagan Dynasty's golden age dawned in 1044 with the accession to the throne of a fiercely ambitious, energetic teenager who seized the crown after defeating his cousin in single combat. Anawrahta "The Ungovernable" (1015–78) immediately embarked on a series of military campaigns that would, in less than two decades, unify the four main kingdoms of medieval Burma. The high point was the conquest, in 1057, of the Mon capital, Thaton, from which Anawrahta returned with 30,000 prisoners, among them the Mon royal family and legions of skilled builders and architects. The talents of these enslaved

---

Mid-7th century Chinese pilgrims Xuanzang and I Ching mention the Pyu city of Sri Ksetra

849 Founding of Bagan by King Pyinbya (817–76) as a walled city with 12 gates and a moat

Ananda, one of the finest temples of Bagan

| 650 | 750 | 850 | 950 | 1050 |

Early 9th century Mranmas/ Myamars, a branch of the Nanzhaos of Yunnan, invade and settle in Upper Burma

832 Destruction of Hanlin

Pyu-era terra-cotta Buddha amulet from the city of Sri Ksetra, c. 8th–9th centuries

1056 The Buddhist monk Shin Arahan travels to Bagan

artisans were put to use during the two remaining decades of Anawrahta's reign, and that of his son and successor Kyanzittha (1030–1112), during which a huge number of monasteries, stupas, temples, and other monuments were erected in the capital, Bagan.

Fueled by wealth from trade and military conquests, the construction boom was coupled with a program of economic, social, and religious reform that would leave an enduring legacy, not least the adoption of Theravada Buddhism by the kingdom. The man credited with originally converting Anawrahta to this relatively austere form of the faith was a monk named Shin Arahan (1034–1115). He had fled his Mon homeland when it was threatened with invasion by the Hindu Khmers from the east, and served as the chief spiritual advisor to four successive Bagan

Well-preserved glazed tiles at the base of the Ananda Temple, built by King Kyanzittha

monarchs. During his lifetime, Theravada became the predominant tradition, overlayering the more arcane practices of Mahayana Buddhism, Hinduism, and the animist worship of nats, or nature spirits.

By the 13th century, however, the Bagan Empire had gone into sharp decline. Laws exempting land grants and other donations to Buddhist monasteries from tax caused the royal coffers to empty. Without enough funds to maintain a large army, rebellion stirred in the kingdom. Then, in 1277 and 1283, during the reign of Kublai Khan (1215–94), Mongol forces invaded northern Myanmar. In 1287 the Mongols advanced to Bagan, with the resulting instability leading to the ruin of the city and its rulers.

The Post-Bagan Era

The decades following the break up of the Bagan Empire were ones of upheaval and strife as the region's powers struggled for overall supremacy. Eventually four main kingdoms emerged from the melee. In the east, a constellation of petty Shan chiefs, who had come to the region with the Mongols, ruled the hill tracts. In the northwest, the kingdom of Arakan, founded in 1430, became in time one of the wealthiest in Southeast Asia, with a writ extending from the mouth of the Ganges to the Ayeyarwady. In Upper Burma, Inwa (Ava) saw itself as the true successor to the Burmese-Bagan Dynasty, but exhausted its reserves trying to reform the empire. Most formidable among its adversaries was the Mon kingdom of Pegu-Hanthawaddy to the southeast, which emerged victorious from the Forty Years' War against Inwa to prosper on trade. The monuments that survive in modern Bago from the kingdom's heyday between the 1420s and 1530s attest to the town's former splendor and its importance as a great center of Theravada Buddhism.

1105 King Kyanzittha builds the Ananda Temple in Bagan

1290s Marco Polo (1254–1324) becomes the first Westerner to visit and write of Burma (Mien)

Marco Polo, the Venetian merchant traveler

1364 King Thadominbya (1345–67) moves capital from Sagaing to Inwa (Ava)

1150   1250   1350   1450

11th–13th centuries Bagan's golden age of temple building

1287 Collapse of the First Burmese Empire after the Mongol invasion

Kublai Khan, the great Mongol leader and grandson of Genghis Khan

1430 Men Saw Mon (1380–1433), also known as Naramithla, founds new Arakanese capital at Mrauk U

The Taungoo Dynasty (Second Burmese Empire)

Pegu's prosperity was being watched covetously by a power emerging to the north, in the landlocked Sittaung Valley. Following the conquest of Inwa (Ava) by a confederacy of Shan states in 1527, many Bamars had fled Upper Burma and settled in this new dynasty's capital, Taungoo, bolstering the power of its redoubtable king, Tabinshweti (1516–50).

Tabinshweti wanted Taungoo to become the hub of an empire, and to further this aim, he captured the Mon port of Pegu (Bago) in 1539, using its wealth to fund further conquests. By 1545 he controlled all of Upper and Lower Burma, except Arakan. Toward the end of his rule, however, the king succumbed to alcoholism, and by the time of his death (by assassination, on his 34th birthday), most of his territorial gains had been lost.

The job of restoring them fell to his brother-in-law and successor, Bayinnaung (1516–81), regarded as the greatest of all Burma's kings for his audacity, ambition, and military prowess. Over the following three decades, he recaptured all of the lost lands and amassed the largest empire in the history of Southeast Asia, encompassing Upper and Lower Burma, Laos, southern Yunnan, Siam, and Manipur. His most lasting legacy, however, was the pacification of the Shan hill states by means of a tributary system which endured until the British annexation of

18th-century illustration of Konbaung nobility in court dress

Burma in 1885, and which made certain that successive capitals around Mandalay remained free from attack from the east.

European Merchants and Mercenaries

The reign of the last powerful Taungoo king, Anaukpetlun (1578–1628), coincided with the arrival on Burmese shores of a new potential threat. European merchants with powerful backers had been making inroads along the coastline of Southeast Asia since the creation of a Portuguese colony in Goa in 1510. Iberian slave traders and renegades had also become a fixture at local royal courts. Impressed by their weapons and modern military tactics, rulers of all the region's major kingdoms had employed European mercenaries to help fight their wars, and in many cases lived to regret the fact. A case in point was the king of Arakan, who, in the early 17th century, recruited the Portuguese adventurer Filipe de Brito e Nicote. Having been given the governorship of Thanlyin, de Brito soon began to use the port as a base from which to plunder the interior, until he was killed by King Anaukpetlun in 1613 (see p82).

Rise of the Konbaungs and the Third Burmese Empire

Toward the end of Anaukpetlun's reign, rebellions throughout the country gravely weakened Taungoo/Burman rule and in 1740, the capital had to be moved from Pegu to the less vulnerable Inwa. Shortly after, however, the Mons

1545 King Tabinshweti unifies Upper and Lower Burma, except Arakan, into one kingdom

1527 Confederation of Shan States conquers Inwa

1500

1551 Bayinnaung crowned king

1569 Siam conquered by Bayinnaung's army

Statue of Bayinnaung, third king of the Taungoo Dynasty

1550

1613 de Brito impaled by Anaukpetlun

1619 British East India Company sends representative to Pegu

1600

Filipe de Brito e Nicote, called Nga Zinga by the Burmese

mounted a successful revolt and sailed up the Ayeyarwady to take the capital in 1752. Watching the Mon advance through his homeland was a young village chief named Aung Zeya who, after a series of daring raids on Mon positions, managed to gather around him a small but highly motivated army. In 1752, at the very moment Pegu's forces were about to breach the defenses of Inwa, Aung Zeya declared himself the new Burman king, taking the honorific title Alaungpaya, the "Embryo Buddha."

It is a name that still stirs great pride among the Burmese, for King Alaungpaya (1714–60) not only managed to expel the Pegu troops left behind to govern his kingdom, but also fended off the inevitable backlash two years later when an army was sent north to retake Inwa. This was followed in 1757 by a counterattack on Pegu itself, at the end of which Alaungpaya slaughtered the city's entire population.

In his short but seminal eight-year reign, Alaungpaya reconquered all of Burma and subdued Manipur and northern Thailand, setting the scene for the third and final Burmese Empire, ruled by the dynasty he founded, the Konbaungs (see pp54–5).

Konbaung Rule

The first major threat to Konbaung rule came in 1767–70, when the Qing Dynasty from Manchuria mounted a series of invasions. Their armies got to within three days' march of Inwa, causing panic in the capital, but were eventually halted by a combination of disease, inclement weather, and dogged resistance from the Burmese themselves. Achieved against all odds, the

Silk painting depicting Konbaung military practice

Konbaung victory conferred a sense of invincibility on the Burmese kings, who thereafter retreated to the cosseted luxury of their palaces on the banks of the Ayeyarwady, and left their generals to do the fighting.

The image of a Konbaung ruler as a sybaritic megalomaniac, a commonplace in the colonial era, first gained currency during the reign of Bodawpaya (1745–1819), Alaungpaya's fourth son, who grabbed the throne after murdering dozens of kinsmen and other potential challengers. Although famous for having 207 queens and concubines and fathering 120 children, Bodawpaya is perhaps best remembered for attempting to construct the world's largest brick stupa at Mingun, and for ordering the audacious attack on Arakan that resulted in the destruction of its capital, Mrauk U. The Burman army returned home from the campaign in triumph, bearing the most sacred of all Arakanese Buddhas, Mahamuni, which was carried over the Rakhine-Yoma Hills to Mandalay city, where it still rests.

Burmese war elephants on a
19th-century temple mural

1666 Mughal Empire defeats Arakan

1740 Mon capital moved from Pegu to Inwa

1752 Konbaung Dynasty established

650

1700

1750

1688 French East India Company opens branch at Syriam

Alaungpaya, founder of the Konbaung Dynasty

1767 Burmese army attacks Siamese capital Ayutthaya

1784 Bodawpaya invades Arakan

The Konbaung Dynasty

The Konbaungs, who dominated Burma from 1752 until the British invasion of 1885, were the country's last independent rulers. Founded by the legendary Alaungpaya, the dynasty had humble beginnings but went on to create an empire stretching from the borders of India to the Gulf of Thailand, even conquering Siam in 1767. The courtly culture and, later, reforms promoted by the Konbaungs have left a lasting effect on Myanmar's government, traditional arts, and sense of national identity.

Bhamarasana, the Bee Throne, was where the king sat during the nomination ceremony of the chief queen

The Court of the Konbaungs

The court was where the king demonstrated his absolute power, embodied most dramatically in the gilded Sihasana, *literally "Lion Throne," before which other royals, the nobility, and courtiers would have prostrated themselves. The ultimate symbol of Burmese sovereignty, the Lion Throne once formed the focal point of the Great Audience Hall of Mandalay Palace (see pp144–5).*

Nine Noble Gems adorned the Lion Throne, each representing a particular attribute or virtue.

The Celestial King represented the monarch's role as protector of the Buddhist faith and the highest judge of his people.

Niches in the doors behind the Lion Throne hold figurines of Kinnara and Kinnari, the bird-humans.

Thibaw and Supayalat
King Thibaw (1859–1916) and his queen are seen as the Lord and Lady Macbeth of Southeast Asian history for their massacre of their royal relatives to consolidate their power.

The base, in the form of two lotus blooms, is carved from yamanay wood *(Gmelina arborea)*, which is light but strong.

Auspicious earth from sacred sites around the kingdom is packed into the base.

Konbaung Art and Architecture

As well as being the kingdom's political hub, the court was also a crucible for the traditional arts, from dance-drama, music, and song to puppetry, poetry, and calligraphy. Burma's finest architects and craftsmen created and embellished wondrous teak buildings in Mandalay's walled city, of which only a few fragments still survive.

Tapestry
Kalagas, velvet panels embroidered with mythological scenes, are still crafted, carrying on a tradition that flourished in the Konbaung era.

Shwenandaw Monastery
This exquisite teak monastery was once part of the palace, and gives a vivid impression of how the vanished city would have looked in its prime.

Carvings
Although most of the elaborately worked teak buildings created by Konbaung artisans have disappeared, the Shwenandaw carvings and the religious images that survive are reminders of their masterly skills.

Konbaung Wars

In common with most Burmese rulers, the Konbaungs were an expansionist dynasty. While its founding father Alaungpaya pushed his kingdom's borders to the limits of modern Myanmar, his successors extended them into India and Siam. Only with the arrival of the British were their territorial ambitions thwarted.

The Burma-Siam War and the Anglo-Burmese Wars
The conquest of Siam in 1767 brought great treasure to the Konbaung court, as well as skilled artists who left a lasting mark on classical Burmese culture. In stark contrast, the 19th-century Anglo-Burmese Wars, and the subsequent punitive reparations forced on the Burmese, crippled Konbaung power forever.

King Thibaw's Exile

To ensure that he never became a martyr in the eyes of his former subjects, Thibaw was exiled by the British following the Third Anglo-Burmese War. An unseasonal rain shower had just ended when, on November 28, 1885, the royals made their way from the palace, past weeping crowds, to the wharf to begin their journey to Ratnagiri, India, where the king eventually died, depressed and penniless. After their departure, Mandalay Palace was comprehensively looted, and the royal apartments commandeered as barracks.

Painting c. 1900 showing British troops escorting the Konbaungs from the palace

Storming of a stockade during the First Anglo-Burmese War

First and Second Anglo-Burmese Wars

Bagyidaw (1784–1846), Bodawpaya's grandson, pursued an equally aggressive policy of expansion, targeting Manipur and Assam in India. The British East India Company regarded these states as a buffer against Burmese invasion of their empire in the subcontinent and reacted by sending troops to support the Assamese and Manipuris. But it was only when the Burmese targeted the hill state of Cacher that direct conflict became inevitable.

Declared in 1824, the First Anglo-Burmese War lasted two years and was a catastrophe for both sides: 15,000 British-Indian troops and many more Burmese perished. The bill, which ran to over £5 million ($19 billion in modern money), nearly ruined the East India Company before its forces prevailed and the Treaty of Yandabo brought the bloodshed to a close. The treaty's terms were punitive: huge swaths of Burmese territory were lost (including all of Arakan) and massive indemnities set, crippling the Konbaung economy for generations.

Heavy-handed gunboat diplomacy was to blame for the Second Anglo-Burmese War of 1852, which erupted after the Burmese governor of Rangoon fined two British captains for customs violations. The ensuing conflict dragged on for a year and only ended when a coup in the Burmese capital, Amarapura, brought to power King Mindon (1808–78), by which time the whole of Lower Burma had been annexed by the British. A devout, scholarly Buddhist, Mindon is most remembered for the splendid monasteries and pagodas he founded in his new capital, Mandalay. He was also a determined modernizer, implementing a program of forward-looking reforms. The changes, however, were to prove powerless in the face of the cataclysmic events about to unfold.

Third Anglo-Burmese War

Mindon died in 1878 without naming a successor. After months of intrigue, the throne went to Thibaw (1859–1916), a prince chosen for his perceived pliability, and because he had fallen in love with Supayalat, the daughter of Mindon's most senior and influential queen. However, the new king and queen proved far from biddable. Shortly after their coronation, to eliminate any potential threat to their rule, the couple oversaw the killing of scores of young royals in a massacre that outraged world opinion. The British called for regime change, but finally it was a dispute over timber taxes on Scottish teak importers that ignited the third, and decisive, Anglo-Burmese war of 1885. This time, the Konbaung king offered no more

British soldiers at the Shwedagon Pagoda, First Anglo-Burmese War

Bahadur Shah Zafar, India's last Mughal emperor

1862 Exiled emperor Bahadur Shah Zafar dies in Rangoon

1800	1825	1850
	1824 First Anglo-Burmese War	**1826** Treaty of Yandabo between the British East India Company and the King of Inwa (Ava)	**1852** Second Anglo-Burmese War; British seize and expand Rangoon	**1859** Mindon moves capital to Mandalay

than token resistance to the army that steamed up the Ayeyarwady. Without a single shot being fired, General Henry Prendergast accepted Thibaw's surrender in Mandalay. As the royal family sailed to exile in India, looters plundered the palace and the country descended into anarchy.

Colonial Rule

Burma was now officially part of British India, ruled by a government from Calcutta which, to keep the Burmese majority in check, deployed similar divide and rule tactics to those used in the subcontinent – a ploy that would have a dramatic effect over the coming century.

Meanwhile, the economy had begun to revive. The Ayeyarwady Delta region was developed, and waves of Indian immigrants poured in to take advantage of the boom. By 1927, Indians were in the majority while the Burmese, denied administrative posts by the British, suffered mounting poverty and unemployment. The consequent growth of Burmese opposition to British rule was spearheaded initially by radical Buddhist monks, and later by groups from Yangon University. Among the latter was an association called the 30 Comrades, led by the young socialist Aung San, future leader of the country and father of Aung San Suu Kyi. Rejecting Gandhian-style nonviolence in favor of military action, they turned to the Japanese for support.

World War II

The main goal of the Japanese invasion of Burma in December 1941 was to close off the "Burma Road," the supply line from Assam to Yunnan by means of which the Allies were able to re-provision Chinese forces. The north of the country was also regarded as a potential back door to British India and total domination of Asia.

As the Japanese forces pressed north, British and Indian soldiers were pushed back 930 miles (1,500 km) to the jungles and mountains of the Indian border. They were accompanied by hundreds of thousands of Indian refugees who were harassed and murdered by the Burmese as they struggled to regain their homeland. Around 12,000 troops and over 30,000 civilians perished in the mass retreat – one of the forgotten disasters of World War II.

Once the Japanese army had been halted at Kohima in northeast India, the Allies were reinvigorated by improved air support and forced the Japanese back across the Chindwin, while deep-penetration units, such as Orde Wingate's Chindits and their American counterparts, Merrill's Marauders, attacked them from behind their own lines. The battle then spilled across the central plains of Burma before the Japanese finally surrendered on August 28, 1945.

A convoy of military trucks on the Burma Road around 1945

1878 King Mindon dies of dysentery

1879 First massacre of royals by Thibaw

British troops entering Mandalay in 1885

1937 Burma granted its own Legislative Council by the British

1941 Japanese invasion

1875

1900

1925

1885 Third Anglo-Burmese War and the British pacification of Burma

1884 About 400 members of the royal family killed in jail by Thibaw

The Burmese Army under British command in 1940

1944 Operation Capital: Allies recapture Burma

1945 Japanese surrender

Independence

During the Japanese occupation, Burma had become a de facto puppet state, with leaders of the former Burmese Liberation Army nominally at the helm. But in March 1945, Aung San switched allegiances, placing his troops at the disposal of the Allies during the final stages of the campaign. After the war, Burma pressed for full independence. Talks were concluded in January 1947, with Britain agreeing to grant Burma its freedom the next year.

Three months later, Aung San's party won the general election, but the celebrations were shortlived: on July 19 gunmen shot dead Aung San and six of his ministers. U Nu, a friend of Aung San's since their student days, took over to become independent Burma's first prime minister. However, the country descended into civil war almost immediately as conflicts erupted between the army and various regional

U Nu, friend of Aung San and first prime minister of independent Burma

forces, from communists and Chinese Kuomintang rebels to former resistance fighters and ethnic minorities such as the Shan, Kachin, and Chin, who had been promised full autonomy but now saw the government dominated by Burmese.

Military Rule and the 8888 Uprising

Meanwhile, the economy went into rapid decline as rice exports plummeted and expenditure on arms rose. U Nu handed over control in 1958 to a temporary military government under General Ne Win, a move

widely welcomed at the time, leading to considerable improvement in Burma's chaotic political situation.

In elections two years later, U Nu was restored to power, but regional calls for autonomy were threatening to drag the country into civil war, so Ne Win and the army stepped in again. The 1962 coup marked the start of radical military dictatorship under the Burma Socialist Programme Party. Private property was confiscated by the state; businesses, agriculture, and the media were nationalized; and foreign aid groups and opposition parties were banned. As a result, Burma became one of the poorest nations in the world. In July 1988 Ne Win resigned after a spate of public protests started by students and monks in Yangon. By August, the demonstrations had spread nationwide, leading to the declaration of martial law. Aung San's daughter, Aung San Suu Kyi, emerged as the popular leader of what became known as the 8888 Uprising (after the date of the strike). In the ensuing crackdown, thousands of protesters were imprisoned, killed, or forced to flee abroad.

SLORC

In September 1988, another army coup brought the hard-line State Law and Order Restoration Council (SLORC) to power under General Saw Maung. The following year, SLORC changed the country's official English name to Myanmar.

1947 Aung San assassinated

1948 Burma gains independence from Britain

1958–60 General Ne Win's caretaker government

General Ne Win, military commander and founder of the Burma Socialist Programme Party

1945   1955   1965   1975

1962 Prime Minister U Nu ousted in military coup

1974 New constitution transfers power to army

U Thant, UN Secretary-General, 1961–71

General Aung San

In 1990, confident that it had the support of the people, and having confined members of the opposition parties under house arrest during the campaign, the military government held free elections, only to lose by a crushing margin, with Aung San Suu Kyi's National League of Democracy (NLD) polling 60 percent of the votes. Instead of respecting the results, the regime rounded up dissidents and NLD activists: many were sent to forced labor camps or "disappeared." Aung San Suu Kyi spent most of the 1990s imprisoned in her own home, as Myanmar became ever more distanced from the outside world.

General Than Shwe dominated politics in the 2000s, and promised a transition to democracy, but is best known for his multi-billion-dollar military and trade deals with the Russians and Chinese, and for moving the capital from Yangon to Naypyitaw.

The Saffron Revolution and Road to Democracy

A dramatic rise in gas and fuel prices in 2007 sparked a popular uprising which, because it was led by monks, was dubbed the Saffron Revolution. Protests were held across Myanmar before the army launched a brutal clampdown in which 31 people were killed and thousands arrested.

A Constitutional Referendum was held in 2008, and although opposition groups condemned the result as a sham, this historic poll paved the way for major political reforms. These included the release of Aung San Suu Kyi in 2010, amnesties for political prisoners, new labor laws, and a relaxation of press censorship. The international

Aung San Suu Kyi, leader of the National League of Democracy

community was quick to respond to the changes: Hillary Clinton and Barack Obama visited for talks, and Myanmar saw a huge surge in foreign tourism. Aung San Suu Kyi entered parliament in 2012 for the first time after by-elections. The same year, ceasefire agreements with several minority groups fighting for autonomy also brought peace.

Since the handover to a nominally civilian government, the country has seen sporadic eruptions of communal strife. In Rakhine State in 2012, thousands of Rohingya Muslims were displaced by rioting and scores left dead, and the entire region was declared off-limits to foreign tourists.

Despite these outbreaks of sectarian violence, Myanmar's prospects look promising. Bowing to international pressure and a need for foreign investment, the government now has a less authoritarian complexion. While full and free elections remain a pipe dream, there seems to be a genuine push for improved human rights and greater transparency. Whether this new openness will survive the challenges posed by greater freedom of speech remains to be seen, but for the time being the spirit in Myanmar is one of optimism for the future.

1989 SLORC declares martial law

1991 Aung San Suu Kyi awarded Nobel Peace Prize

2005 Naypyitaw announced as new capital

2011 Thein Sein elected president

2012 NLD win seats in elections; government signs peace accord with Karen rebel army

1985 1995 2005 2015

1988 8888 Uprising; Aung San Suu Kyi speaks at the Shwedagon

Rioting in Yangon during the 8888 Uprising

2008 Cyclone Nargis devastates the Delta region

President Thein Sein

2013 Communal disturbances in Meiktila; Thein Sein announces release of political prisoners

MYANMAR AREA BY AREA

Myanmar at a Glance

Myanmar stretches from the Himalayas in the north to the intensely tropical regions of the south. Between the two, the mighty Sittaung and Ayeyarwady Rivers drain across vast arid valleys bounded by jungle-clad hills, while in the east, the Thanlwin cuts through the Shan Plateau, dividing China from the Andaman Sea. The rivers meet the ocean at deltas where patchworks of paddy are interlaced by winding canals and rivulets, but where devastating cyclones also regularly wreak havoc. A storehouse of art and culture, Myanmar offers sights ranging from the ethereal ruins of Bagan to the faded structures of colonial Yangon, and rich traditions of music and dance nurtured in the conservatories and theaters of Mandalay.

Hkakabo Razi *(see p185)*, lying at the head of remote river valleys, is Myanmar's highest mountain and perfect for adventure trekking.

Bagan *(see pp116–35)*, on the banks of the Ayeyarwady River, is one of Southeast Asia's greatest archeological treasures. Dotted across sandy plains, these exquisite remnants of the medieval Bagan Empire's lost city remain, despite natural disasters and neglect, an unforgettable sight.

Hakha

WESTER
MYANM
(see pp100–

Mrauk U

Sittwe
(Aykab)

Mrauk U *(see pp110–14)*, set deep amid the hills of Rakhine State, holds the evocative remains of the medieval kingdom of Arakan, once famed across Asia for its riches of its kings and the splendor of its palaces and temples. Today only a few ruined stupas and ordination halls remain.

The Shwedagon Pagoda *(see pp74–7)*, Myanmar's most venerated Buddhist shrine, soars above Yangon's skyline from a complex of shining gold and marble. Despite being vandalized by colonial invaders and suffering earthquake damage, it has been beautifully restored and looks resplendent today.

◄ View of the sunset over the Ayeyarwady and the stupas of Mandalay city from Mandalay Hill

Mandalay city *(see pp142–9)* holds the last surviving vestiges of the Konbaung Dynasty, including the richly carved teak Shwenandaw Monastery.

Inle Lake *(see pp166–8)* in the Shan Hills is renowned for its Intha stilt villages, crumbling stupa complexes, and lotus silk weaving workshops.

Ngapali *(see p106)*, with its golden sand and transparent turquoise water, is the country's most alluring beach resort.

Bago *(see pp92–5)*, former capital of Lower Burma, retains a crop of exceptional Buddhist monuments, including Myanmar's best-loved reclining Buddhas.

The Kyaiktiyo Golden Rock Pagoda *(see pp190–91)* is Myanmar's most popular pilgrimage spot after Yangon's Shwedagon Pagoda and Mandalay's Mahamuni Temple.

Hkakabo Razi

Putao

NORTHERN MYANMAR *(see pp178–85)*

Myitkyina

Bhamo

nywa

Lashio

Mandalay

Pyin U Lwin

EASTERN MYANMAR *(see pp162–77)*

Kengtung

BAGAN ARCHEOLOGICAL ZONE *(see pp116–37)*

Taunggyi

MANDALAY REGION *(see pp138–61)*

Naypyitaw

Loikaw

Pyay

Taungoo

BAGO REGION *(see pp88–99)*

Bago

YANGON *(see pp64–87)*

Hpa-an

Yangon

thein

Mawlamyine (Moulmein)

Shwedagon Pagoda

SOUTHEASTERN MYANMAR *(see pp186–95)*

Dawei

Myeik (Mergui)

Ayeyarwady (Irrawaddy)

0 kilometers   150

0 miles   150

Kawthaung

YANGON

Although it was superseded by Naypyitaw as the official capital in 2005, Yangon, overlooking the confluence of the Hlaing and Bago Rivers, remains Myanmar's largest and most populous city, as well as its diplomatic, economic, and cultural hub. The city has retained a great deal of its colonial charm, but with its chic five-star hotels, restaurants, car showrooms, and air-conditioned shopping malls, Yangon is also where Myanmar's re-entry into the mainstream of modern Asian life is most clearly discernible.

Until the British invasion of 1852, the city was a ramshackle port of only 20,000 people, distinguished less by its flagging maritime trade than by the presence of the Shwedagon Pagoda, Myanmar's principal religious monument. However, both trade and the population expanded rapidly in the wake of the British annexation, bolstered by waves of immigration from India. The new rulers called the town Rangoon, an anglicized version of the Burmese Yangon (literally "End of Strife"), the name chosen by Alaungpaya following his devastating conquest of Lower Burma between 1755 and 1757. By the early 1900s, it had become one of Asia's richest and most cosmopolitan capitals.

A grid plan of grand municipal buildings and multistory tenements was laid out on land close to the riverfront, where the colonial-era British authors Rudyard Kipling and Somerset Maugham sojourned en route to more far-flung postings in the empire. The Japanese bombings of World War II, and seven decades of neglect since, have taken their toll on the architecture, but the flaking, mildewed facades create a charismatic backdrop for the busy street life of the modern city, where commuters breakfast on bowls of steaming *mohinga* (noodle soup) at sidewalk stalls, and new hatchbacks vie for space with old-style trishaws.

Close to the waterfront, the Botataung and Sule Pagodas are worth visiting, perhaps combined with trips to the traditional markets. North of downtown, the soaring golden Shwedagon Pagoda is deservedly the city's main visitor attraction; farther north, the broad, park-lined avenues and lakes of the suburbs provide welcome respite from the heat and traffic.

Monks taking a *Tipitaka* examination in the Mahapasana Guha at the Kaba Aye Pagoda, Yangon

◀ The Middle Terrace of the Shwedagon Pagoda, with a host of ornately decorated subsidiary shrines surrounding the main stupa

Exploring Yangon

Yangon's principal sights are mostly concentrated in the south of the city, between the river and the Shwedagon Pagoda. Apart from the colonial quarter and the stretch of Bogyoke Aung San Road from the Sule Pagoda to the market area, both of which make for interesting walks, the downtown area is too congested and spread out to be easily covered on foot. A quick taxi ride, however, will access the sights around the Shwedagon. It is best to leave the pagoda itself until sunset, when it looks most spectacular. The walkway around Kandawgyi Lake, whose waters reflect the great gilded stupa, is good for an evening stroll. The Kyauk Htat Gyi and Nga Htat Gyi Pagodas are midtown highlights, while toward the airport, the Kabe Aye Pagoda and Lawka Chantha Abhaya Labha Muni are worth visiting.

The colossal reclining Buddha statue at the Kyauk Htat Gyi Pagoda

Getting Around

Taxis are inexpensive and only difficult to come by during rush hour. Trishaws are still common, though losing ground to motorcycle taxis. Buses cover all of Yangon, but for non-Burmese speakers they are not an easy option – there are no route maps; numbers and destinations are written in Burmese; and while cheap, services are usually very crowded. Given the heat, traffic, and distances, walking can be tiring, except in the markets and colonial district, which are best explored on foot.

Sights at a Glance

Temples, Pagodas, and Tombs

- ❶ Sule Pagoda
- ❺ Botataung Pagoda
- ❼ Bahadur Shah Zafar's Dargah
- ❽ Maha Wizaya Pagoda
- ❾ *Shwedagon Pagoda pp74–7*
- ⓫ Nga Htat Gyi Pagoda
- ⓬ Kyauk Htat Gyi Pagoda
- ⓮ Koe Htat Gyi Pagoda
- ⓰ Kaba Aye Pagoda
- ⓱ Lawka Chantha Abhaya Labha Muni

Towns

- ⓳ Thanlyin
- ⓴ Kyauktan

Museums and Historic Sights and Buildings

- ❷ City Hall
- ❹ Strand Hotel
- ❻ National Museum
- ❿ Martyrs' Mausoleum
- ㉑ Taukkyan War Cemetery

Parks and Lakes

- ❸ Mahabandula Garden
- ⓭ Kandawgyi Lake
- ⓯ Inya Lake
- ⓲ White Elephant Pagoda
- ㉒ Hlawga National Park

Worshippers praying under the vividly painted ceiling of the Maha Wizaya Pagoda

For hotels and restaurants in this region see p202 and pp210–11

Buddhist nuns feeding terrapins at the Botataung Pagoda

Greater Yangon

Hlawga Lake

Mingaladon

East Dagon

Insein

Yangon Mingaladon

Mayangone

Thingangyun

YANGON

Thaketa

Dala

Thanlyin

Yangon River

Kyauktan

0 kilometers   10

0 miles   10

Key

Area of the main map

Main road

Other road

Railroad

LANTHIT ROAD

OAK KALA ROAD

INSEIN BUTA KYON ROAD

INSEIN ⑰

⑱

E GYO GONE ST

TAW WIN RD

MINGHAMMA ROAD

MYANMAR GOLF CLUB

THUDHAMMA ROAD

Tadalay

INSEIN ROAD

KYAIK WAING PA GODA ROAD

SWE TAW MYAT RD

PYAY ROAD

Yaegu

WAI ZA YAN TAR ROAD

HLAING

MAYANGONE

AMAING BUTAR YONE ROAD

PARAMI ROAD

⑯

KABA AYE

PARAMI ROAD

Oakkyin

BAHO ROAD

PARAMI ROAD

INSEIN ROAD

THANINE COLLEGE ST

YAN GYI KYAUNG ST

PAGODA ROAD

Parami

Thiri Myaing

BAYINT NAUNG ROAD

Kamayut

STATION

ROAD

PYAY ROAD

INYA ROAD

Inya Lake

⑮

KANBE ROAD

Kanbe

YANKIN

AUNG ZE YA ROAD

Hledan

HLEDAN RD

University of Yangon

UNIVERSITY AVENUE

KABA AYE PAGODA ROAD

WAI ZA YAN TAR ROAD

Bauk htaw

KAMAYUT

PYAY ROAD

INYA ROAD

INYA MYAING RD

THALLWIN RD

U CHIT MANG RD

E RACE COURSE RD

Hanthawaddy

HANTHAWADDY RD

SAN CHAUNG

BAHAN

SHWEGONDAING RD

THA MEIN BA YAN RD

Tamwe

TAMWE

Kyee Myin Daing

KYEE MYIN DAING KYEE MYIN DAING KANNER RD

LOWER KYEE MYIN DAING RD

BAGAYAR RD

BAHO ROAD

U WISARA ROAD

DHAMMAZEDI RD

⑫

⑪

ZOOLOGICAL GARDEN ST

Myittar Nyunt

⑭

PYAY ROAD

⑩

NAT MAUK ST

NYA BANYA DALA RD

KYAIK WAING RD

Ma Hlwa Kone

Pan Hlaing

⑨

⑬

UPPER PAZUNDAUNG RD

Ahlone Rd

SHWEDAGON PAGODA RD

⑧

Kandawgyi Lake

KAN YEIK THA

MINGALAR TAUNG NYUNT

⑥

⑦

Pazundaung

DAGON

Shan Rd

AHLONE

Pyay Rd

Lanmadaw

Phaya Lan

Yangon Central

LANMADAW

PHONE GYI STREET

LANMADAW ST

BOGYOKE AUNG

ANAWRAHTA

SAN PYA ROAD

THEIN PHYU ROAD

PAZUNDAUNG

②

MAHABANDULA ROAD

①

③

ROAD

MERCHANT ROAD

BOTATAUNG PAGODA ROAD

Pazundaung River

Pazundaung River

STRAND ROAD

④

STRAND ROAD

⑤

BOTATAUNG

Hlaing River

0 km   1

0 miles   1

For additional map symbols *see back flap*

Street by Street: the Colonial Quarter

Following the Third Anglo-Burmese War of 1885, the colonial capital on the banks of the Yangon River witnessed a dramatic building boom, with the Sule Pagoda its centerpiece and the riverfront its grandiloquent gateway. Today, this group of late-19th- and early-20th-century buildings in downtown Yangon is the largest of its kind in the world, a miraculous vestige of the era when old Rangoon was one of Asia's most affluent, cosmopolitan cities. However, after decades of neglect, several of the once grand edifices have become derelict, and the 2011 move of the Myanmar government to Naypyitaw has left many of them empty. In recent years, dozens of century-old structures have also been demolished to make way for modern concrete blocks.

Mohinga stalls

Shwedagon Pagoda & train station

❶ ★ Sule Pagoda
The gilded linchpin of Yangon cuts a striking silhouette in the center of a busy intersection. Uniquely, the stupa's octagonal layers extend to the bell section, which is normally smoothly curved.

❸ ★ Mahabandula Garden
Originally called Fytche Square after Lieutenant-General Albert Fytche, a 19th-century Chief Commissioner of Burma, this memorial park near the Sule Pagoda forms a peaceful enclave in the heart of downtown.

Yangon Division Court

Customs House

Colonial buildings
Many of Yangon's once grand colonial buildings are now dilapidated, with weed-choked flaking facades, while squatters occupy former department stores, banks, and government offices.

SULE PAGODA ROAD

BANK ST

MAHABANDULA GARDEN ST

MERCHA

MAHABANDULA

STRAND ROAD

Hlaing River

Key
— Suggested route

Pansodan Jetty

❷ ★ City Hall
This was among the first large civic buildings in the former capital designed by a Burmese architect, and the style is noticeably more vernacular than that of earlier British-era landmarks.

Samosa stalls

Myanmar Travels and Tours (MTT)

0 meters 100
0 yards 100

Immanuel Baptist Church
This 1830 church is one of Yangon's oldest. The Baptist faith was brought to Burma by American missionaries in 1812 and still has a fervent following among the Karen.

PANSODAN STREET

MAHABANDULA ROAD

★ High Court
The Queen Anne-style building, formerly the High Court, was completed in 1911, and with its municipal red-brick facade and lofty clock tower epitomizes the pomposity of the Raj at its height.

38TH STREET

SEIKKANTHA STREET

39TH ST

BO AUNG KYAW ST

British Embassy

❹ ★ Strand Hotel
After years of neglect during the post-colonial period, Yangon's most prestigious hotel was restored to an immaculate state by Burmese and Indonesian entrepreneurs.

Australian Embassy

Botataung Pagoda

● Sule Pagoda

City Map D5. Junction of Sule Pagoda Rd and Mahabandula Rd.
Yangon Central Train Station.
Mahabandula Park Terminus.
Open 5am–9pm daily.

Hundreds, and possibly thousands, of years before the British set out their orderly trellis of streets around it, the Sule Pagoda served as an important place of pilgrimage and worship. Buddhist legend asserts that its central stupa encloses a sacred hair of the historic Buddha, Gautama, and that it was founded in 230 BC by Sona and Uttara, a pair of missionary monks dispatched from India to the court of nearby Thaton. The pagoda's name, however, most likely derives from that of Sulerata, the guardian spirit of the site, who is said to have guided the monks to nearby Singuttara Hill, where three other hairs of the Buddha were enshrined and which is now the site of the Shwedagon Pagoda.

Whatever the actual origins of the monument, it was certainly reconstructed several times before the Mon Queen Shin Sawbu of Pegu-Hanthawaddy (1394–1471) had the central

zedi (stupa) enlarged to its present height of 144 ft (44 m). The stupa is unusual for the fact that its octagonal layers encompass the normally smoothly curved bell section.

The pagoda's central position, at the hub of Lt. Alexander Fraser's colonial-era street layout, make it the city's most prominent landmark after the Shwedagon Pagoda *(see pp74–7)*, which explains why it has played such an important role in Myanmar's political life. During the pro-democracy demonstrations of 1988 and 2007, the intersection that surrounds it was the scene of bloody encounters between scores of unarmed protesters and the Tatmadaw (military).

Dwarfed by the phalanx of skyscrapers surrounding it, the pagoda is ringed by Internet cafés, print studios, and dozens of shops; the four entrances lie at the cardinal points, aligned with the main streets. The best vantage point overlooking the pagoda is the Sky Bar at the top of the Sakura Tower, located a few blocks north on Sule Pagoda Road, from where the view of the *zedi* is particularly striking after dark.

The massive City Hall, built in a fusion of British and Burmese styles

● City Hall

City Map D5. Mahabandula Rd.
Mahabandula Park Terminus.
Closed to the public.

Located to the northeast of the Sule Pagoda, City Hall dates from the 1920s and ranks among the more grandiose edifices erected by the British. Its design, by the Burmese architect U Tin, incorporates traditional Myanmar motifs, such as multitiered roof pagodas *(pyatthats)*, peacocks, lotus flowers, and serpents, while somehow retaining the stolid appearance of a typical British municipal building. The focus of many mass demonstrations since the 1960s, it has in recent years been the target of a succession of bomb attacks.

The richly gilded Sule Pagoda rising from a busy intersection at the heart of Yangon

The elegant lobby of the colonial-style Strand Hotel

❸ Mahabandula Garden

City Map D5. Sule Pagoda Rd.
🚌 Mahabandula Park Terminus.
Open daily. ♿

Facing the City Hall is a small park named after the hero of the First Anglo-Burmese War, General Mahabandula, who masterminded a valiant, but ultimately unsuccessful, resistance to the British invasion of 1824. The defense ended after the general was killed by a mortar shell while parading around the front line dressed in full regalia under a gilded parasol to boost the morale of his men. The obelisk at the center of the park is a memorial to those who died in Burma's 20th-century independence struggle. Early morning is the best time to visit, when the neatly cropped, flower-lined lawns are sprinkled with serene Tai Chi practitioners.

Mahabandula Garden, offering a pleasant respite from the city's bustle

❹ Strand Hotel

City Map E5. 92 Strand Rd.
Tel (01) 243377. 🚌 Bogalay Zay, 650 ft (200 m) SE. ♿ ✏ 🖥 📷
W hotelthestrand.com

Since its gala opening in 1901, the Strand has served as the city's most prestigious hotel – frequently mentioned in the same breath as the Taj Mahal Palace in Mumbai, Raffles of Singapore, and the Eastern & Oriental in Penang – although one with a checkered history. It was originally the creation of the famed Sarkies brothers, Armenian entrepreneurs who were the first to recognize the need for luxury accommodations in Rangoon after the opening of the Suez Canal. During its colonial heyday, the Strand was visited by and immortalized in the writings of Somerset Maugham, Rudyard Kipling, and George Orwell. The hotel went into sharp decline following Burmese independence in 1948, and was only restored in the mid-1990s.

Elegant teak and marble floors, mahogany and rattan furniture, paddle fans, and the absence of a swimming pool or a modern wing preserve the Raj-era ambience and charm. It is worth sampling the hotel's timeless atmosphere over high tea in the famous Strand Café, accompanied by the soothing strains of the *saung gauk* (the traditional Burmese harp) and the xylophone.

❺ Botataung Pagoda

City Map F5. Strand Rd, 10 min walk E of the Strand Hotel. 🚌 Botataung Pagoda stop. **Open** 5am–9:30pm daily. 🎆 📷 Nov/Dec: annual pagoda festival in the month of Nadaw.

The beautiful Botataung Pagoda is revered by Buddhists as the resting place of some of the country's most sacred relics. Two millennia ago, all eight of the Buddha's hairs said to have been brought to Burma from India during his lifetime were kept here, protected by a 1,000-strong armed guard – in old Mon, *bo* means "soldier," and *tataung* "one thousand." Only one hair remained which, alongside many other precious objects, was secreted inside the stupa until the building was hit by a bomb during World War II. Reconstruction work revealed precious reliquaries, with one containing pieces of bone and a single strand of hair. These are now installed in the golden *zedi*'s hollow interior.

Built in classic Mon style, the new 131-ft (40-m) high bell-shaped stupa has a shining coat of gold leaf. Planetary shrines mark the cardinal points, while a side hall houses a gilded bronze Konbaung-era Buddha, which originally sat inside Mandalay's famous Glass Palace. Carried off to London after the British invasion of 1885, it was returned to Burma in 1951.

Gilded Buddha at the Botataung Pagoda, one of Yangon's main pagodas

Statue of King Bayinnaung of the Taungoo Dynasty outside Yangon's National Museum

❻ National Museum

City Map C3. 66/74 Pyay Rd, Dagon Township. **Tel** (01) 2825634. 🚌 Pegu Club stop. **Open** 10am–4pm daily. 📷 ✉ 📷

A short taxi ride north of Yangon's downtown area, the National Museum is an essential stop on any city tour. Despite the poor lighting and labeling, it is worth visiting just to see the resplendent *Sihasana*, or Lion Throne, of the Konbaung Dynasty, housed in a gallery on the first floor. Less a seat than a raised ceremonial doorway on which Mindon and Thibaw used to preside over audiences with their courtiers and ministers at Mandalay Palace *(see pp144–5)*, the sumptuously gilded and richly carved object is topped with flaring ornaments inspired by the shape of ox horns. Divine

beings, astrological symbols, floral motifs, glass mosaic, and the eponymous lions feature in the elaborate decoration, which was intended to express the links between the monarch and the heavenly realm of Thagyamin, the king of the *nats* (nature spirits). Sealed in glass cases around the edges of the gallery are miniature reproductions of the other thrones that once adorned the halls of Mandalay Palace.

Displays of jewel-encrusted courtly regalia in an adjacent gallery underline just how ornate and refined Konbaung culture was at the twilight of the Yadanabon era in late-19th-century Mandalay.

Standout exhibits in the Prehistory Hall on the second floor include treasures found at the archeological site of Sri

Ksetra *(see pp98–9)*, including silver reliquaries, carved votive tablets, and a group of exquisite bronze figurines of musicians, dancers, and clowns, rare survivors from the Pyu civilization (1st century BC–9th century AD). The third floor has traditional puppets and musical instruments, including a magnificent *hsaing waing* ensemble and a couple of superbly decorated *saung gauk*, or Burmese harps. The fourth floor holds a dimly lit but fine collection of ancient gold and silver jewelry, while the uppermost floor has a collection of Buddha images spanning 1,500 years of Burmese history, along with costumes from Myanmar's ethnic minorities.

❼ Bahadur Shah Zafar's Dargah

City Map D3. Zi Wa Ka St, off U Wisara Rd. 🚌 No. 43 from Sule Pagoda to the Shwedagon Pagoda South Gate stop. **Open** 8am–8pm daily.

Tucked away down a residential side street is the final resting place of Bahadur Shah Zafar II, the last Mughal emperor of India, whom the British deposed and exiled to Rangoon following the great Indian uprising of 1857. Held under house arrest with his wife, Begum Zeenat Mahal, and other family members, the former ruler survived only four years of imprisonment.

Upon his death in 1862, his body was hastily interred in an unmarked grave in the garden, a move which the British

Bahadur Shah Zafar's mausoleum, a place of pilgrimage for Myanmar's Indian Muslims

officials at the time vainly hoped would discourage pilgrims. A *dargah* (mausoleum) was eventually constructed on the site of the old house, but the location of the grave remained unknown. It was only in 1991, when workers were digging trenches for a new building on the site, that a brick structure was found 3.5 ft (1 m) below the surface containing the graves of Bahadur Shah and his wife and grandson. The spot has since been enshrined in a style more befitting a monarch renowned to this day as a polymath, fine calligrapher, inspired poet, and Sufi mystic: with a covering of gilt-edged silk and a scattering of fragrant rose petals.

The exterior of the Maha Wizaya Pagoda, with its 11-tiered *hti* (finial)

Sufi musicians performing at the *dargah* of Bahadur Shah Zafar II in Yangon

❾ Maha Wizaya Pagoda

City Map D3. opposite Shwedagon Pagoda's south entrance. 🚌 No. 43 from Sule Pagoda to the Shwedagon Pagoda South Gate stop. **Open** daily.

This plain, though finely proportioned, modern stupa, located opposite the southern stairway of the Shwedagon Pagoda on the other side of U Htaung Bo Road, was built in 1980 using public donations. It celebrated the unification of all of the country's Theravada Buddhist monastic orders under one supervisory body.

The king and queen of Nepal donated sacred relics from their personal collection for the relic chamber. They also gifted the main image for the circular central shrine inside the main stupa. The rotunda's domed ceiling has vivid murals and painted stuccowork depicting episodes from the life and enlightenment of the Buddha.

The splendid *hti* (finial) that crowns the structure consists of 11 tiers – two more than the nearby Shwedagon Pagoda – and was gifted to the stupa by Burma's former military dictator, General Ne Win.

India's Last Mughal

An undistinguished wooden house on the northern fringes of Rangoon is a far cry from the splendor of Delhi's Red Fort. But this is where the deposed Mughal emperor of India, Bahadur Shah Zafar II, spent the last few years of his life, stripped of his riches and privileges, without even a pen to write his beloved Urdu poetry. The indignity was his punishment for his role in the events of 1857, when a force of *sepoys* (Indian soldiers) rose up against their British overlords. By the time the rebellion was suppressed, hundreds of thousands had lost their lives and the magnificent Mughal capital, with its refined Sufi-inspired culture, had been reduced to ruins. Recounted in William Dalrymple's *The Last Mughal*, the role Bahadur Shah actually played was more of a bewildered,

Portrait of the Mughal emperor Bahadur Shah Zafar II, c. 1838

reluctant puppet than a steely warlord. Manipulated into supporting a war for which he had no stomach by an army who had no respect for his rule, the emperor looked on powerlessly as the terrible events of 1857 unfolded, and paid a high price for his acquiescence. At his trial, British prosecutors implicated him in the events of what was called the Great Mutiny by some historians and the War of Independence by others. Bahadur Shah's sentence was exile, and he was sent to Rangoon with the surviving members of his family. There, attended by his wife Zeenat Mahal, he spent his last days writing despairing verses on the walls of his prison with lumps of charcoal. Since his death, his *dargah* has become a place of pilgrimage for Myanmar's Indian Muslims, while his poetry continues to be read across South Asia.

Shwedagon Pagoda

The chimeric Shwedagon Pagoda is Myanmar's most sacred Buddhist shrine. At 325 ft (99 m), the stupa dominates Yangon's skyline, and looms even larger in the consciousness of the country's Buddhists. No site is more revered, nor visited in such numbers. Legend says that the shrine encloses the relics of four Buddhas, including eight hairs of Gautama believed to have been brought here during his lifetime. Successive rulers enlarged and embellished the complex, adding countless shrines, halls, and lesser stupas. Despite earthquake damage and several acts of vandalism by colonial invaders, it has been lovingly restored several times and today looks resplendent.

The Shwedagon Pagoda at dusk, with its gently glowing gilded surfaces

Eastern Devotional Hall holding a Kakusandha Buddha statue

★ **Maha Tissada Bell**
King Tharrawaddy (1787–1846) had this 80,000-lb (36,000-kg) bell cast in 1841. The ceiling of its pavilion is made of superb lacquerwork that is inlaid with glass mosaic.

KEY

① **The Naungdawgyi Pagoda** was built where the Buddha's hairs were kept before being placed in the stupa.

② **The Mahabodhi Pagoda**, a replica of its namesake in Bodh Gaya, India, where the Buddha achieved enlightenment, is noticeably different in style from the other structures.

③ **The Bo Bo Aung shrine** is believed to have been created by a wizard with miraculous powers.

④ **The ruby-eyed Tawa Gu Buddha** is one of the nine miracle-working wonders of the pagoda.

⑤ **The banana bud** is covered with more than 13,000 solid gold plates, unlike the lower parts of the stupa, which are covered in gold leaf.

⑥ **The octagonal upper terrraces** are only open to monks.

⑦ **64 pagodas** encircle the stupa, eight for each *bo bo gyi*, or planetary post (*see p33*).

⑧ **The Maha Gandha Bell**, cast in 1779, was raised in 1825 from the Yangon River, into which it had fallen during a British attempt to steal it.

Northern Devotional Hall
A statue of the historical Buddha, Gautama, is enshrined in the northern devotional hall, which is flanked by the planetary posts for Venus.

★ Southern Entrance and Devotional Hall
This chamber is centered on a statue of Konagamana, second of the five Buddhas of the present era. Its roof has some exceptional iron tracery work.

VISITORS' CHECKLIST

Practical Information
City Map C2. Singuttara Hill, 2.5 miles (4 km) N of Sule Pagoda.
Open 4am–10pm daily.
via elevators at the south gate; the east also has elevators; the west has an escalator.
Mar: annual pagoda festival.
shwedagonpagoda.com

Transport
Yangon Mingaladon.
No. 43 from Sule Pagoda.

Memorial honoring the 1920 student uprising that led to the Independence struggle

Rakhine Tazaung
Commissioned by two wealthy Arakanese traders, this hall has some wonderfully intricate wood carving on its eaves and a large reclining Buddha inside.

Western Devotional Hall featuring a statue of the Kassapa Buddha

The *Sein Bu*

The topmost point of the Shwedagon Pagoda, the *sein bu* or "diamond bud" crowning the tip of the spire, is set with a priceless 76-carat diamond. The gem refracts the sun's rays into rainbow colors on the terrace below that change as the viewer steps forward and back at a certain spot of about 6.5 ft (2 m) in length, which local guides and monks identify for visitors.

0 meters 50
0 yards 50

Mahabodhi Tree, grown from a cutting of the original banyan in Bodh Gaya, India

★ Wish Fulfilling Place
Devotees kneel and pray facing the great stupa at this star-shaped open space in the belief their wishes will be granted. The view of the stupa from here is the finest in the complex.

Exploring the Shwedagon Pagoda

Thousands of visitors stream through the Shwedagon Pagoda every day to pray at the shrines clustered around its base. Approaching from one of the four principal stairways, the majority proceed in a clockwise direction, pausing to make offerings at various landmarks along the way, or to savor the spectacle of the great stupa from the shaded comfort of the covered halls encircling the marble-lined middle terrace. The atmosphere is especially intense at dusk, when the crowds peak, red-robed monks encircle the upper tiers of the golden spire, the air is filled with the scent of incense and candles, and the gilded *zedi* glows an ethereal color. Dress codes apply (no shorts, miniskirts, or plunging necklines), but otherwise the mood is surprisingly relaxed and inclusive for a place of such religious significance – a testament to the tolerant, hospitable nature of the Burmese.

The Mahabodhi Tree, grown from a cutting of the tree under which the Buddha sat

🏚 The *Zaungdan*

The great stupa and its surrounding terrace may be approached via four different covered stairways, or *zaungdan*, aligned with the cardinal points. Each is lined with stalls selling religious paraphernalia, floral offerings, incense, Buddhas, colored flags, streamers, souvenirs, and other curios, but they all have a slightly different feel. Damaged by fire in 1931, the western stairway leading from the People's Park is the most modern, with new escalators and a pair of giant shiny *chinthe*, or leogryphs. The northern approach dates from 1460 and has 128 steps, while the eastern one, a continuation of Bahan Bazaar, has the most traditional ambience, due to the elaborate wood carving and paintwork of its pillars and roofs. This entrance has an elevator. The southern stairway, leading up from the city side of the monument, also has an elevator and tends to be the busiest of all, especially in the evenings and on weekends.

🏛 The Middle Terrace

Emerging for the first time from the entrance halls to the glare of white marble and gold of Shwedagon's Middle Terrace is an experience few visitors forget. The principal monument, towering ahead, is surrounded by a forest of elaborately gilded and decorated subsidiary stupas, shrines, and pavilions (*tazaung*), ranged around a processional walkway built in the 15th century by the Mon kings, who leveled the top of Singuttara Hill for the purpose. Worshippers generally proceed in an auspicious clockwise direction (*let ya yit*), replicating the movement of the heavens.

The first stop is usually the *bo bo gyi* or planetary post corresponding to the day of their birth (*see p33*). Eight in total – Burmese astrology recognizes eight days, with Wednesday divided into two – these take the form of little white Buddha statues to which devotees offer water, flowers, and paper umbrellas. Each day is associated with a different animal, represented beneath the statue: a winged gryphon for Sunday, tiger for Monday, lion for Tuesday, tusked

One of the Shwedagon Pagoda's four massive stairways, or *zaungdan*, lined with a variety of shops and stalls

The Shwedagon Pagoda's Middle Terrace, with elaborately decorated subsidiary shrines

Naypyitaw, where the ruling generals built an exact replica on the outskirts of the capital.

The arresting spectacle of the golden tower soaring from the summit of Singuttara Hill astonished the British troops who used the complex as a cannon emplacement in the Anglo-Burmese Wars of 1824 and 1852, although this didn't stop them from pillaging the shrines in search of treasure and attempting (unsuccessfully) to carry off the great Maha Gandha bell to be melted down for cannonballs.

In modern times, the pagoda has served as a rallying point for the pro-democracy struggle. Aung San Suu Kyi addressed a massive crowd here in 1988 during the uprising of that year, and in 2007 the stupa was occupied by protesting monks during the Saffron Revolution.

elephant for Wednesday morning, tuskless elephant for Wednesday afternoon, mouse for Thursday, guinea pig for Friday, and mythical dragon-serpent for Saturday. The larger statues behind are the planetary posts' guardian spirits, or *nats*.

Other popular sites around the Middle Terrace are the Nine Wonders of the Shwedagon: mostly miracle-working statues of Buddhas, saints, wizards, and necromancers believed to be capable of creating beneficial, or counter-acting malevolent, spells. In the evening, hundreds of people file between them, then kneel at the open court to the northwest of the enclosure, known as the Wish Fulfilling Place, to murmur prayers and prostrate themselves before the stupa. Often there are also large family groups attending their children's *shin pyu* or coming-of-age ceremony, the children dressed in white silk suits and wearing elaborately sequined hats on their heads, and their elders sporting the finest silk *longyis* and *htameins*.

As the stupa's floodlights are illuminated after sunset, thousands of candles and bundles of incense are lit at the table lining the base of the monument, filling the air with fragrant smoke.

🔟 The Great Stupa
Originally built to enshrine eight hairs of the Buddha, along with other precious relics, the great stupa is believed by Myanmar Buddhists to be 2,500 years old,

although archeologists maintain that it more probably dates from the Mon era of the 4th–9th centuries AD. Earthquakes and fires have toppled the mighty tower on several occasions, leading to ever larger and more beautiful reconstructions. Queen Shin Sawbu of Pegu-Hanthawaddy (1394–1471) first covered the stupa in gold leaf, donating her own body weight in gold for the purpose. She was later outdone by her son-in-law, King Dhammazedi, who gave four times his weight, plus that of his wife, to re-clad the stupa. Its present imposing height of 325 ft (99 m), though, was achieved only in 1769.

The pagoda's design follows a standard Burmese archetype (*see pp32–3*), which has since been often copied throughout the country, most recently in

The beautifully illuminated *zedi* (stupa) of the Shwedagon Pagoda

The Legend of the Shwedagon Pagoda

A much-loved Burmese legend attributes the foundation of the stupa to the brothers Pu and Tapaw, also known as Tapusa and Hpalika, who were once sent to India by their father, a rich merchant, to buy rice for famine victims in Bengal. While traveling along the Ganges, they were taken to meet the Buddha and became his disciples. On hearing the brothers were from Okkalapa (west of Yangon), the Buddha asked them to take back eight hairs from his head and bury them with relics of his predecessors secreted under a tree at Singuttara Hill. The 27-ft (8-m) tall *zedi* they built on the hilltop to encase the relics is recorded in ancient inscriptions as dating from 588 BC. It is quite possible that the hairs, the gold casket holding them, and the original stupa lie below the present structure, but no one is ever likely to find out, there being a strict taboo against excavation work on the site.

Gilded Buddha

❿ Martyrs' Mausoleum

City Map C2. Arzani St, near North Gate of Shwedagon Pagoda.
No. 43 from Sule Pagoda to Shwedagon Pagoda North Gate.
Open 8am–6pm Tue–Sun.

In a wooded park just north of the Shwedagon Pagoda, on the far side of Arzani Street, stands the Martyrs' Mausoleum. It was erected in honor of General Aung San, the first leader of independent Burma, and six of his ministerial colleagues, who were assassinated while holding a cabinet meeting of the interim government in 1947. Each year on July 19, the anniversary of the attack, the country's leaders gather in the park to lay wreaths at the curved red wall on its southern side. General Aung San's daughter, pro-democracy leader and Nobel laureate Aung San Suu Kyi, has attended the ceremony since her release from house arrest in 2010. She was only two years old at the time of her father's death; he was 32. The gunmen, along with U Saw, the rival politician who allegedly masterminded the killings, were captured and hanged the following year. Other than the iconic red wall, set on a raised marble terrace amid manicured lawns and landscaped grounds, there is little to see here, although the site is an atmospheric one.

Nga Htat Gyi Pagoda's Buddha, seated against a grand carved wood backdrop

⓫ Nga Htat Gyi Pagoda

City Map E1. Shwegondaing Rd.
Bandarpin stop, Shwegondaing Rd. **Open** 7am–10pm daily.

One of Myanmar's most imposing seated Buddhas resides in a temple crowning a low hill a short taxi ride to the northeast of the Shwedagon Pagoda. Sometimes called the "Five-Story Buddha," the pale-faced statue dates from 1558, although the polished hall in which he rests was built only in the 1930s. As well as his richly bejeweled crown and intricately carved golden robes, the figure is famous for the ornate, flame-like armor that emanates from his body, and the sumptuous carved wood backdrop against which he sits. Glass windows set in the raised ceiling above his head illuminate the Buddha to superb effect.

⓬ Kyauk Htat Gyi Pagoda

City Map E1. Shwegondaing Rd.
Kyauk Htat Gyi (or Chauk Htat Gyi) stop, Shwegondaing Rd.
Open 7am–10pm daily.

A bit further up Shwegondaing Road is a less well known temple housing a colossal reclining Buddha. Constructed in 1966 using funds donated by a wealthy local businessman, the 230-ft (70-m) tall figure rests in a vast hangar made of red corrugated iron and steel girders. A stepped platform at its northern end provides a useful vantage point from which to view the Buddha's giant feet, divided into squares and inscribed with 108 auspicious symbols. The adjoining monastic complex is home to around 500 monks and also holds a renowned Vipassana meditation center.

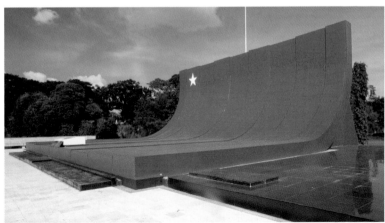

Martyrs' Mausoleum, commemorating the deaths of seven independence heroes including General Aung San

For hotels and restaurants in this region see p202 and pp210–11

⓭ Kandawgyi Lake

City Map E3. Kan Yeik Tha Rd/Bahan Rd, Dagon Tsp. 🚌 3 St on Bahan Rd. **Open** daily. 🎐 Nov: annual regatta.

Convoluted Kandawgyi Lake forms a refreshing oasis in the heart of the city. It is a 20-minute walk east of the Shwedagon Pagoda, whose gilded profile is reflected to dramatic effect in its shimmering waters. Created by the British as a source of clean water for Yangon, it is fed by Inya Lake (*see p80*) to the north and is only a few feet deep. Kandawgyi means "Royal Lake," and its elegant wooden walkways and bridges resting on stilts in the water are popular places for an evening stroll. In November, leg rowers from across the country descend on the lake to race in the annual regatta, sponsored by the government. The road skirting the southern shore of the lake, site of a luxury hotel, also hosts large, decorated pavilions during the Thingyan water festival celebrations in April. In 2010, ahead of the national elections, the festivities here were marred by a triple bomb attack in which nine people lost their lives and more than 60 were injured.

The leafiest area of Kandawgyi Lake is along its northern shore, encompassed by the **Bogyoke Aung San Park**. This public garden is laid out around the two-story former home of General Aung San and his wife Daw Khin Kyi; it now holds a small museum dedicated to the memory of the man who was the architect of Burmese

The iconic Karaweik Palace, modeled on the royal barges of the Konbaung kings

independence. A bronze statue of Aung San stands at the entrance to the gardens.

The lake's southeastern shore is the site of the **Kandawgyi Nature Park**, a massive sprawl of woodland encompassing walkways, children's play enclosures, picnic areas, a mini zoo, and cafés. Crowded with young families during the daytime, it becomes a party zone during the evening, where the city's young, hip, and rich come to eat, drink, and relax with the rippling reflection of the floodlit Shwedagon as a backdrop.

Inside the nature park, the most iconic landmark on the lake is the somewhat surreal **Karaweik Palace**, a giant, bird-shaped edifice seemingly afloat on the water. It was built by the government in the 1970s to resemble the royal barges on which the Konbaung kings used to travel on the Ayeyarwady River, complete with multitiered

roof and mythic Hindu *karaweik* birds. The sumptuous interior holds a restaurant, handicrafts emporia, and a performance space where shows of traditional Burmese music and dance are staged most nights for visiting tour groups.

🏛 **Bogyoke Aung San Park**
15, Bogyoke Museum Lane, Natmauk Rd, Bahan Township. **Open** 9am–5pm daily. 🚻 ♿ 🖥

🏛 **Kandawgyi Nature Park**
Kan Yeik Tha Rd, Bahan Tsp. **Open** 6am–10pm daily. 🚻 ♿ 🍴 🖥

🏯 **Karaweik Palace**
Kandawgyi Nature Park, Kandawgyi Lake. **Open** noon–10pm daily. 🚻 ♿ 🍴 🌐 **karaweikpalace.com**

⓮ Koe Htat Gyi Pagoda

City Map A2. Bagayar Rd. 🚌 Koe Htat Gyi stop on Bagayar Rd. **Open** 6am–8pm daily.

Famed for his eerily life-like eyes, the huge Koe Htat Gyi – which translates literally as "Nine-Story Buddha" – sits within an airy corrugated-iron structure with a traditional nine-tiered roof on Bagayar Road, not far from the east bank of the Hlaing River in central Yangon. The Buddha, dating from 1905, measures 72 ft (22 m) from head to toe. His famous eyes, made from blown glass, gaze impassively into space from beneath a beautifully decorated gold and black ceiling.

The leafy shores of Yangon's serene Kandawgyi Lake

The tree-lined shores of Inya Lake, a popular spot with residents of Yangon

⓱ Inya Lake

West Yankin/Sin Way Tin/Lava Hill Tsp.
🚌 Kaba Aye Pagoda Rd stop. **Open**
daily. 🚻 ♿ 📷 🎫 Feb: Irrawaddy
Literature Festival, Inya Lake Hotel.

The main source of water for
the city of Yangon, Inya Lake is
a sprawling reservoir originally
laid out by the British in 1882
beyond what was then the
northern edge of the city, but
which has long since been
subsumed by residential neighborhoods. Lying approximately
6 miles (10 km) from the downtown area, Inya Lake is the site
of the city's university campus,
the US Embassy, and a string of
exclusive waterfront properties.
Among the latter are the residence of General Ne Win and
the much photographed home
of Aung San Suu Kyi, where she
spent many years under house
arrest prior to her release in
2010. Her residence was one

of many built to accommodate
high-ranking British officials in
the colonial era, and which now
constitute some of Southeast
Asia's most valuable real estate.

Yangon University's campus
once held classes for all categories of students, although it
is almost empty today. Only
graduate studies are conducted
here, with undergraduates having been dispersed in the 1990s
to newer institutions on the
fringes of the city to disrupt
possible student activism.

Lining the southern shore of
the lake near the university is
the 37-acre (15-ha) **Inya Lake
Park** with floral displays set out
on sloping embankments.
Featured in countless Burmese
movies, the location is a favorite
with young couples and has
long been emblematic of love
and romance in the popular
imagination. In stark contrast,
the **White Bridge** (Tada Phyu),

abutting the western shore of
the lake, is synonymous with
the brutality of the military
government. In March 1988,
hundreds of student protesters
were gunned down or drowned
by security police after being
trapped between barbed wire
barricades, the lake, and nearby
houses. This incident fueled
support for nationwide demonstrations and the start of the
8888 Uprising a few months
later (so named because it took
place on August 8, 1988). The
tragedy is commemorated by
Burmese dissidents as Red
Bridge Day, referring to the
blood which is said to have
stained the walkway.

⓲ Kaba Aye Pagoda

Kaba Aye Pagoda Road,
Chawdwingone District. 🚌 Kaba
Aye stop, Kaba Aye Pagoda Road.
Open 6am–8pm daily. 🎫 Jun: Kaba
Aye scripture recitation.

This unusual pagoda northeast
of Inya Lake was built by U Nu,
the first prime minister of independent Burma, in the 1950s
ahead of the Sixth Buddhist
Synod. Enshrined inside its main
temple are the relics of two of
the Buddha's principal disciples,
presented to the Myanmar
government by the British
Museum, where they had been
deposited in 1854 as war plunder. Around 1,100 lb (500 kg) of
silver was used in the creation

Entrance to the Yangon University campus at Inya Lake

For hotels and restaurants in this region see p202 and pp210–11

Buddha statues seated against the great hollow central pillar of the Kaba Aye Pagoda

Mindhamma Hill, where it now stands as one of the city's best loved religious destinations. The statue can easily be visited en route to or from the nearby Mingaladon International Airport, or from guesthouses or hotels in the north of the city.

⑱ White Elephant Pagoda

Mindhamma Road, opposite the Lawka Chantha Abhaya Labha Muni, Insein Township. 🚆 Insein Station, Yangon Circular Railway. 🚌 Sawbwar Gyi Kone stop on Pyay Road. **Open** 9am–5pm daily.

of the central image in the inner shrine. Dozens more statues adorn the rest of the complex.

In the pagoda's grounds, and also built for the Sixth Synod of 1954, is the **Mahapasana Guha**, a cavernous structure intended to resemble the cave in India where the First Buddhist Synod was convened shortly after the death of the historic Buddha, Gautama. It holds an enormous assembly hall capable of accommodating 10,000 worshippers and is said to have been built by volunteers in only three days and nights.

⑰ Lawka Chantha Abhaya Labha Muni

Mindhamma Road, Insein Township. 🚆 Insein Station, Yangon Circular Railway. 🚌 Sawbwar Gyi Kone stop, Pyay Rd. **Open** 6am–9pm daily.

Throughout history, Burmese kings have considered boulders of flawless white marble particularly auspicious material from which to sculpt monumental Buddhas. In 1998, when an exceptionally large one came to light at the Sangyin quarry, 21 miles (34 km) north of Mandalay, the government lost no time in commissioning the country's most acclaimed religious sculptor, U Taw Taw, to produce a statue. It took the artist over a year to complete the Buddha, which measures 37 ft (11 m) from head to toe and weighs 600 tonnes.

The colossal Lawka Chantha Abhaya Labha Muni is now housed in a glass-sided shrine atop Mindhamma Hill in the northern suburbs. Painted panels inside the temple recount the extraordinary events surrounding the transportation of the huge statue from the workshop near Mandalay where it was carved to the then capital, Yangon. To ship the figure, a special eight-rail track had to be laid from the Sangyin quarry to the Ayeyarwady River. A ceremonial golden barge with *karaweik* heads was used to carry it south, watched by vast crowds of excited onlookers from the riverbank. The barge stopped at one town every day on its 12-day journey to allow public obeisance. Yet another specially built rail line took the statue from the docks to the 37-acre (15-ha) garden site at the top of

White elephants are considered auspicious in Southeast Asian tradition, and for centuries the region's rulers have prized albino pachyderms, which are believed to confer good luck, prosperity, and a long reign for Burmese kings (*see p107*). The custom has endured into the modern era. In a small temple set in a park in the north of the city, out toward the airport, Myanmar's former Tatmadaw (military) rulers have housed three white elephants that were discovered in the forests of Rakhine. The trio, not so much white as reddish-brown, have a specially built waterfall in which to bathe and a shaded enclosure to protect their skin from the sun. However, many people – encouraged to visit by the city's tour guides – find the sight of these large animals kept hobbled on chains undignified.

White elephants, thought to bring luck and prosperity

Farther Afield

A handful of sights dotted on the flat, riverine countryside around Yangon offer a number of pleasant escapes from the city. The most popular is the trip across the river to Thanlyin and Kyauktan, where an ancient hilltop stupa and island temple can be visited in an easy half-day excursion. To the north, the journey to Bago or Kyaiktiyo may be broken at the Taukkyan War Cemetery, the final resting place of thousands of Commonwealth soldiers who died in Burma during World War II, or at the nearby Hlawga National Park, a rare pocket of undeveloped, forested land on the fringes of the city.

Subsidiary stupas encircling the terrace of Thanlyin's Kyaik Khauk Pagoda

⓳ Thanlyin

10 miles (17 km) SE of Yangon. 🏔 62,000. ✈ Yangon Mingaladon. 🚉 Oak Pho Su Station. 🚌 No. 173 or 189 from Sule Pagoda.

Archeological remains dating from the Andhran period of the 2nd century BC have been unearthed at Thanlyin (formerly known as Syriam), across the river from Yangon, but it wasn't until the appearance in the 16th century of Portuguese adventurer Filipe de Brito e Nicote that the port flourished as a city in its own right. He had traveled east from Lisbon as a cabin boy, taking advantage of the wave of Portuguese expansion from Goa to the Moluccas (Spice Islands) before arriving in Arakan when it was at the height of its powers. De Brito established a fort at Syriam, ostensibly on behalf of the Arakanese king, but in fact to carve out a kingdom of his own.

From here he made pillaging raids inland and controlled shipping in the area, amassing a fortune in the process. However, his force of 3,000 mercenaries, drawn from Europe, Asia, and Africa, was no match for the great flotilla of 4,000 vessels dispatched in 1613 by King Anaukpetlun to destroy Syriam and its impudent Portuguese overlord. After a bloody, protracted siege, the port was captured and its ruler impaled.

The tumbledown ruins of a solitary Catholic church, half a mile southeast of the river in an overgrown, weed-choked plot off Kyaikalot Pagoda Road, are all that remain of this brief period of European rule on the coast of Burma.

Thanlyin's renaissance came about in the 1980s after the construction of an iron bridge connecting it to Yangon. Since then, its modern container port at **Thilawa** has become the busiest in the country, handling the bulk of Myanmar's maritime trade. However, apart from the ruined church, this bustling town of broad, leafy streets and low-rise concrete houses has little to detain travelers.

Environs

Crowning a low hill called Hlaing Pote Kone on the southern edge of Thanlyin is **Kyaik Khauk Pagoda**, an 800-year-old Mon stupa which resembles Yangon's Shwedagon Pagoda. The shrine is believed to contain hairs of the Buddha, originally enshrined here in the 3rd century BC by King Sulathrima of Thaton. Now beautifully gilded, the stupa has been rebuilt five times after being destroyed by earthquakes. Its terrace, ringed by smaller *zedis*, offers a spectacular view over the surrounding fields, stretching to the east bank of the Yangon River.

Buddha statues at the 800-year-old Kyaik Khauk Pagoda in Thanlyin, near Yangon

For hotels and restaurants in this region see p202 and pp210–11

Kyauktan's "floating" Ye Le Pagoda, built on a small island in the Hwaw Wun Creek

⑳ Kyauktan

13 miles (20 km) S of Thanlyin.
🏔 28,000. ✈ Yangon Mingaladon.

On the banks of Hwaw Wun Creek, Kyauktan is best known for its uniquely situated temple, the "floating" **Ye Le Pagoda**, which rests on a tiny islet midstream. Beautifully decorated in traditional style, with gold paint and multitiered roofs, the shrine is a popular half-day excursion from Yangon, a couple of hours away by road. A special launch is on hand to ferry visitors across to the temple (Myanmar nationals can take the cheaper local boats). The complex also has a small pond teeming with catfish, which worshippers feed with little bags of puffed rice that are on sale nearby.

🛕 Ye Le Pagoda
Open 7am–9pm daily. 🚗

㉑ Taukkyan War Cemetery

21 miles (35 km) N of Yangon on the Yangon–Bago Rd. 🚌 No. 9 from Aung Mingalar Bus Terminal.
Open 7–11am, 1–4:30pm daily. ♿

This immaculately maintained cemetery on the northern outskirts of Yangon holds the graves of 6,374 servicemen who lost their lives during World War II, along with memorials to the 27,000 others whose remains were never reclaimed,

the majority of them from the Indian subcontinent and Africa. Set amid lawned gardens, the rows of polished stones are a moving tribute to the fallen, most of whom perished in unimaginably harsh conditions fighting the Japanese in the early 1940s. Lying just off the highway, it makes a worthwhile stop on the journey to Bago, Mawlamyine, or Kyaiktiyo.

A memorial to the fallen of World War II at the Taukkyan War Cemetery

㉒ Hlawga National Park

Yangon–Bago Rd. ✈ Yangon Mingaladon. 🚌 No. 9 from Aung Mingalar Bus Terminal.
Open 8am–6pm daily. 🚗 💻 📷

Encompassing just over 1,500 acres (6 sq km) of wetland, semi-evergreen, and mixed-deciduous forest on the northern fringes of Yangon, Hlawga National Park was created in 1982 to preserve the green belt

around the Kokanabe and Hlawga Lakes, the city's principal water supply. The national park offers a pleasant escape from the nearby city, although wildlife is thin on the ground – the only animals that can reliably be seen are monkeys, various species of common deer, including sambar and barking deer, and occasionally the odd pangolin. The park is also home to a variety of reptiles, from monitor lizards and pythons to kraits and cobras.

A network of hiking trails provides access to the forest, and short elephant rides are offered, as well as boat trips on the lake. A play area for children, with a large model dinosaur, will appeal to visitors with young families. The national park tends to be particularly busy on weekends, when Yangon residents drive out on National Highway 1 (the main road to Bago and Kyaiktiyo) for family picnics.

Children playing on a model dinosaur at the Hlawga National Park outside Yangon

YANGON STREET FINDER

Navigating Yangon can be a challenge. The lack of standard Burmese transliteration means that street names appear with different spellings even on the same maps, and may not always correspond to those in this guide. Some roads are also known by more than one name, having been renamed after Independence. Except in the downtown area, street numbers are not often displayed, and those that are tend to be in Burmese script.

The map references given for all hotels, restaurants, shops, and sights in this guide refer to the Street Finder maps on the following pages. The letter and number in the map reference give the grid reference on the main map. The key map below shows the area covered by the main map. Symbols used on the map are given in the key below. The opposite page has an index of street names and places of interest marked on the Street Finder map.

The golden *zedi* of Yangon's Sule Pagoda at night

Key

- Major sight
- Other sight
- Other building
- 🚆 Train station
- ⛴ Ferry jetty
- 🚢 Riverboat jetty
- ℹ Visitor information
- 🚓 Police station
- ✚ Hospital
- Buddhist pagoda
- Buddhist temple
- Hindu temple
- C Mosque
- Church
- Synagogue
- Railroad

Scale of Maps 1–2

0 meters   500

0 yards   500

Street Finder Index

BAGO REGION

Bago Region's vast stretches of alluvial plain and jungle were the setting for one of Southeast Asia's most splendid cities, the port of Bago (Pegu), before successive invasions and the shifting of the Sittaung River sent the settlement into decline. Although little more than a scruffy market town today, Bago boasts a spectacular crop of monuments spanning more than 1,400 years of history. They include several remnants from its medieval heyday, among them the magnificent Shwemawdaw Pagoda, a stupa even larger than Yangon's Shwedagon.

Legend has it that the city was founded in AD 573 by a pair of Mon princes after they spotted a female *hamsa* bird resting on the back of its mate on an islet *(see p92)*. The capital they built on the spot, Hanthawaddy, later rose to become the hub of a far-reaching Mon empire whose riches proved too strong a temptation for the Burmese kingdom in Taungoo, farther north. In 1539, the Taungoo king Tabinshweti invaded the city, by then known to European traders as Pegu, and his successor, Bayinnaung, made it the capital of the Second Burmese Empire.

The Mon briefly reoccupied Bago in 1740, but the city was again brutally sacked 17 years later, this time by the redoubtable King Alaungpaya, who massacred the entire population. The ensuing decline only accelerated once the Sittaung shifted course in the 1790s,

leaving Bago a day's journey inland from the sea and cut off from the maritime trade that had always been its lifeblood. Today Bago makes a rewarding day trip from Yangon, or a stopover on longer journeys up the Sittaung Valley.

Taungoo holds a few impressive remnants of Tabinshweti's reign, but given its location at the foot of the Bago-Yoma Hills, the town serves primarily as a springboard for forays into what remains of the once vast teak forest that cloaked the region's hills. Purpose-built and working timber camps provide accommodations in the thick of the jungle, where elephants can be seen at work. Access is via a poorly maintained road that winds west across the hills to Pyay, on the Ayeyarwady River, where the enigmatic ruins of ancient Sri Ksetra, strewn across expanses of mustard fields and scrubland, are the principal attraction.

A row of statues depicting the Buddha's disciples at Shwedaung's Shwemyetman Pagoda

◀ Detail of a brightly colored *chinthe* (leogryph) at the spectacular Shwesandaw Pagoda in Pyay (Prome)

Exploring Bago Region

Bago city is a 90-minute drive northeast of Yangon, making it an easy day trip. To reach Taungoo, there is either the old Mandalay road, National Highway 1, passing through a string of Burmese market towns, or the new concrete expressway, more direct but with little of interest along the way. Running west of Taungoo, the infamous Oktwin–Paukkhaung logging road is a fragile artery through the Bago-Yoma Hills to Pyay. In the rainy season it is all but impassable, but can be tackled in chartered 4WDs the rest of the year. The main incentive to brave the trip is for the chance to overnight in forest camps, watching elephants extracting timber. Pyay is a popular start-ing point for river cruises but few visitors use it as a waystage on longer journeys north via Bagan, as onward transport is scarce. Apart from its splendid Shwesandaw Pagoda, the key attraction is ancient Sri Ksetra, centuries older than Bagan.

The Payama Pagoda in Sri Ksetra, one of the major sights near Pyay

Getting Around

A fleet of beaten-up local buses and faster luxury buses run along the four-lane Yangon–Bago Highway, although most visitors based in Yangon hire taxis for the day trip. Buses run north up the Sittaung Valley to Mandalay, pausing at Taungoo. For anyone not traveling in their own chartered vehicle, transport across the Bago-Yoma Hills is sporadic and rough, limited to local trucks that depart only when full. Pyay, on the Ayeyarwady, can be reached by bus, government ferry, or train; private operators also run cruises from here.

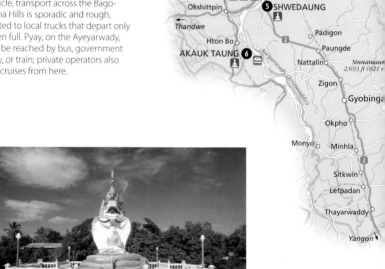

Statue of the Buddha under a serpent's hood at the Nawdawgyi Myathalyaung Buddha, Bago

For hotels and restaurants in this region see p203 and p211

Giant *chinthe* at the entrance to the pavilion housing the massive Shwetalyaung Buddha, Bago

Sights at a Glance

1 *Bago pp92–5*
2 Taungoo
3 Pyay (Prome)
4 *Sri Ksetra (Thayekhittaya)*
pp98–9
5 Shwedaung
6 Akauk Taung

View from the terrace of Bago's Mahazedi Pagoda

Key

- ═══ Highway
- ─── Main road
- ═══ Other road
- ╌╴ Railroad
- ─── Regional border
- △ Peak

0 kilometers   30

0 miles   30

For additional map symbols *see back flap*

❶ Bago

Former capital of the Mon kingdom and the Second Burmese Empire, Bago (Pegu) had its golden age between the 1420s and 1530s when its treasuries were filled with gold amassed from trade in silk, spices, and slaves across the Indian Ocean. With close trading links to India and Sri Lanka (Ceylon), the city also became an important center for Theravada Buddhism. Spectacular religious monuments are scattered across the modern town, all of them in pristine condition, having been upgraded in typically contemporary Burmese style with layers of gilt and vibrant gloss paint which belie their considerable antiquity. The sights are concentrated in two main groups: one in the grid-planned old quarter to the east, the other farther west across the creek.

The mighty golden pinnacle of the Shwemawdaw Pagoda in Bago

🕌 Shwemawdaw Pagoda
Pagoda Rd. **Open** 7am–9pm daily. 🎫 day ticket.

No monument in the region conveys the power and wealth of the lost kingdom of the Mons as dramatically as the Shwemawdaw Pagoda, whose gilded pinnacle soars 374 ft (114 m) above Bago's old palace quarter. It was built to enshrine relics of the Buddha, including two hairs said to have been gifted by Gautama himself during his lifetime. The original structure erected here has been rebuilt or enlarged on several occasions, both by the city's own Mon rulers in times of prosperity, and by repentant Bamar monarchs as atonement for the loss of life incurred by their conquests. Bayinnaung even donated his crown jewels to make a new *hti*, or finial, in

the 1550s. Several devastating earthquakes and storms in the early 20th century nearly destroyed the pagoda, before it was overhauled by public subscription in 1947. It is now officially Myanmar's tallest *zedi* (stupa). Four covered *zaungdan*, or stairways, lead to the main terrace, where a small museum houses antique Buddhas recovered from the rubble after a strong earthquake in 1930. Remnants of the old banana bud, which also fell during that temblor, can be seen near the eastern approach. As the area's most important religious site, Shwemawdaw is visited in great numbers year around, but deluged during April when thousands of local farmers take advantage of the pre-monsoon lull in the rice calendar to attend the pagoda's annual festival.

🕌 Hintha Gon
Hintha Gon Paya Rd. **Open** 7am–9pm daily. 🎫 day ticket.

The top of a low hillock next to the Shwemawdaw is believed to be the spot where the *hamsa* birds of Bago's origin myth landed. Statues of the pair stand at the entrance to the Hintha Gon, a temple built to mark the auspicious event. It can be reached via a staircase at the east side of the Shwemawdaw. The summit is a great place from which to admire the sun setting over the golden stupa to the west. The temple is also an important center for *nat* (nature spirit) worship and the venue of a lively *nat pwe* festival, when transvestite dancers perform spirit possession rituals to raucous musical accompaniment.

🏛 Kanbawzathadi Palace
Myin Taw Tar Rd. **Open** 9am–6pm daily. 🎫 day ticket.

No sign of the original Mon palace has been found at Bago, but in 1990, traces of huge post holes and brick foundations were discovered in parkland just south of the Shwemawdaw. Archeologists identified this area as the site of Bayinnaung's royal palace. One of the most powerful kings of Burma, Bayinnaung (1516–81) took the great city in 1551 with a combined force of his own elephant corps and Iberian mercenaries. Court chronicles record that in a last bid to save his capital, the Mon ruler, Smim

The *Hamsa* Bird

Legend has it that the site of Bago was chosen by two Mon princes after a pair of golden-necked *hamsa* birds landed on an islet which was so small that the female had to rest on the back of her mate. The *hamsa* – or *hintha* in Burmese – is an aquatic bird that crops up throughout the folklore and mythology of South Asia. It seems to have symbolized virility, strength, purity, divine knowledge, and spiritual accomplishment since Vedic times. Widely depicted in ancient Buddhist art, it is often featured on reliquaries found inside stupas. No one is sure why, but it is likely that the bird – whose Latin name *hansar* is the root of the German *gans* and English *goose* – is revered for being equally at home in the three elements of water, air, and earth.

Antique Burmese *hamsa* opium weight c. 1900

For hotels and restaurants in this region see p203 and p211

The gates to the Kanbawzathadi Palace, ornately decorated with stuccowork

Htaw (r. 1550–52), challenged
his Burmese adversary to single
combat on elephant back, a
duel that Bayinnaung is said to
have won with ease.

Among the travelers dazzled
by the splendor of the palace
built in the wake of this victory
was the Englishman Ralph Fitch,
who visited in 1586 and spoke
of sumptuously gilded wooden
buildings of great workmanship.
The somewhat gaudy, fanciful
reconstruction of the palace
installed by the Tatmadaw government probably bears little
resemblance to the original, but
it does convey a sense of the
scale of the lost buildings.

🐍 Snake Monastery
Bandula Rd. **Open** 8am–8pm daily.
A popular diversion for both
local Buddhist pilgrims and
foreign visitors is the Thatana
Lin Yaungshwe, or Snake
Monastery, which is located
near the Hmorkan Tank, a
couple of blocks southwest of
the Kanbawzathadi Palace area.
Its pride and joy is a 30-ft (9-m)
python that is believed to be
the reincarnation of a famous
abbot from the Shan Hills.
Streams of devotees come
every day to pay their respects
to it by leaving cash donations
or food, particularly during the
period of Buddhist Lent. Five

monks are required to carry
the snake between enclosures.
Visitors are sometimes allowed
to touch the reptile, which is
said to be around 110 years old,
except during the Burmese
month of Waso (June-July),
when it is said to be fasting.

The python at Bago's Snake Monastery,
believed to be a reincarnated abbot

Sights at a Glance

① Shwemawdaw
　Pagoda
② Hintha Gon
③ Kanbawzathadi
　Palace
④ Snake Monastery
⑤ Nawdawgyi
　Myathalyaung
　Buddha

⑥ Shwetalyaung
　Buddha
⑦ Kalyani Sima
⑧ Mahazedi Pagoda
⑨ Shwegugle
　Pagoda
⑩ Kyaik Pun Pagoda

For map symbols *see back flap*

Nawdawgyi Myathalyaung, Bago's largest reclining Buddha statue

🏛 Nawdawgyi Myathalyaung Buddha

Shwetalyaung Rd. **Open** 7am–9pm daily. 🎟 day ticket.

On the west side of town is a monumental Buddha, the Nawdawgyi Myathalyaung, oriented east to west facing a rectangular tank. Built only in 2002, it is even longer (250 ft/ 76 m) than its better known neighbor, the Shwetalyaung Buddha, although it receives a lot less attention. The figure makes for a great photo opportunity in the early morning, when it is reflected in the glassy waters of the adjacent reservoir.

🏛 Shwetalyaung Buddha

Pagoda Rd. **Open** 7am–9pm daily. 🎟 day ticket.

Immediately north of the Nawdawgyi Myathalyaung Buddha is Shwetalyaung, Bago's superb reclining Buddha, the star attraction among the monuments on the west side of town. Measuring 180 ft

(55 m) from head to toe and 52 ft (16 m) in height, the figure is thought to have been built in 994, although by the time of Alaungpaya's sack of 1757, it lay wreathed in jungle and all but forgotten. It was only in the 1880s, after a British survey team spotted the head of the statue protruding from the foliage below, that the Buddha was renovated. A corrugated-iron *tazaung* (pavilion) was erected over it soon after to protect the paintwork, which has since been maintained in pristine condition. The mosaic pillow is a 19th-century addition. While this is not the largest reclining Buddha in the country – that honor goes to the one near Mawlamyine (*see p193*) – it is the best loved, thanks to its particularly serene expression. The statue's countenance is meant to convey to worshippers the joy the Buddha experienced on his deathbed at the moment of entering *parinirvana*, as well

as the meaning of his final words to his assembled disciples: "All living things are subject to decay; strive with diligence for your liberation."

🏛 Kalyani Sima

Kalyani Sima Rd. **Open** 7am–8pm daily. 🎟 day ticket.

As part of a wider effort to revive the monkhood following the demise of the First Burmese Empire, King Dhammazedi (1412–92) constructed this grand ordination hall close to the Shwetalyaung Buddha. Its name derives from the Kalyani River in Sri Lanka, site of a famous Mahavira monastery, to which a mission of 22 monks was dispatched by the king to be reordained. Dhammazedi's reasons for wishing to do this are set out on a series of ten inscription stones erected to the west of the hall, dominated by expressions of dismay at the sectarianism that had taken hold of the faith in the late 15th century. Some of the stones were damaged in attacks by de Brito in 1599 (*see p52*) and others during the sack of Bago by Alaungpaya in 1757 (*see p53*), when the hall was totally destroyed. The tablets, written in Pali and Mon, are of value primarily as a testament to the close links between Burma and Ceylon in medieval times.

The hall itself, used as a model for over 400 similar structures erected by Dhammazedi across his kingdom, was rebuilt after

The 10th-century Shwetalyaung, Bago's serene-faced reclining Buddha

collapsing in the earthquake of 1930, and now has a modern appearance, with gleaming marble floor tiles and glass mosaic adorning the main chamber. Mirror-encrusted *nat* figures stand beneath the pillared arches lining the side walls. The Kalyani Sima remains in use for twice-monthly confessional assemblies, in which monks are publically asked whether they have committed any offences against the strictures of their monastic order. Elaborate instructions for the rituals carried out on these occasions are contained in the Dhammazedi inscriptions.

The massive seated Buddhas at the Kyaik Pun Pagoda

Mahazedi Pagoda, which once held the fake tooth relic brought from Sri Lanka

🔱 Mahazedi Pagoda
Mahazedi Rd. **Open** 7am–9pm daily. 📷 day ticket.

Less than a mile west of the Shwetalyaung Buddha stands the whitewashed Mahazedi stupa in which King Bayinnaung famously interred the gold and diamond-encrusted relic he had been tricked by the Ceylonese into believing was the tooth of the Buddha. King Anaukpetlun removed the tooth in 1599, and in later centuries the stupa was destroyed both by Alaungpaya's attack and the great earthquake of 1930. Mahazedi has since been restored to its former glory, along with Bayinnaung's Victory Ground and the miniature Bagan-style Ananda Temple, also in the complex. The former features vibrantly painted statues of Bamar troops posing in full battle dress with an auspicious white elephant (writing in 1586, the English traveler Ralph Fitch reported seeing four albino pachyderms in the compound of King Bayinnaung's palace).

🔱 Shwegugle Pagoda
Shwegugle Pagoda Road.
Open 8am–9pm daily. 📷 day ticket.

This less-visited stupa, a short distance south of the Mahazedi Pagoda, is noteworthy for the vaulted chamber encircling the base of the monument in which 64 seated Buddhas were installed. The building was constructed in 1494 during the reign of King Byinnya Ran II (r. 1491–1526).

🔱 Kyaik Pun Pagoda
Kayik Pun Pagoda Rd, around 3 miles (4.5 km) S of the train station, just off the main Yangon–Bago Highway.
Open 8am–9pm daily. 📷 day ticket.

The Kyaik Pun Pagoda – literally "Four Figures" pagoda – rises from the scrubby southern outskirts of Bago. Built by King Migadippa in the 7th century AD and restored in 1476 by King Dhammazedi, it consists of four colossal seated Buddhas. Placed back to back facing the cardinal points around a square central pillar, they are said to represent Kakusandha, Konagamana, Kassapa, and the historical Buddha, Gautama. The figures measure an impressive 90 ft (27 m) from head to toe.

The Fake Tooth Relic

Bayinnaung was the despotic, expansionist king who created the Second Burmese Empire in the mid-16th century. An acquisitive megalomaniac, he was obsessed with symbols of power, and for Theravadans none was more potent than the tooth relic of Sri Lanka. The king was so keen to bring home the prized object that when, in 1560, he heard that the Portuguese had carried it off, he sent a ship full of gold and precious stones to the Portuguese colony of Goa to buy it. Low on funds at the time, the Portuguese viceroy, Constantino da Bragança, couldn't believe his luck when the Burmese arrived. But Goa's religious authorities ruled that such a sale would be idolatrous. Rather than risk the wrath of the Inquisition, the viceroy had the tooth destroyed. However, Bayinnaung's dismay faded when he learned the stolen tooth was a

Bayinnaung, National Museum, Yangon

decoy. He later bought the original from the Ceylonese and had it interred in Bago's Mahazedi Pagoda. Alas, this one too turned out to be a fake (along with the princess he bought as part of the deal). The king refused to accept the fact, attributing all kinds of magical powers to it. Stolen by Anaukpetlun in 1599, it is now in Sagaing *(see p153)*.

Taungoo's richly gilded 16th-century Shwesandaw Pagoda and its subsidiary shrines

❷ Taungoo

Road Map D4. 177 miles (286 km) N of Yangon. 66,000. Naypyitaw, 55 miles (90 km) north.

Nestled amid the teak and bamboo forests along the foothills of the Shan Plateau, Taungoo is the largest town in the lower Sittaung Valley. However, since the founding of Naypyitaw farther north, it has rather lost its importance as a stopover on the long haul between Yangon and Mandalay. The few visitors who pause here do so to admire the scant remains of a powerful post-Bagan dynasty whose capital this was 500 years ago.

Founded in 1280, Taungoo had its heyday during the reign of Tabinshweti (1516–50), the ruler who masterminded the unification of Burma's kingdoms and principalities, beginning with the sea port of Bago (Pegu), which he made his capital in 1539. Few remnants of medieval Taungoo survive intact, but it is possible to gain a sense of the town's former prominence from the extent of the square moat and fragments of wall running around it, and the ornamental Kandawgyi Lake on the southwest edge of its old quarter.

Far and away the most impressive monument, however, is the late-16th-century **Shwesandaw Pagoda**, in the center. Believed to hold sacred hair relics of the Buddha, it is richly gilded and rises from a precinct at the end of whose covered northern entrance stand statues of the region's seven dynastic rulers. Side halls house various large Buddhas, including a 12-ft (3.5-m) high seated statue cast in bronze and silver in 1912.

A couple of blocks southeast of the Shwesandaw stands the 19th-century **Myasigon**

Pagoda, with a gilded stupa atop a brick *pahto* (temple) that features glass mosaic arches and a seated Buddha circled by *bo bo gyi*. Statues displayed in subsidiary shrines include Chinese goddesses gifted by a visiting German Buddhist in 1901. Taking pride of place in the pagoda's small museum are a bronze image of Erawan, the three-headed elephant who is the mount of Indra, and a standing Buddha plundered by Bayinnaung during his attack on the Siamese capital, Ayutthaya.

🛈 Shwesandaw Pagoda
Pagoda Rd. **Open** 5am–9pm daily.

🛈 Myasigon Pagoda
Near Taungoo Train Station.
Open 5am–9pm daily.

Environs

Taungoo today serves as a springboard for trips into the wooded hills to its northwest, to government-owned forest camps and Karen villages where it is possible to watch domesticated working elephants and their *oozies* (mahouts) extracting teak in time-honored tradition. Despite decades of sanctions, Myanmar's timber industry continues to thrive, not least thanks to the contribution of the tuskers, who are able to work in terrain inaccessible to machines *(see p107)*.

Visitors may travel out to the camps for the day or stay overnight. Among the purpose-built camps is the 20-acre (8-ha) **Pho Kyar Forest Resort**. Guests can take elephant rides into the bush, watch the animals at work, and help bathe the calves. Visits to working **timber camps** deeper in the forest, which move around following the logging, are also available.

🏠 Pho Kyar Forest Resort
31 miles (50 km) NW of Taungoo, 10 miles (16 km) E of Thargaya, near Thaing Creek, Swa Forest Reserve.

🏠 Timber camps
Various in the hills around Taungoo. 🛈 Dr Chan Aye, Myanmar Beauty Hotel, 7/134 Bo Hmu Po Kun St, Taungoo.
🅦 myanmarbeautyhotel.com

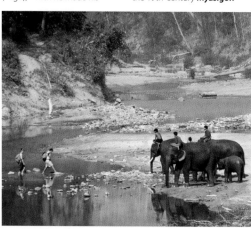

Domesticated working elephants in Myanmar's Bago-Yoma Hills

For hotels and restaurants in this region see p203 and p211

❸ Pyay (Prome)

Road Map C4. 173 miles (280 km) N of Yangon. 🏛 110,000. ✈ Yangon Mingaladon. 🚃 🚌 🚤 🛥
🎪 Nov: Shwesandaw pagoda festival.

In the late 19th century, Prome, on the Ayeyarwady's east bank, was founded as the headquarters of the Irrawaddy Flotilla Company, whose paddle steamers served as the main link between Yangon and Mandalay from 1865 to the 1940s. Today known as Pyay, the town is a bit of a backwater, and the trickle of foreign travelers who stop off each year usually do so en route to other destinations along the river. However, the place is full of Burmese atmosphere, with a lively riverside market and one of the country's most spectacular stupas.

The magnificent gilded **Shwesandaw Pagoda** crowns a low hill on the southeast side of town. Said to be a full meter taller than Yangon's Shwedagon Pagoda, the stupa looks especially dramatic around sunset, when its gilded surfaces glow beautifully against the backdrop of the distant Ayeyarwady. A series of inscriptions housed inside a brick *tazaung* in the pagoda complex record that the *zedi* (stupa) was originally sited here in 589 BC, but substantially enlarged during the reign of Kyanzittha of Bagan in 1083. However, it was King Alaungpaya, founder of the Konbaung Dynasty, who gilded the monument and added its distinctive double *hti*, or finial, which he intended as a symbol of Burmese unity after his bloody military campaigns of the mid-18th century.

One of the best views of the Shwesandaw Pagoda is to be had from the terrace encircling the giant **Sehtatgyi Buddha** (literally "Ten-Story Buddha"), a short walk to the east, whose head rises above the treeline to almost the same height. Access to the statue is via a covered walkway on its western side.

The ruins of the ancient city of Sri Ksetra (see pp98–9), capital of the Pyu kings, lie about 5 miles

The bespectacled Buddha at the Shwemyetman Pagoda in Shwedaung

(8 km) to the east of Pyay and, by staying overnight in the town, it is possible to explore them on a day trip.

🏯 **Shwesandaw Pagoda**
Pagoda St. **Open** 7am–9pm daily.

🏯 **Sehtatgyi Buddha**
Pagoda St. **Open** 7am–9pm daily.

View of the Sehtatgyi Buddha from the Shwesandaw Pagoda in Pyay

❹ Sri Ksetra (Thayekhittaya)

See pp98–9.

❺ Shwedaung

Road Map C4. 9 miles (14 km) S of Pyay. 🏛 21,000. 🚌

In a land of countless Buddhas, the figure enshrined at the **Shwemyetman Pagoda** in the town of Shwedaung stands out, thanks to its pair of enormous gold-rimmed spectacles. The first set is said to have been gifted during the Konbaung era. They were stolen shortly after, and since then the statue has had a series of replacements (thieves keep stealing them). The Shwemyetman Buddha is believed to have the power to cure ailments related to the eyes, and the temple is a popular pilgrimage destination for Myanmar's visually impaired.

🏯 **Shwemyetman Pagoda**
Shwedaung, Pyay Township.
Open daily.

❻ Akauk Taung

Road Map C4. Near Hton Bo (Tonbo) village. 🚌 by car 36 miles (58 km) south from Pyay to Hton Bo village, then by local riverboat for the remaining 45-minute trip by water.

Another popular excursion out of Pyay is the day trip to Akauk Taung, a sandstone cliff on the Ayeyarwady where hundreds of Buddhas have been carved into niches in the rock. The figures were the handiwork of long-distance boatmen, who used to pause here to pay tolls, or to wait for whirlpools in the river to abate. Viewed from the water, the shrines, with their whitewashed surrounds and fringe of tropical foliage straggling above them, rank among the most photogenic sights on the Ayeyarwady River.

❹ Sri Ksetra (Thayekhittaya)

The distinctively shaped stupas, dried-up moats, and earthworks in the fields a few miles east of the Ayeyarwady River at Pyay are all that remains of what was, 1,200 years ago, one of Asia's grandest fortified settlements. Capital of the Pyu kings, Sri Ksetra ("City of Splendor"), also known as Thayekhittaya, grew wealthy by controlling trade down the river and across the Bay of Bengal to India. Between the 4th and 9th centuries, the walled town was known to travelers from as far afield as eastern China and India, and is thought to have been the largest in the country, supporting a population of thousands. No one is sure why Sri Ksetra went into decline (invasion by the Mon is the current theory) but by the 10th century it had been squarely eclipsed by Bagan. Today its ruins lie all but forgotten, visited by only a handful of foreigners each year.

Pyu-era terra-cotta Buddha amulet, c. 8th–9th centuries

0 kilometers   1

0 miles   1

KEY

① **The Payagyi Pagoda** dates from around the 5th century. This large brick stupa is surrounded by three ambulatory terraces, of which the uppermost is only open to men.

② **The Nat Bauk Gate** is the main entrance into Sri Ksetra. The road from Pyay passes through it.

③ **Archeology Field School**

④ **Old canal**

⑤ **The railroad line to Yangon** cuts through the middle of Sri Ksetra.

⑥ **The small museum** displays Buddha statues, beads, and other artifacts uncovered at the site.

⑦ **Throne stone**

⑧ **A large cluster of ruins** have been excavated near the south gate.

⑨ **The Lemyethna Temple** contains four original Buddha reliefs.

⑩ **The "royal cemetery"** is where a concentration of large funerary urns and coins have been unearthed.

⑪ **The 11th-century Rahanta Pagoda** holds a handful of Bagan-era Buddhas, facing the palace area. The Rahanta Gate nearby has been excavated and partially rebuilt.

★ **Bawbawgyi Pagoda**
This late-4th-century cylindrical-sided, elongated stupa is the site's largest and most striking. It served as a prototype for Bagan's earliest pagodas (see pp120–21).

★ **Payama Pagoda**
A survivor from the 4th–5th centuries AD, this stupa is one of the oldest monuments in the country and has been well restored.

The royal palace complex
At the center of the city stood the royal palace complex. Recently excavated brick foundations reveal its impressive scale. Sri Ksetra has been put forward by the Myanmar government to UNESCO as a potential World Heritage Site.

The Khin Ba stupa mound, dating from the 5th–6th centuries AD, is the oldest undisturbed Buddhist relic chamber in Southeast Asia and has yielded several precious objects, including this silver Pyu coin.

Yangon ↘

Bei Bei Pagoda
Mounted on a raised plinth, the hollow Bei Bei shrine dates from the early 10th century, when the ancient city was already in decline.

WESTERN MYANMAR

Western Myanmar encompasses two very different regions, each with its own distinctive geography and culture. The Delta, immediately west of Yangon, has since British times served as the country's rice bowl – a vast patchwork of green paddy fields crisscrossed by canals fed by the silty waters of the Ayeyarwady as it splits into a myriad tributaries on its way to the ocean. Farther north, a spine of jungle-covered hills separate the Delta region from the narrow coastal strip of Rakhine State, heartland of the former kingdom of Arakan.

In the Delta, travel generally means long boat journeys for local people, but since the sinking of a government ferry in March 2012, foreign tourists have been obliged to reach the region's capital, Pathein, by road. Apart from the chance to sample the atmosphere of the coastal wetlands, the main incentives to make the trip are Ngwe Saung and Chaungtha, a pair of low-key beaches on the Bay of Bengal, the nearest seaside resorts to the city of Yangon. The fertile Delta region was the area that, in May 2008, bore the brunt of Cyclone Nargis, the worst tropical storm to have hit Myanmar in living memory. It caused catastrophic damage and left more than 138,000 people dead.

Rakhine State, in the far northwest corner of the country, has always maintained an uneasy relationship with the Burmese population of the central plains.

The region remains one of the least developed parts of Myanmar, despite the fact that it holds two of the country's prime visitor attractions: the evocative archeological site of Mrauk U, and Ngapali beach, whose vivid turquoise water and gleaming white sand eclipse every other coastal resort in the area.

Ngapali's relaxed feel can make it hard to believe that towns farther north have seen outbreaks of communal violence in recent years. In 2012, attacks on Rakhine Muslims, known as Rohingyas, left scores of people dead and forced thousands to flee their villages; clashes in 2013 spread as far south as Thandwe. This has led to curfews and occasional travel restrictions in the Rakhine capital, Sittwe (Aykab). At the time of writing, however, no permits were required to visit Mrauk U, a day's journey up the Kaladan River from Sittwe.

Fields of golden rice stubble spread below the misty blue ridges separating Mrauk U and the Lemro River

◄ The clear blue waters of the Bay of Bengal at the exquisite Ngapali beach near Thandwe

Exploring Western Myanmar

Exquisite Ngapali beach is what tempts most travelers across the Rakhine-Yoma Hills to this little-visited, far northwest corner of the country, although few venture to make the trip overland – the road is impassable for much of the year. Taking a flight from Yangon is the best approach to Thandwe, the jumping-off spot for Ngapali. All of this area's visitor facilities are strewn in the coconut groves immediately behind the beach, which serves as a springboard for snorkeling and diving trips to offshore islets. Flying is also the easiest way to reach Sittwe, at the mouth of the Kaladan River, the most popular access point for the ruined medieval city of Mrauk U.

■ Area illustrated

Getting Around

Delta towns are accessible by road. There is also a ferry from Yangon to Myaungmya, an hour's bus journey away from Pathein. Flights from Yangon to Sittwe and Thandwe operate daily, year round, but they tend to be overbooked between December and February. Boats from Taungup (north of Thandwe) to Sittwe do the nine-hour journey five times a week. Ferries (government and private) and boats leave Sittwe each morning for Mrauk U; the journey takes between five and seven hours, depending on the vessel. Taxis make the same trip, but are substantially more expensive.

The stone entrance of Sittwe's Lokhananda Pagoda

Sunrise viewed from the Shwetaung Pagoda in the ancient ruined city of Mrauk U

Paletwa

Nat Ma Taung (Mt Victoria)
10,016 ft (3,053 m)

Ingyaung

CHIN

Kyauktaw

10 DHANYAWADI

9 WETHALI

8 MRAUK U

Rathedaung

Min Bya

Wunwa

7 SITTWE (AYKAB)

Myebon

Dalet

Ann

Kyun Thaya Island

RAKHINE

Kyaukpyu

Letpan

Lamu

Zinchaung

Ramre

Munaung

Ramree Island

Taungup

Ywapaga

Okshittpin

Pyay

5 THANDWE

6 NGAPALI

Kyangin

Yangon

Mawion

Kyeintali

Tugyi

Myogwin

Bay of Bengal

Gwa

Gwa Bay

Hinthada

Ngathaing

Danson Bay

AYEYARWADY

Kyaunggon

Danubyu

Zalun

CHAUNGTHA **3**

Thongwa

Yangon

Pantanaw

NGWE SAUNG **4**

2 PATHEIN

TWANTE **1**

Myaungmya

Maubin

Kyonmangay

Bogale

Dedaye

Labutta

Pyapon

Kyauk Chaung

Setsan

Cape Puriyan

Tangon

Ama

Magway

Datkon

Sights at a Glance

1 Twante
2 Pathein
3 Chaungtha
4 Ngwe Saung
5 Thandwe
6 Ngapali
7 Sittwe (Aykab)
8 *Mrauk U pp110–14*
9 Wethali
10 Dhanyawadi

Fishing boats moored at Ngapali in Western Myanmar

Buddha statue at the top of the hill
in Mya Pyin village, Ngapali

Key

— Main road

═ Other road

⋯ Railroad

▬ International border

▬ Regional border

△ Peak

| 0 kilometers | 50 |
| 0 miles | 50 |

For additional map symbols *see back flap*

The gilded, bell-shaped *zedi* of Pathein's Shwemokhtaw Pagoda, surrounded by dozens of subsidiary stupas

❶ Twante

Road Map C5. 28 miles (46 km) W of Yangon, an hour by road via the Hlaing River bridge, or 30 mins from the Dalah ferry dock. 🔼 42,000. ✈ Yangon Mingaladon. 🚌

A typical small Ayeyarwady Delta town known primarily for its pottery, Twante is an easy day trip from Yangon and makes a good introduction to the region. Buses and Jeeps leave for the town at regular intervals from Dalah, on the south bank of the Yangon River, which may be crossed by a short but enjoyable ferry ride from the Pansodan Jetty on Strand Road.

Stacked with a range of goods in various stages of completion, the pottery workshops lining Twante's canals are hard to miss, and their staff delight in guiding visitors through the manufacturing process. The town's other main sight is the 11th-century **Shwesandaw Pagoda** on its southern outskirts. The stupa is said to enshrine hairs of the Buddha. Although Twante was one of the worst hit areas during Cyclone Nargis in May 2008, the pagoda came through the violent storm unscathed, unlike many of the other religious monuments in the town.

❷ Pathein

Road Map C5. 🔼 132,000. ✈ Yangon Mingaladon. ✈ Pathein Airport, on the northeast edge of town near the university. 🚌 🚌 to Myaungmya, then bus to Pathein.

Also known as Bassein, Pathein is the capital of the Delta region and one of Myanmar's most populous cities. Its enduring prosperity comes from the flat expanses of green paddy fields spread across the surrounding wetlands. In the British era, hundreds of thousands of acres of jungle, swamp, and marsh in the area were cleared to create cultivable land. As rice became Burma's main cash crop, people poured in from across India and the rest of the country to cash in on the bonanza. Exports from the Delta supplied Europe during the American Civil War and fueled the growth of Calcutta and Straits Settlements plantations in what was then Malaya. By the 1930s, half of the country's rice was sold overseas. However, production has plummeted since Independence due to antiquated agricultural practices, impoverished soil, and the vulnerability of local farmers to drought and flooding.

Pathein's pride and joy is the 153-ft (47-m) **Shwemokhtaw Pagoda**, whose golden, bell-shaped *zedi* (stupa) soars above the bend in the river at the center of town. Believed to have been founded in the 3rd century BC, it has since been enlarged many times, notably by the peripatetic king of Bagan, Alaungsithu (1089–1168), who sponsored the construction of many major temples, ordination halls, forts, and reservoirs across his domain. Shwemokhtaw's

A range of goods on display at a pottery workshop in Twante

crowning glory is a particularly resplendent *hti* (finial) made of three layers: the first of bronze; the second of silver; and the third of solid gold weighing 3.9 lb (6.3 kg), with 843 rubies, 829 diamonds, and 1,588 semi-precious stones.

The nearby waterfront is a good spot for a stroll. Dotted with Chinese and Burmese temples, its banks are lined with wooden boats used to transport pottery and other merchandise around the Delta and to and from the city market.

Also worth a visit is the **Settayaw Pagoda**, on the northeast edge of town, where a Konbaung-style Buddha image cast in bronze presides over a footprint of the historical Buddha, Gautama. The temple can be reached via a pretty, red and white bridge, which is a favorite backdrop for local wedding photographs.

Currently, foreign nationals are not permitted to travel on the daily riverboat from Yangon to Pathein; check in advance with Myanmar Travels and Tours to see if the situation has changed and restrictions lifted.

🛕 **Shwemokhtaw Pagoda**
Shwezedi Road. **Open** 4am–9pm daily. ♿ partial access via the south entrance.

🛕 **Settayaw Pagoda**
Mahabandula Rd.
Open 8am–9pm daily.

Trishaw carrying a monk in Pathein, capital of the Ayeyarwady Delta region

Pathein Parasols

A traditional Delta industry that has witnessed a sharp decline elsewhere in Myanmar, parasol making still thrives in Pathein thanks to the recent revival of tourism. Several workshops around the city make umbrellas in the traditional way, using bamboo, paper, waxed cotton, and silk. Renowned for their striking colors and delicately painted decoration, the parasols, known as *Pathein hti*, became desirable fashion accessories among the Victorian and Edwardian British aristocracy, and were exported in huge numbers from Burma. Many of the parasol workshops welcome visitors. Over green tea and nibbles, the artisans demonstrate the various stages of the production process, from carving the bamboo spokes and carefully blending the natural pigments used to color the parasols, to embellishing them with traditional floral patterns and bird designs.

Colorful parasols decorated with traditional designs

❸ Chaungtha

Road Map C5. 25 miles (40 km) W of Pathein. 🚌 900. 🚐

Ox-cart rides, picnics, and copious seafood lunches, rather than sunbathing and swimming, are what tend to occupy the droves of Yangonites who descend on Chaungtha beach on sunny weekends. From Monday to Friday, however, the few foreign tourists who take the winding road west of Pathein can expect to have the mile-long stretch of golden sand largely to themselves. Accommodations are offered in a string of lackluster, mostly mid-scale hotels behind the beach, whose most distinctive landmark is a small pagoda crowning a plant-covered rock in the middle of the bay. The islet just off the headland to the southwest – Chaungtha Kyun, dubbed "White Sand Island" – can be explored in a day trip. The water around it is clearer and better for snorkeling, and local fishermen run trips to it every hour or so.

❹ Ngwe Saung

Road Map C5. 29 miles (48 km) W of Pathein. 🚌 4,000. 🚐

Located a couple of bays south of Chaungtha, Ngwe Saung has marginally whiter sand and bluer water than its near neighbor, and although neither are on a par with the beach at Ngapali *(see p106)*, in distant Rakhine, the resort makes for a pleasant stop. The area was closed for a few years after 2008's devastating Cyclone Nargis, which, together with the long journey time from Yangon, has slowed the pace of development. Confined to the north end of the 6-mile (10-km) beach, resort complexes are still few in number; more low-key hotels and budget guest-houses cluster in the south. Various small islands offshore and a more distant cove to the south beyond Sinma village are offered as day trips by local boatmen. The water becomes clearer away from the coast and most of the hotels offer masks and snorkels to rent.

Sandoway Resort, located on the beautiful beachfront at Ngapali

❺ Thandwe

Road Map C4. 231 miles (372 km) NW of Yangon. ⊞ 105,000. ✈ Yangon Mingaladon. ✈ Thandwe Airport, 3 miles (5 km) W on the coast. ⊟ daily except public holidays.

The thousands of visitors who stream through Thandwe (formerly known as Sandoway) each winter en route to Ngapali rarely see more of the town than its airport. But it is well worth jumping in a taxi or pick-up truck for the 45-minute drive from Ngapali to visit Thandwe's bustling **market**, located in a former British jail. People from the surrounding villages pack the covered area from around 7am to shop for fresh produce, textiles, and a typically Burmese array of hardware. Souvenirs are also on sale.

On the surrounding hilltops are three gilded stupas offering great views over the town and nearby coast. A brisk 20-minute walk west of the market, the largest, **Nandaw Pagoda**, dates from the late 8th century and is said to have been erected by King Minbra to enshrine a bone relic of the Buddha. **Sandaw Pagoda** is believed to house a hair of the Buddha, and **Andaw Pagoda** a tooth relic.

In October 2013, communal violence from farther north in Rakhine State spread as far south as Thandwe, but the area has stabilized and there are currently no travel restrictions.

❻ Ngapali

Road Map C4. 4 miles (6 km) SW of Thandwe. ✈ Yangon Mingaladon. ✈ Thandwe Airport. ⊞

With its translucent turquoise water, white sand, and backdrop of gently inclined palm trees, Ngapali is one of the country's most stunning beaches, which is why Myanmar's Tatmadaw (military) government earmarked it for high-end development back in the 1990s. As a result, the accommodations here are a bit more chic than at resorts on the Delta coast. Tariffs are sky high by Southeast Asian standards, and infinity pools, stylish teak-built chalets, and sun terraces with uninterrupted sea views are the norm.

For the time being, villagers from the fishing settlement of Gyeiktaw, around the headland to the south of Ngapali's 3-mile (5-km) stretch of sand, still outnumber foreign visitors, even during the peak season. However, this looks set to change when a crop of larger resort complexes currently being built are completed.

Beachside cafés and restaurants at Ngapali beach

❼ Sittwe (Aykab)

Road Map B4. 553 miles (890 km) NW of Yangon. ⬛ 152,000. ✈ Yangon Mingaladon. ➡ Sittwe Airport, 2.5 miles (4 km) SW of the center. 🚌 from Taungup. 🚌 to Mrauk U 🚢 Mon–Sat.

The Rakhine capital, Sittwe (also known as Aykab, its Bengali name), occupies a strategic location at the mouth of the Kaladan River, in the far northwest of the country. The British developed the town as a port and trade hub in the 19th century, but since Myanmar gained independence, political friction between the Arakanese and Burmese has marginalized the region, which now ranks among the most impoverished in the country.

A major setback to the town's economic prospects was the spate of communal clashes between Buddhists and the local Muslim Rohingya minority in 2012 and 2013, following which the government temporarily suspended all travel to the area. Hundreds died in the violence, and many thousands were forced into makeshift camps in safe havens, or across

The gilded interiors of the Lokhananda Pagoda in Sittwe

the border in Bangladesh. The situation has stabilized since, and a permit is no longer required to visit Sittwe.

For passing time between boat connections, visitors can explore the huge fish market at the east end of town, where some exotic merchandise is on sale from first light, or try the View Point, a mile south, which is a popular spot for a breezy sunset stroll and a cold beer.

Less inspiring is the lackluster collection of inscriptions and other minor archeological finds in the **Rakhine State Cultural Museum**. Sittwe's principal

stupa is the gigantic, gilded **Lokhananda Pagoda** on the southern edge of town, commissioned by General Than Shwe in 1997. An ordination hall on its northern side houses an intriguing bronze and brass Buddha thought to date from 24 BC, which local fishermen hauled out of the Kaladan.

🏛 Rakhine State Cultural Museum
Main Rd. **Open** 9:30am–4:30pm Tue–Sun. 📷 🚫

🛕 Lokhananda Pagoda
Ball Lone Quin Quarter, near airport. **Open** 6am–9pm daily. ♿

Myanmar's Elephants

The vast teak forests of Myanmar have always been prime elephant territory, and the animal features prominently in the country's folklore and mythology. Used to represent the Buddha on ancient stupas, tuskers traditionally symbolized spiritual power and vitality. Particularly prized were white (albino) animals, which kings throughout history have gone to great lengths to acquire. Their presence in royal palaces was supposed to assure long and fruitful reigns for their owners, a belief that continues to this day – Myanmar's former military leaders collected white elephants which are now kept in special enclosures in Yangon and Naypyitaw.

From an estimated peak of around 10,000 in the last century, the numbers of wild elephants have plummeted to around 2,000. Poaching for ivory and habitat loss due to mining, hydroelectric schemes, and deforestation have played their part, but research has revealed that the main culprit is the country's state-owned timber industry.

Around 4,750 elephants presently work in Myanmar's forests. However, reproduction rates among domesticated animals are very low, and the working population has to be

A domesticated working elephant

supplemented with captured animals. Between 50 and 100 elephants are currently caught each year using tranquilizer darts, and this is having a damaging impact on the viability of the wild population. Once trapped, elephants suffer a traumatic regime to break them in, involving food and sleep deprivation, physical restraint, and beatings. The training process can last as long as 20 years. Several camps offer visitors the chance to see domesticated elephants at work, but sightings of wild ones are rare, as areas where they survive in healthy numbers are remote and inaccessible to casual visitors.

Sunrise over the mist-shrouded stupas and shrines of the ancient ruined city of Mrauk U ▶

❽ Mrauk U

Occupying a sliver of lush coastal land, Arakan – precursor of modern Rakhine State – was in the 16th century the hub of a trade network in spices and slaves that extended from south India to Indonesia, and brought fabulous riches to the Arakanese kings. The grandeur of their capital, Mrauk U, was renowned across Asia. Merchants from Persia, Afghanistan, Abyssinia, China, Japan, Portugal, and Holland settled here. The arts flourished, and the markets were full of precious stones and perfumes. However, after the Burmese sacked the city in 1784, the population of 16,000 fled and it fell into ruins. Now only a scattering of stupas and temples remain, rising from a carpet of bleached grass and scrub – a sight that is especially beautiful in the mist of early morning.

Lemyethna Temple
Men Saw Mon, the first king of the Mrauk U Dynasty, built this temple in 1430, and lived only just long enough to see it completed.

★ Dukkan Thein
Built in 1571 by King Minphalaung, this ordination hall has an upper terrace accessed by three monumental stairways. The eastern entrance leads to a spiral passageway lined with some of Mrauk U's finest stone carvings.

Dhanyawadi & Wethali *(see p115)*

Wa Ze Creek

KEY

① **Bandula Kyaung** is a shrine housing the precious Sanda Muni statue, which was hidden inside a cement block for centuries.

② **The palace museum** has a modest collection comprising Buddha images, stone inscriptions, coins, and a scale model of the site.

③ **The royal palace** of Mrauk U was among Asia's most magnificent royal abodes, but only a few wall fragments remain.

④ **Andaw Thein** was renovated in the 1530s by King Minbin, then enlarged into a temple by King Min Razagyi (1557–1612) in 1596 to house a tooth relic of the Buddha.

⑤ **Ratanamanaung Pagoda**

⑥ **Sakyamanaung Pagoda**

⑦ **Peisi Daung Pagoda**

⑧ **The Shwetaung Pagoda** is a stupa site on a hilltop to the south, reached via a winding path. One of the finest views of Mrauk U is to be had from here at dawn.

★ Sittaung Temple
The highlight of Minbin's temple lies hidden deep inside its walls, where stone passages are lined with splendid bas reliefs and Buddhas.

Let Se Kan

Anuma Moat

Ratanabon Pagoda
Centered on an elegantly curved stupa, Ratanabon resembles a huge bell. Its name suggests it was originally designed to house treasures that may have been looted when the Burmese sacked the city in 1784.

VISITORS' CHECKLIST

Practical Information
Road Map B3. Five–seven hrs by boat NE of Sittwe. **Open** temples: 7am–5:30pm daily; museum: 10am–4pm Tue–Sun. 🎫 tickets sold in dollars at jetty or at the Sittaung Temple; separate fee for museum. 🎫 guides arranged via hotels or at Sittwe Airport. 🎫 🎫 Apr/May: Sittaung annual festival.

Transport
🛪 Yangon Mingaladon. 🛬 Sittwe Airport. 🚢 from Sittwe. Taxis & cars available from Sittwe. Hotels can arrange Jeeps for excursions. Tuktuks & horse carts available at Mrauk U for tours.

★ **Koethaung Temple**
This impressive 16th-century pagoda on the site's eastern fringes is said to have had 90,000 Buddha statues placed within it. It is also the largest building in all of Mrauk U.

City of the Monkey Egg

Mrauk U is often translated as "Monkey Egg," a curious name attributed to the site's mythical origins when a monkey and a peacock are said to have mated on the banks of the Lemro River. In fact, the name derives from the Burmese tendency to mispronounce Mrauk U as "Myauk U," which does indeed mean "Monkey Egg." The original Arakanese, however, means "Holy City of the North," an altogether more plausible moniker.

Mandalay's Mahamuni, originally from Mrauk U

⑤

⑥ ⑦

0 meters   600
0 yards   600

Exploring Mrauk U

The remains of the former Arakan capital, Mrauk U, straddle the Lemro River – a tributary of the broader Kaladan – amid an area of low, scrub-covered hills. Connected by sandy tracks, the principal monuments lie close enough together to be explored on foot or by horse cart, although the heat tends to limit serious sightseeing to the mornings and early evenings. Entry tickets must be paid for in dollars, either on arrival at the boat jetty or at the Sittaung Temple.

The entrance to the palace museum, which displays artifacts found in Mrauk U

Monk walking down a path next to the walls of the royal palace at Mrauk U

🏛 Royal Palace and Museum

The royal palace at the center of Mrauk U was constructed by the founder of the Mrauk U Dynasty, Men Saw Mon (1380–1433), also known as Naramithla. Built in 1430, it was once the city's most spectacular edifice – a huge, ornately decorated wooden structure set on three receding levels and surrounded by three interlocking walls. Only parts of the outermost rampart remain, along with fragments of a gateway and central platform, but several contemporary descriptions survive, including one by Augustinian monk Sebastian Manrique, who lived in the capital for eight years from 1629. Manrique wrote of the vast gilded pillars inside, and rooms "made of odiferous woods... which thus gratify the sense of smell by their own natural fragrance. There was one room known as the 'House of Gold' for being entirely ornamented from top to bottom in that metal."

On display at the palace museum inside the western walls is a collection of Buddha statues, inscriptions, and coins – many of them reproductions – found during archeological excavations across the site.

🏛 Sittaung Temple

Some of Mrauk U's most impressive monuments are con-centrated in the area immediately north of the palace ruins, at the foot of the ridge of hills running north from the site. Connected by broad dirt tracks, they are all easily reachable on foot.

The stand-out building in this northern group is the Sittaung Temple, built in 1535 by King Minbin (1493–1554) to mark his victorious Bengal campaign. Its suitably triumphant center-piece is a grand, bell-shaped stupa surrounded by scores of subsidiary *zedis*. Inside, the central ambulatory passage around the main shrine is lined with thousands of carved stone Buddhas and bas reliefs of the *Jatakas*, showing scenes from the Buddha's life, which have been heavily restored and are now floodlit. The latter draw much of their inspiration from contemporary life in the Arakan capital, and are a priceless window on this lost medieval world. The profusion of sculpture has earned the building the

The bell-shaped stupa of the Sittaung Temple, surrounded by subsidiary shrines

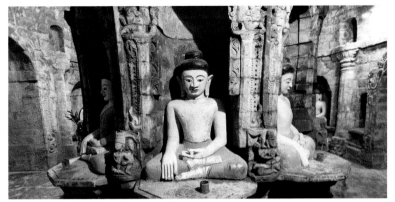

Painted Buddha statues in the central shrine of the Andaw Thein ordination hall

nickname "Temple of 80,000 Buddhas." At the main entrance, a 10-ft (3-m) tall inscribed pillar, originally from the settlement at Wethali *(see p115)*, recounts in Pali the dynastic history of the rulers of Arakan between the 5th and 8th centuries AD.

Andaw Thein

A short distance northeast of Sittaung, the slightly older, smaller Andaw Thein (literally "Tooth Shrine") has a very similar layout to its neighbor, with a central stupa encircled by 16 smaller ones rising from an octagonal base. This gem of a temple dates from the 1520s and was originally built as a monastic ordination hall; it was later enlarged by King Min Razagyi to house a tooth relic of the Buddha brought back from a pilgrimage to Ceylon.

Ratanabon Pagoda

The third structure in this sequence, the Ratanabon Pagoda, a short way farther north, dates from 1612 and is the most picturesque of the trio. Its elegantly curved central stupa was destroyed by a Japanese bomb in World War II but has since been restored.

Dukkan Thein

Farther west stands the impressive Dukkan Thein (or Htukkanthein) ordination hall, whose distinctive stupa, topped by a mushroom-shaped finial, rests on two imposing, fortress-like terraces atop a low hillock. A flight of steps on its east side leads inside to three vaulted chambers connected by a passageway lined with 179 Buddha statues in niches. Flanking these are carved figures thought to be

depictions of the Arakanese donors and their wives who sponsored the construction of the temple, each with a different hairstyle. The main Buddha figure in the central shrine is illuminated at dawn by light filtering through a square window in the dome above.

Lemyethna Temple

The final monument of note in this northern group is the Lemyethna Temple, in which eight Buddhas are seated on thrones around the base of an octagonal column. Facing them are empty niches where another 20 figures formerly sat. Square in plan, with four projecting vaulted porches in the style of classical Bagan, the temple dates from the reign of Men Saw Mon and is one of the oldest on the site.

The Chin Villages

A popular half-day excursion from Mrauk U is the two-hour boat ride north up the Lemro River to a cluster of settlements inhabited by Chin minority people. Until the practice was banned by the government in the 1960s, Chin women used to tattoo their faces with intricate spiderweb designs. One popular hypothesis suggests they did so as a form of disfigurement to avoid being kidnapped into slavery or concubinage, while another says the tattoos were a mark of beauty. A few elderly women in these villages retain the markings, allowing visitors to photograph them in exchange for donations. Discouraged by Baptist missionaries after World War II, facial tattoos have become rare, even in the Chin heartland near the Bangladesh border, where an ongoing insurgency has led to the displacement of thousands of Chin. The group living near Mrauk U are among these refugees and welcome the money received from visitors to supplement the meager income they derive from fishing and subsistence farming.

Chin woman with tattooed face, Kyi Chaung village

A panoramic view of the massive Koethaung Temple, Mrauk U's largest structure

Koethaung Temple

The cluster of monuments scattered across the low hills, rice paddies, and marshes at the eastern end of Mrauk U are dominated by the iconic Koethaung Temple, the largest on the site. Given the dearth of shade along the lanes leading to this group, it makes sense to start sightseeing early in the morning, or hire a horse cart, tuktuk, or Jeep for the trip.

Oriented toward the east, Koethaung is square in plan with an exterior composed of five receding terraces, each holding rows of small stupas. It was built by Minbin's son, Mintikka (r. 1554–6), who attempted to outdo his father by building a larger temple with an even greater number of

Animal statues around the "bell" of Koethaung

Buddhas – there are allegedly 10,000 more here than at the Sittaung Temple, hence its name, which means "90,000".

Peisi Daung Pagoda

One of the best views of the eastern group of monuments, and Koethaung in particular, is to be had from the unexcavated pagoda crowning the hilltop immediately to the south. Five Buddhas are enshrined at the dusty Peisi Daung Pagoda (four facing the cardinal points and one on top), each depicted with large white eyes. Some effort is required to push through the undergrowth shrouding the hill to reach the monument, but the views over the surrounding banana groves and rice fields are well worth

Buddha statues at the unexcavated Peisi Daung Pagoda

the effort. Traces of the third, outermost belt of city walls are also visible from this splendid vantage point.

Ratanamanaung Pagoda

Located around half a mile northeast of the palace site, Ratanamanaung was built by King Sandathudam Raza in 1652. The pagoda is a solid stone structure – plain and octagonal in shape from the base to the tip of its spire. Brightly painted planetary figures astride elephants and mythical creatures are installed at intervals on the ambulatory path surrounding the monument. On the northwest side of the stupa stand the remains of a hall known as the Gupru, or "White Cave," where in 1696 a resident monk, Marone Pyi Ya, was ritually crowned as the symbolic ruler of Mrauk U, a title he retained for a full year.

The unusual geometric tiers of the Sakyamanaung Pagoda

Sakyamanaung Pagoda

Thanks to its lofty spire and finial, which peak at 280 ft (82 m), the other prominent landmark in this eastern area is the Sakyamanaung Pagoda, which stands roughly midway between the palace and the Koethaung Temple. Attributed to King Thiri Thudhamma (r. 1622–38), Sakyamanaung was one of the last major projects undertaken at Mrauk U and is unusual for being made up of a mixture of circular and octagonal tiers. The overall effect is one of elegant symmetry, although its graceful appearance is somewhat at odds with the grinning, sword-wielding ogres guarding the entrance.

The Great Payagyi Buddha statue, one of the main sights in Wethali

❾ Wethali

Road Map B3. 6 miles (10 km) N of Mrauk U. ✈ Yangon Mingaladon. ✈ Sittwe Airport. 🚢 Sittwe to Mrauk U, then by hired Jeep.

Faint traces of one of Mrauk U's forerunners litter the fields 6 miles (10 km) north of the archeological site, where sections of ancient walls and the foundations of partly excavated monasteries and temples are all that is left of ancient Wethali. Founded in AD 327 by King Devan Sanda, the settlement is thought to have been occupied for around 700 years and bears close similarities to the contemporaneous Pyu cities of the Ayeyarwady Valley. Most of the key finds unearthed here have been removed. They included a famous inscribed obelisk, which now stands at the entrance to Mrauk U's Sittaung Temple (see p112), and a handful of coins and sculpture pieces on display at Mrauk U's palace museum (see p112). But one noteworthy object remains in situ: a 17-ft (5-m) seated Buddha hewn from a single block of stone, known locally as the **Great Wethali Payagyi**. It is believed to be one of Myanmar's oldest surviving Buddhas.

Silver coin of King Chandra Surya

❿ Dhanyawadi

Road Map B3. 20 miles (32 km) N of Wethali. ✈ Yangon Mingaladon. ✈ Sittwe Airport. 🚢 Sittwe to Mrauk U, then by hired Jeep.

Another 20 miles (32 km) to the north, Dhanyawadi is the site of a second lost city, which local legend asserts was visited by the Buddha in 554 BC. The event, which took place during the reign of King Chandra Surya, is believed to have been marked by the casting of a huge bronze Buddha statue – the illustrious Mahamuni. The figure was enshrined inside the **Mahamuni Temple** here until Bodawpaya's invading army carried it over the Rakhine-Yoma Hills to Mandalay in 1784 (see p142). Its presiding image may have gone, but the temple, now thoroughly modernized and housing three fine Buddhas, still attracts pilgrims from all over the country. A little museum near the southern walls of the shrine displays fragments of pottery and Pali inscriptions attesting to the antiquity of Dhanyawadi, which archeologists believe reached its peak between the 4th and 6th centuries AD.

The faint outlines of oval perimeter walls, similar to those of the Pyu cities, and a square palace are invisible to visitors at ground level but may clearly be seen on satellite images.

The Lost Kingdom of Arakan

Although virtually forgotten by the rest of the world today, Arakan at its height ranked among Asia's most illustrious kingdoms, with a seaborne empire that stretched from the Ganges to the Ayeyarwady. The key to its wealth lay in trade, particularly in slaves, bought from Portuguese slavers preying on Bengal's coastal settlements and sold in prodigious numbers to the Dutch colony of Batavia (now Jakarta), along with shiploads of rice. Tax revenue from territorial conquests also helped fill Mrauk U's coffers.

Fortune seekers from across Asia and Europe traveled to the city during its heyday, when its population peaked at around 160,000. They discovered a sophisticated, refined culture blending Islamic influences from northern India with indigenous Buddhist tradition. This syncretic style was a legacy of the 25-year exile of the dynasty's founder, Men Saw Mon, in the court of the Sultan of Bengal. The prince had fled there to escape repeated attacks by the Burmese, and during his enforced stay became fluent in Persian and a connoisseur of the region's Afghan-influenced Indo-Islamic culture, particularly its poetry, music, and architecture. On his return to Mrauk U, Bengali artists became a prominent feature

The ruins of Mrauk U, capital city of the Arakan kingdom

of his own court, founded in 1430, where the royal attire had more in common with Mughal fashions than the Thai-influenced styles of Burmese kings in Inwa (Ava). Sadly, precious few artifacts survive from what was undoubtedly one of Southeast Asia's great cultural flowerings, other than the exquisite Mahamuni Buddha image, which Bodawpaya's army carried off in 1784 and is now in Mandalay.

BAGAN ARCHEOLOGICAL ZONE

Lost cities abound in Myanmar, but none approach the splendor of Bagan. Scattered across an arid plain in a bend of the Ayeyarwady are the ruins of around 2,000 monasteries, temples, shrines, and stupas – remnants of an imperial capital that reached its peak between the 11th and 13th centuries. Viewed at sunrise or sunset, with the warm light intensifying the red-brown hues of their brickwork, the hundreds of tapering, elegantly symmetrical towers and finials rising from the dusty sand flats create a superb spectacle.

Once a thriving metropolis of between 50,000 and 200,000 people, Bagan dazzled Marco Polo, who described its gilded skyline as "one of the finest sights in the world." Monks and scholars from across Asia came here to study philosophy, law, grammar, astrology, and medicine, and religion permeated every aspect of life. Under the influence of Shin Arahan (see p51), Bagan's kings gradually began to favor and promote Theravada Buddhism. But the faith overlayered a complex blend of arcane beliefs rooted in the Tibetan-influenced Mahayana tradition and Hindu cults of Shiva and Vishnu, as well as in the worship of local nature spirits, or *nats*.

It is possible to chart this cultural shift in Bagan's religious architecture, where small, dark shrines swirling with Tantric murals were, over time, superseded by towering temples and giant, bell-shaped stupas. While a handful of these remain active places of worship, visited in great numbers by Burmese pilgrims, many more stand all but forgotten in the scrub. Virtually none, however, remain in a ruinous state. Since the 1990s, the government has pursued a massive renovation program, restoring even smaller, off-track monuments. Local villages have been forcibly relocated, an unsightly viewing tower set up, and ruins rebuilt, often from scratch and with little regard for original appearances, much to the dismay of UNESCO, which has denied Bagan coveted World Heritage Site status. The heavy-handed government control of the site, however, is effortlessly eclipsed by the phenomenal beauty of the monuments themselves, which are one of the true wonders of the medieval world.

Villagers herding goats through the fields surrounding the ancient temples and stupas of Bagan

◀ Detail of one of the Buddhas at the Htilominlo Temple, one of the greatest of Bagan's shrines

Exploring the Bagan Archeological Zone

Bagan's 2,000 or so surviving monuments are spread over a 26-sq-mile (50-sq-km) area called the Bagan Archeological Zone. Entry tickets to the site can be bought on arrival at the airport or jetty, or at some of the larger temples, and must be paid for in US dollars. Nyaung U village, the main market and transport hub, has most of the budget and mid-scale accommodations. Overlooking the bend in the river and connected via surfaced roads, Old Bagan has restaurants and a handful of mostly high-end hotels, while New Bagan is where most of the tour groups stay. Although major monuments are open from dawn to dusk, less frequented ones may be locked. Key keepers usually live nearby and will unlock the gates when tourists appear – a service for which they'll expect a small tip.

Mural at the refined Sulamani Pagoda showing a scene from the Buddha's life

Sights at a Glance

Getting Around

To get around Bagan, Chinese-made gearless bicycles may be rented from most hotels, although they puncture easily and can be hard work in the heat. A more relaxing option is to hire a horse cart for the day. Drivers know the zone well and provide a commentary on the monuments, although their English may not be fluent. Taxis can also be hired for the day. Electric bikes (e-bikes) are a popular option, but you have to pedal if they run out of power midway. Pick-up trucks run a regular route between Nyaung U, Old Bagan, Myinkaba, and New Bagan. For Popa Taung Kalat, taxis are the most convenient option. Alternatively, pick-up trucks leave from Nyaung U market, but some only go as far as Kyaukpadaung, where you have to change for Popa. All travel agents sell tickets for the Malikha 2, Nmai Hka, and Myanmar Golden River Group ferries to Mandalay. Departures are from the Nyaung U jetty, or the Old Bagan jetty in the dry season. The slower IWT ferries leave twice weekly; tickets are sold from their office near the Nyaung U jetty, and by all travel agents.

Souvenirs for sale and exhibits at the small Thanaka Museum in Nyaung U

Detail, Tuyin Taung temple,
Popa Taung Kalat

Key

— Main road
═ Other road
-- Track
— Railroad

The Sacred Architecture of Bagan

Bagan's golden era of sacred building spanned 250 years, during which time architectural styles evolved in a dramatic fashion. Initially imitating the cylindrical structures of the ancient Pyu city of Sri Ksetra, Bagan's stupas gradually grew more slender and bell-shaped, culminating in the elaborately embellished, tapering spire that remains the classical Burmese archetype today. Temples changed from simple replicas of wooden shrines to soaring masterpieces with entrances on four sides, cavernous interiors, and spectacular roof finials – innovations enabled by the emergence of the pointed arch in Bagan. Charting this stylistic metamorphosis and piecing together the historical shifts it represents is one of the great pleasures of a visit to the site.

Fresco at the Sulamani Temple, Bagan Archeological Zone

Bagan's Stupas

Myanmar's oldest surviving stupas are those at the city of Sri Ksetra (see pp98–9). Their cylindrical, elongated shapes influenced the forms of Bagan's first pagodas. These slowly became more bell-like, with squat middle sections and tapering spires, and grew larger and higher, set on grand stepped terraces (see pp32–3).

Bupaya
Early gourd-shaped stupas such as Bagan's Bupaya had gently swelling sides and tapering spires.

Lawkananda
The design gradually evolved to have straight flanks and rounded tops, a bit like the early Pyu stupas.

Sapada
Some of Bagan's pagodas showed Sinhalese influence in the design of the square relic chamber above the bell.

Shwezigon
The scale of the pagodas gradually became grander. Stupas had broad bells and were set on high bases.

Mingalazedi
With the majestic stupas of the 13th century, the Burmese pagoda reached its most colossal, imposing form.

Painting and Stucco

Bagan's brick monasteries and temples were originally encased in a shell of stucco which was applied wet, molded, and allowed to dry. Patches on surviving structures reveal how sophisticated this plasterwork was, combining figurative forms of mythical creatures and saints with floral borders and geometric shapes. Mural fragments also adorn temple interiors; the oldest of them date from the 10th century, when Tantricism and Hinduism greatly influenced Burmese Buddhist iconography. New paintings in a more graphic, folk-art style were also added to several shrines by the Konbaungs.

Detail of stuccowork at the Upali Thein ordination hall

Bagan's Temples

Taking their cue originally from Indian architecture, Bagan's temples grew slowly more imposing, ethereal, and distinctively Burmese over time, culminating in the giant, double-storied shrines that tower above the northern plain to this day.

Pointed arch and door guardians, Nagayon

Floor plan of Nagayon

Mon: Nagayon Temple

Dating from the reign of King Kyanzittha (1030–1112), the earliest temples in Bagan are in Mon style, with a single entrance opening onto a vestibule and a central inner sanctum which contains a Buddha image.

Transitional: Ananda Temple

Kyanzittha's masterpiece still shows Mon influence, but is in the form of a perfect Greek cross, with four entrances and projecting porticoes. Vaulted concentric corridors encircle the inner shrines.

Floor plan showing the Greek cross layout of the Ananda Temple

The graceful exterior of the Ananda Temple

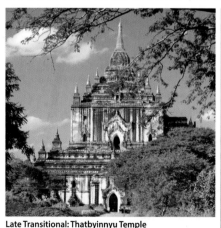

Late Transitional: Thatbyinnyu Temple

Taller, more slender, and lighter inside thanks to the addition of larger doors and windows, the refined Bamar style of the 12th century introduced the concept of "hollow" or *gu*-style cubes placed on top of each other.

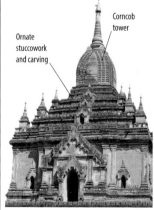

Corncob tower

Ornate stuccowork and carving

Late Bagan: Htilominlo Temple

The last of the great temples erected in Bagan in the 13th century, such as Htilominlo, take the *gu* principle and embellish it with more complex roofs, ornate decor, and elongated towers.

❶ Old Bagan

The area of sandy scrub beside the bend in the river, known as Old Bagan, formed the hub of the medieval city. Traces of the fortified walls and gateways that once encircled it on the landward side are still visible in many places, but it is the great concentration of temples and stupas dating from Bagan's heyday – including two of the site's giants, the Gawdawpalin and Thatbyinnu Temples – that make this a particularly rewarding area to explore on foot or by bicycle. In 1998, the villagers who lived among the ruins were forcibly relocated a mile or two south in New Bagan, so there are few opportunities for refreshment between the monuments. The nearest stalls cluster along the main road east of the Tharabar Gate.

View over the temples of Bagan with the Rakhine-Yoma Hills in the distance

★ **Gawdawpalin Temple**
Built by King Narapatisithu (1138–1211), Gawdawpalin is one of Bagan's largest and most ethereal temples. It is of the "hollow," or *gu*, type, with porticoes on four sides and a vaulted inner corridor.

Lacquerware
Museum

KEY

① **The Bagan Golden Palace** is a reconstruction of the original.

② **The diminutive Pitakat Taik** once held Anawrahta's library, a collection of Buddhist scriptures looted after the attack on Thaton. It reportedly took 30 elephants to carry the books back to Bagan.

③ **The 20-ft (6-m) Thandawgya Buddha** sits in *bhumisparsha* mudra.

④ **Ngakywenadaung Pagoda**, a small bulbous structure, is similar to the early Pyu pagodas.

⑤ **The 11th-century Nathlaung Kyaung** was in its day the most important Hindu temple at Bagan. Its presiding deity, stolen in the 19th century, is now in a Berlin museum.

⑥ **Pahtothamya Temple** contains Mon-style paintings.

⑦ **The site museum** holds a poorly lit and labeled collection of stone Buddhas and inscriptions culled from Bagan's monuments.

Mimalaung Kyaung
This late-12th-century shrine became known as "the temple that does not catch fire" after it survived unscathed a devastating blaze in 1225.

Mataungta
Gate

Tharabar Gate

The last surviving gateway in the old city walls, Tharabar is flanked by a pair of brick-walled shrines dedicated to the *nats*, or nature spirits, Min Mahagiri and Hnamadawgyi.

VISITORS' CHECKLIST

Practical Information
Road Map C3. 7 miles (11 km) west of airport. **Open** museum: 9am–4:30pm Tue–Sun; temples: dawn–dusk daily. 🗺 covers all of Bagan; separate admission fee for museum. 🎧 guides can be hired through most hotels; horse cart drivers also provide commentary.

Transport
🛫 Mandalay Intl. 🛬 Nyaung U Airport. 🚐 Pick-ups run between Nyaung U, Old Bagan, Myinkaba, & New Bagan. Bicycles, e-bikes, taxis, horse carts available for hire.

Shwegugyi Temple

This fine early-Bamar-style temple was erected by King Alaungsithu in 1131. Inscriptions inside record that it took just seven months to complete. Large windows and doors create a light, airy feel inside.

Kalay Gate

★ Thatbyinnyu Temple

Visible from all over Bagan, Thatbyinnyu, which means "omniscience," is the tallest structure on the site, rising to a majestic 210 ft (61 m). It was the first to adopt the double-story "hollow" *(gu)* style.

Key

— Suggested route

0 meters — 200
0 yards — 200

❷ Ananda Temple

Surmounted by a classically proportioned corncob tower, the whitewashed Ananda Temple is among the most stylistically refined and impressive temples in Bagan. It is also the most revered by Burmese Buddhists. Its grand entranceways lead to four beautiful gilded Buddhas standing in huge recesses, interconnected by corridors that are adorned with wonderful stone sculpture and painting. The exterior surfaces are no less sumptuously embellished, featuring bands of green-glazed terra-cotta plaques showing scenes from the *Jatakas*, episodes from the Buddha's life. From afar, however, the golden spire is Ananda's most readily identifiable feature, as spectacular today as it was when Kyanzittha commissioned the building in 1105.

Door guardians, made of exquisitely carved and painted hardwood, flank the entrances on the east and west.

Outer wall and arched gateways
A high wall with arched gateways at the cardinal points encloses the whole complex. Inside the entrances, guardian deities in the seated *lalitasana* position, denoting spiritual ease, welcome worshippers.

KEY

① **The long north and south porticoes** are 19th-century Konbaung additions.

② **The gable-arched entrances** to the temple are decorated with exuberant stuccowork. Only those on the east and west sides are open.

③ **The upper terraces**, which are currently not open to the public, contain Ananda's finest paintings.

④ **The central roof** consists of six receding terraces.

⑤ **Corner stupas** adorn the roof.

⑥ **Over 1,000 stone sculptures** line the outer corridor, many of them set in niches.

⑦ **Carved stone reliefs** lining the inner ambulatory corridor recount the story of the Buddha's life.

Stone *chinthes*, or grinning leogryphs, stand guard at all the corners of the temple building.

★ Central tower
The splendid corncob tower, soaring 170 ft (52 m) above the sandy plains, underlines the fact the shrine was designed by Indian architects. It is crowned by a gleaming golden umbrella finial, or *hti*.

Jataka **tiles**
Thousands of green-glazed terra-cotta tiles encrust the base, sides, and terrace of the temple, depicting scenes from the *Jatakas*.

★ Four Buddhas
One of the temple's most famous features are the four gilded wooden Buddhas standing in the main shrines. Only those in the north and south are original, the other two having been destroyed by fires.

South-facing Kassapa

North-facing Kakusandha

East-facing Konagamana

West-facing Gautama

❸ Ananda Oak Kyaung

Road Map C3. Old Bagan, W of Ananda Temple's northern entrance.

In ancient Pali-Sanskrit, "oak" means "brick," and this small *vihara* (chapel or sanctuary) is one of only a few brick monasteries surviving from the early Bagan period. The building is best known for the exceptionally well-preserved frescoes that cloak its interior walls and ceilings. Rendered in earthy reds, greens, blacks, and browns, these are particularly rich with scenes of everyday life in the 11th century: market shopping, Arab traders, soldiers marching, and people bathing, cooking, and playing musical instruments, including the *hsaing waing* (Burmese musical ensemble) and *saung gauk* (Burmese harp). There is also some erotica. Although Ananda Oak Kyaung is locked as a rule, the caretaker who has the key lives in a house next to the compound and will open it for visitors.

❹ Sin Myar Shin

Road Map C3. N of the Shwesandaw Pagoda.

One of a trio of shrines standing in a neat row just south of the main road, this double-story

Frescoes surrounding a statue of the Buddha in the tiny Upali Thein ordination hall

temple is capped by a richly gilded corncob spire. Two Buddha images preside over the main hall on the first floor, while four Buddhas facing the cardinal points sit in the upper chamber. Traces of original murals remain throughout, along with paintings from the Konbaung era of the 18th and 19th centuries.

However, the best reason to come to this shrine is for the chance to scramble up to its high terrace below the main tower for glorious views of the sunrise or sunset. Very few visitors to Bagan realize that the authorities still permit people to climb Sin Myar Shin, so the terrace rarely has more than a handful of people. This is a particularly good place to come to admire the Thatbyinnyu and Ananda Temples, both located only a short distance north, and floodlit to spectacular effect in the evenings.

❺ Upali Thein

Road Map C3. 1 mile (1.5 km) NE of Ananda, Old Bagan–Nyaung U Rd. ✉

This diminutive ordination hall dating from the 13th century forms part of a larger monastic complex whose wooden portions have long since disappeared. It is noteworthy for the way its exterior mimics the design and decor of the now lost wood structures, and for the frescoes inside. Painted during the Konbaung era, they show scenes from the lives of past Buddhas as well as from the hall's consecration. The building was erected during the reign of King Kyazuco (r. 1234–50), known as the Philosopher King for his piety and knowledge of the Theravada canon. Kyazuco named the building after a famous monk, Mahasiha Upali, who was originally invited to Bagan by his father.

A Historical Theme Park?

The efforts of Myanmar's military government to restore the ancient ruins of Bagan after centuries of wear from weather and earthquakes were described by UNESCO as "[a] Disney-style fantasy version of one of the world's great religious and historical sites… [using] the wrong materials to build wrongly shaped structures on top of magnificent ancient stupas." Since 1995, an estimated 1,299 stupas, monasteries, and temples have been speculatively rebuilt from piles of bricks scattered across the site of the medieval city, while another 668 have seen major renovations, funded largely by merit-making donations from wealthy Burmese. Archeologists, heritage architects, and UNESCO have been unanimous in their condemnation of the program, claiming that the results bear little relation to what the original structures would have looked like, and criticizing the use of cement and other modern materials. In reply, the Burmese authorities claim it is the government's "duty to preserve, strengthen, and

Ancient temples and pagodas scattered across Bagan

restore" Bagan's monuments, and have flown in the face of foreign disapproval by permitting the construction of an unsightly observation tower and gigantic museum complex that now dominate horizons where once only temple towers rose from the plains. The controversy, however, seems not to have deterred tourists, and, since 2010, foreign visitors have flocked to the archeological zone in record numbers to view the spectacular reconstructions.

The soaring lines of Htilominlo, one of the last great temples built in Bagan

❻ Htilominlo

Road Map C3. SE of Upali Thein, Old Bagan–Nyaung U Rd.

One of the greatest of all Bagan's temples, Htilominlo dominates the northern group of monuments and is the very antithesis of the nearby Upali Thein: a soaring, triumphant building whose tapering central spire reaches 150 ft (46 m) into the sky. King Nantaungmya (r. 1211–34), son of a concubine and therefore several notches down the line of succession, commissioned it to mark his ascent to the throne after a divination ritual involving a tilting white umbrella. Built in splendid late-Burmese style, with a main vestibule that is oriented to the rising sun, the temple is the last example of its kind erected in Bagan. Patches of ornate stone carving and stucco survive around the doorways, arches, and pediments outside. The interior houses four gilded Buddhas on each of its two floors, facing the cardinal points.

❼ Shwe Leik Too

Road Map C3. Outskirts of Wetkyin village, midway between Nyaung U and Old Bagan.

The 13th-century Shwe Leik Too is a midsized temple in late-Bamar style with four projecting porticos and a corncob tower, enclosed by a low perimeter wall. The temple is of interest primarily because it is among only a handful of monuments in Bagan which the government still allows visitors to climb. A low-roofed passageway leads from the vaulted inner chamber, which holds both standing and seated Buddhas, to the upper terrace from where fine panoramic views extend over the northern half of the archeological zone. To the southwest, Htilominlo looks resplendent in the dawn light, while the myriad temples and pagodas to the east form striking silhouettes as the sun rises behind them.

The 13th-century Bamar-style Shwe Leik Too Temple with its corncob tower

❽ Gubyauknge and Gubyaukgyi

Road Map C3. Wetkyin village.

East of Htilominlo, the 11th-century Gubyauknge, one of Bagan's oldest temples, retains some fine original stuccowork on its exterior. A pair of *nats*, or nature spirits, flank the doorway to the main shrine, reflecting the syncretic nature of Buddhism in the medieval city.

Gubyaukgyi, a stone's throw northeast, is a 13th-century building with a distinctive, pyramidal sanctuary tower surmounting its roof. Usually called the Wetkyin Gubyaukgyi to distinguish it from its namesake in Myinkaba, the temple retains some fine mural traces around the entrance ceiling.

Mural at the 13th-century Wetkyin Gubyaukgyi temple in Bagan

❾ Nyaung U

Road Map C3. 2.5 miles (4.5 km) NW of airport. 🏠 55,000. ✈ Mandalay International. ✈ Nyaung U Airport. 🚐 🚌 🚎 Pick-ups run a regular route between Nyaung U, Old Bagan, Myinkaba, and New Bagan. 🚍

Bagan's central market area lines the main street of Nyaung U village. Most visitors who travel up here do so to eat in one of the many restaurants flanking Thiripyitsaya 4 Street. Many also stop off at the quirky **Thanaka Museum**, which has displays showing how *thanaka*, the quintessentially Burmese face paste, is produced. The museum shop sells cosmetics made from this fragrant wood powder.

🏛 **Thanaka Museum**
Corner of Thiripyitsaya 4 St and Main Rd. **Open** 9am–9pm daily. 📷

⑩ Kyanzittha Umin

Road Map C3. Nyaung U.

A cave temple in a plot just southwest of the Shwezigon Pagoda, Kyanzittha Umin was originally part of a small monastery. The cave's exterior was encased in a brick facade, while inside it was excavated to create corridors whose walls and ceilings were decorated with murals, many of which survive intact. Although named after King Kyanzittha (1030–1112), the site was probably developed during the reign of his father, King Anawrahta (1015–78). A flashlight is recommended for a visit as the cave has no interior lighting.

⑪ Shwezigon Pagoda

Road Map C3. Western edge of Nyaung U. Oct/Nov: Shwezigon pagoda festival.

The gilded Shwezigon Pagoda, on the outskirts of Nyaung U in the northeastern corner of the archeological zone, was Bagan's most important religious site during the reign of King Anawrahta, founder of the Bagan Empire *(see pp50–51)*, and his son, King Kyanzittha, who completed work on this complex. Over the span of their two lifetimes, military conquests

and land reforms brought peace and prosperity to the kingdom, enabling an intense period of temple construction of which this, along with the Ananda Temple, is the shining example. It was Anawrahta's enthusiastic promotion of Theravada Buddhism, coupled with a tolerant attitude to *nat* worship, that also forged the distinctive religious culture of Burma in the 11th century – one that endures to this day. Evidence of this is to be found in the southeast corner of the pagoda's enclosure, where the Shrine of the 37 *Mahagiri Nats* is dominated by a stone statue of Thagyamin, the king of the *nats*.

Believed to enclose a bone and tooth relic of Gautama Buddha, as well as a gold image of Anawrahta and a Chinese emerald Buddha, the main *zedi* (stupa) measures 160 ft (49 m) high and 160 ft (49 m) across its base, with four smaller stupas at its corners and bands of 500 beautifully enameled *Jataka* plaques around its sides. Four other subsidiary shrines at the *zedi's* cardinal points house beautiful cast copper Buddhas dating from 1102. Also worth a close look, on the eastern facade of the pagoda near the great lion images, are the Edicts of King Kyanzittha, recounting the ruler's coronation and the foundation story of the site.

The unusual Sapada Pagoda, with a square relic chamber in the spire

⑫ Sapada Pagoda

Road Map C3. Junction of the main and airport roads, Nyaung U.

Standing incongruously at the intersection of the airport road and Nyaung U's main street, this late-Bagan-style pagoda owes its unusual shape to the career of the young monk after which it was named. Sapada was one of 20 novices dispatched to an illustrious monastery in Ceylon, where he spent ten years. His teachings later had a great influence on Theravada philosophy in the Burmese capital. In honor of the monk's formative sojourn abroad, the stupa has a Sinhalese-style square *harmika*, or relic chamber, between its bell-shaped bottom and top spire.

The grand Shwezigon Pagoda, believed to contain relics of the Buddha

For hotels and restaurants in this region see pp203–4 and p212

⑬ The Southern Plain

Road Map C3. Minnanthu village.

The temples spread across the southeastern extremity of the archeological zone, around Minnanthu village, are the most remote on the site, but their superb murals, which include some of the oldest and best preserved in Bagan, warrant the effort needed to reach them.

On the west side of the lane winding through Minnanthu is the whitewashed **Lemyethna Temple**. This single-storied edifice is built in late Bagan style on a square raised platform with four projecting porches and an upper section of receding terraces, surmounted by an Indian-style curvilinear spire and gilded pagoda. Dating from 1222, it is said to have been built in honor of a prime minister who, having been sentenced to execution by the king, wrote a famous poem expressing equanimity at the prospect of his death, described as merely part of the "ineluctable cycle of Karma." Lemyethna contains some well-preserved paintings, particularly around the arches framing the Buddha shrines, although many of these have been lost under a recent coat of limewash.

A short way north, on the opposite side of the lane, stands a trio of shrines conjoined by

Buddha images with hands positioned in the *dharmachakra* mudra, Payathonzu Temple

narrow vaulted passageways. **Payathonzu Temple** was never completed but is renowned for its wonderful 12th-century paintings dominated by floral motifs into which mythical animals, birds, and human figures are woven. Shown under the bodhi trees where they gained enlightenment, the 28 Buddhas of the Past also feature prominently. Several murals reveal a marked Tantric influence. Some scholars attribute this to Payathonzu's proximity to the last of Bagan's Ari monasteries. These were home to forest-dwelling monks who practiced Tantric rituals regarded as debauched by the Theravada order.

More wonderful paintings adorn the walls and arched ceilings of the **Nandamannya Temple**, a short walk north down a sandy track off the lane. Framed by decorative scrolls are a series of large panels showing scenes from the life of Gautama Buddha.

These include the Birth, with Prince Siddhartha coming forth from the right hip of his royal mother, and the Renunciation of the World, symbolized by the Buddha cutting off his hair. A small rectangular panel on the shrine's western side depicts the famous *Temptation of Mara*. Here the demon Mara, the personification of unwholesome influences and temptation, tries in vain to seduce the Buddha out of the meditation that led to his enlightenment by showing him visions of beautiful young women, who, in some legends, are said to be Mara's daughters.

A hot-air balloon floating past the exquisite temples of Bagan

Ballooning in Bagan

The sight of hot-air balloons drifting serenely over Bagan's otherworldly skyline has become almost as iconic of the archeological zone as the temples themselves. Operated by a company known as Balloons Over Bagan, also called Eastern Safaris (balloonsoverbagan.com), these magical flights run every morning and evening through the winter season from October to March. The rides allow visitors an unrivaled perspective over the sprawl of Bagan, from the monuments and surrounding plain to the Ayeyarwady River and Rakhine-Yoma Hills. After an hour in the air at an easy 15 mph (24 kmph), the balloons come to a gentle halt in the fields on the fringes of the site, where a champagne breakfast awaits, followed by a ride back to base in a vintage Burmese bus. Tickets can be booked online or at the Balloons Over Bagan sales desk in Wetkyin village, on the southwestern edge of Nyaung U.

The temples and pagodas of Old Bagan, with the great Thatbyinnyu Temple soaring up behind them ▶

⓮ New Bagan

Road Map C3. 5.5 miles (9 km) SW of Nyaung U Airport. ✈ Mandalay International. 🚍 Nyaung U Airport. Pick-ups run between Nyaung U, Old Bagan, Myinkaba, and New Bagan.

Bagan Myothit, or New Bagan, was created in the 1990s to house villagers relocated by the Tatmadaw (military government) from Old Bagan. Of the monuments around the village, the largest and most impressive is the **Dhammayazika Pagoda**. It was built in 1196 by King Narapatisithu (1138–1211), during whose peaceful reign Burmese culture first began to supersede that of the Mon and the ancient Pyu. The gilded stupa rests on three hexagonal terraces studded with five smaller gilded shrines that contain Konbaung-era Buddhas. Dhammayazika was one of many prominent sites in Bagan to receive a radical makeover by the government in the 1990s.

The **Anauk** (west) and **Ashe** (east) **Petleik Pagodas**, in New Bagan's southern neighborhood of Thiripyitsaya, date from the 11th century. Neither would be of more than passing interest were it not for their superb collection of unglazed terracotta *Jataka* tiles discovered in vaulted corridors surrounding

Souvenir stalls lining the path to the gilded 12th-century Dhammayazika Pagoda

the stupas during excavation work carried out in 1905. The tiles are now protected by newly built brick walls and roofs.

At Bagan's southern edge, the **Lawkananda Pagoda** stands on a bluff above the river. Attributed to Anawrahta (1015–78), it dates from the 11th century and enshrines one of the four tooth relics of the Buddha that are said to have magically replicated themselves from the one set within the Shwezigon Pagoda (*see p128*). The stupa, whose gold leaf and marble-tiled terrace are recent additions, stands on a platform that affords fine views over the river.

🛈 Dhammayazika Pagoda
Between New Bagan and Minnanthu village, north side of main road.

🛈 Anauk and Ashe Petleik Pagodas
Southern edge of Thiripyitsaya, New Bagan.

🛈 Lawkananda Pagoda
Southwest of New Bagan.

⓯ Myinkaba

Road Map C3. Between Old Bagan & New Bagan. 🏠 800. ✈ Mandalay International. 🚍 Nyaung U Airport. Pick-ups run between Nyaung U, Old Bagan, Myinkaba, and New Bagan. 🎉 Sep: Manuha festival.

After the conquest of Thaton in 1057, King Anawrahta exiled the Mon King Manuha to the village of Myinkaba. The most stately and well preserved of the temples that sprang up around the displaced royal family is the **Nagayon Temple**. It was built by King Kyanzittha (1030–1112), allegedly at the spot where he took refuge from his brother and predecessor Sawlu (1050–84) during a feud in the 1080s. Kyanzittha had the temple built after he became king as an act of thanksgiving to a snake deity that protected him during his flight; a cobra hood above the head of the gilded standing Buddha in the main shrine underlines the connection. The ambulatory corridor retains some impressive 11th-century paintings, along with sculpted figures of previous Buddhas.

The 11th-century Lawkananda Pagoda overlooking the Ayeyarwady River

For hotels and restaurants in this region see pp203–4 and p212

The 11th-century Abeyadana Temple with a classical square base

The foundation myth of the nearby **Abeyadana Temple**, on the opposite side of the road, is linked to the same snake-related story, only in this version, the site was where the fugitive prince met Abeyadana, his Bengali lover, before fleeing Bagan. Some of the site's finest murals adorn the interior of the shrine, featuring images of Hindu deities and Mahayana Buddhist bodhisattvas, interpreted as reflecting the Bengali origins of the queen.

The **Nanpaya Temple**, a short way north on the edge of the village, is believed to have been the residence (some say prison) of King Manuha, accounting for the *hamsa* bird images on the outside of the building – the *hamsa* was the heraldic symbol of the Mon nation (*see p92*).

Four pillars inside the pagoda are decorated with some of Bagan's most beautiful stone carvings, including one showing Brahma, a deity of the Hindu trinity, holding lotus flowers.

The **Manuha Temple**, still farther north, was built by the eponymous king in 1059 while he was in exile, using funds raised by the sale of his remaining crown jewels. A somewhat nondescript square block on the outside, the pagoda holds an extraordinary quartet of outsized Buddhas – three giant gilded sitting figures, and a huge reclining one – whose disproportionate scale and cramped confines are believed to have been intended to express the discomfort of the Mon king's incarceration and exile from his homeland.

Buddhist pilgrims pour through Manuha's compound during holiday periods, and the next stop on their itinerary is usually the **Gubyaukgyi Temple** beside the main road at the north end of Myinkaba. Built in 1113 by Prince Yaza Kumaya, it is famed for its murals, which were restored by UNESCO in the 1980s. The paintings lining the main hall illustrate scenes from 550 *Jataka* stories, including the 16 Dreams of Kosala. On the outside of the building, some exceptionally fine stucco decoration survives on the surrounds of the pierced-stone windows.

Adjacent to the temple stands a small structure enclosing a four-sided carved pillar. The oldest surviving text from medieval Bagan, the famous Myazedi Inscription is written in Pali, Pyu, Mon, and Burmese, and is one of a pair – the other is at the site museum at Old Bagan.

The Gubyaukgyi Temple, featuring some fine stuccowork around its windows

Artisan working on a laquerware pot, Bagan

Lacquerware

Myanmar has been a center for fine lacquerware since Bayinnaung's invasion of Siam in 1563, when skilled Laos-Shan artisans were brought back to his court. Bagan became the industry's main hub in the 20th century, and in the 1920s the British founded a lacquerware school in the ruined city to foster the craft. The largest concentration of workshops and showrooms is around Myinkaba and New Bagan. There visitors can watch the various stages of lacquerware production, from the weaving of bamboo and rattan frames, through the molding and drying of the lacquer putty, to the careful engraving and polishing required to finish the pieces. Prices are high, primarily because it can take a few months to complete even a small bowl; a large object with elaborate designs requires up to a year of work. The finer the detail, and the more colors and layers of lacquer that are applied – 15 coats is the norm for a quality article – the more the product will cost.

The graceful five-terraced Shwesandaw Pagoda, a popular sunset-viewing spot

⓰ Mingalazedi Pagoda

Road Map C3. NE of Myinkaba village to the west of the road.

This giant pagoda between the main road and riverbank was the last major building project at Bagan before the Mongol invasion of 1287. Nothing about the structure, however, suggests an empire on the decline. The scale, complexity, and precision of the stonework is exceptional, and the number of expensive ceramic plaques adorning its three receding terraces unrivaled. It is a testament to the extravagance for which its sponsor, King Narathihapate (1238–87), was renowned – in a donatory inscription, the king boasts of commanding an army of 36 million men and eating "300 dishes of curry each day."

Yet beneath the bravado, the city's coffers were emptying fast and the king's grip on power slipping away. The black hole in the treasury's finances had grown during Narathihapate's reign. Even as his slaves toiled on the lavish Mingalazedi, Kublai Khan's Mongol army were attacking Bhamo, gateway to the Ayeyarwady and central Burma. Only a couple of years after work on the building was completed, the king fled in panic to Pyay (Prome), where he was arrested and forced to take poison, earning for himself the unflattering epithet Taok Pyay Min, "the king who ran from the Chinese."

Until 2012, it was possible to scale the steep flights of steps that lead to the cylindrical base of Mingalazedi's bell-shaped stupa, but access has since been forbidden.

Mingalazedi Pagoda, the last of the great stupas built at Bagan

⓱ Shwesandaw Pagoda

Road Map C3. S of Anawrahta Rd/ Yangon–Mandalay Hwy.

One of the few monuments that the Bagan authorities allow visitors to climb is the Shwesandaw Pagoda, a ten-minute ride by horse cart to the northeast. Built by King Anawrahta in 1057, the enormous *zedi* was one of four that Bagan's founding father constructed outside the city walls to provide cosmic protection for the capital (Shwezigon was another).

The pagoda comprises five square terraces topped by a cylindrical stupa with a recently added *hti*, or finial. The old one toppled in an earthquake in 1975 and still lies where it landed, crumbling in the dusty compound below.

A hair relic of the Buddha that the king of Bago presented to Anawrahta for his help in repelling a Khmer invasion of the Mon kingdom is believed to be secreted inside the stupa. Flights of steep steps ascend the whitewashed monument on four sides, leading to a spacious terrace at the base of the stupa. The panoramic views from here over the archeological zone are magnificent, although at sunset, when a souvenir bazaar springs up in the enclosure below, the crowds and noise of camera shutters can be oppressive.

Environs
Housed in a long, rectangular, redbrick chamber on the west side of the Shwesandaw compound is a serene Buddha known as **Shinbinthalyaung**. Measuring 60 ft (18 m) from head to toe, the reclining figure was installed during roughly the same period as the nearby stupa. Broken traces of original frescoes adorn the plaster walls of the temple.

A two-minute walk north of the Shwesandaw Pagoda, the little-visited **Lawkahteikpan Temple** is a beautifully proportioned structure dating from the reign of Kyanzittha's successor, Alaungsithu (1089–1168). Inside, the walls and ceilings above the gilded, seated Buddha are decorated with well-preserved and intricate mid-12th-century frescoes. They require a flashlight to be viewed as there is no lighting in the building.

⓲ Dhammayangyi Temple

Road Map C3. SE of the Shwesandaw Pagoda.

Rising from the sand and scrub, Dhammayangyi, a massive walled temple a short walk southeast of the Shwesandaw Pagoda, is the largest and best preserved of all of Bagan's monuments. The temple was built in the late 1160s, during the short three-year reign of King Narathu (1118–71). The king was said to be a violent psychopath who ascended to the imperial throne after murdering his father, Alaungsithu, by smothering him with a pillow, and elder brother, Min Shin Saw, by poisoning him on his coronation day. The temple's colossal size is often interpreted as a gesture of atonement for the killings, though it seems to have done little to erase Narathu's nasty streak. He later strangled his Bengali queen, allegedly because he took objection to her Hindu rituals. Her father promptly dispatched an eight-strong suicide squad to exact revenge in 1171. Court chronicles record that the assassins were able to gain access to the palace by disguising themselves as Brahmin astrologers, hiding their swords beneath their robes. Having killed the king, they slit their own throats.

Similar in layout to Ananda, Dhammayangyi is thought to have the best masonry and brickwork in the archeological zone. King Narathu is said to have overseen construction work himself, threatening with summary execution any mason who left between the bricks a gap wide enough for a needle to be inserted.

The colossal Dhammayangyi, the largest temple in Bagan

The Sulamani Temple, one of the most beautiful structures of Bagan's late period

⓳ Sulamani Temple

Road Map C3. Central Bagan Plain.

The most refined of the temples of Bagan's late period, Sulamani forms a striking silhouette in the center of the archeological zone. Fusing the monumental verticality of structures such as Thatbyinnyu (see p121) with the horizontal planes of Dhammayangyi, it fully deserves its name, which translates as "Crowning Jewel." The temple was built on two major levels, with porches at the cardinal points, and seven tiers of ascending terraces whose corners are crowned by delicate tapering stupas. Surmounting the whole is a beautifully designed sikhara tower, comprising a pagoda placed on top of a curvilinear corncob base.

Only the first floor is open to the public. Encircling the inner shrine, where four Buddhas face the four directions, is an inner ambulatory with niches for Buddha statues on pedestals and murals depicting scenes from the life of the Buddha and a menagerie of mythological beasts, snakes, and sea creatures. Some of these are original, but most date from the Konbaung era of the 18th–19th centuries. Also of note are the exceptionally fine carved stucco moldings adorning the pediments over the exterior doorways and windows, and the glazed ceramic plaques lining the temple's base and terraces.

⑳ Popa Taung Kalat

The most popular day trip from Bagan is the drive to Popa Taung Kalat, or Mount Popa as the sheer-sided volcanic plug is more commonly known. Myanmar's most revered center of *nat* worship, it is visited in huge numbers by local people, who come to pray at the Mother Spirit shrine at the foot of the hill. Opposite the temple, a flight of covered steps winds up Taung Kalat to a small Buddhist monastery on the summit plateau. From here, stupendous views extend west across the plains of Bagan to the Ayeyarwady and the distant Rakhine-Yoma Hills, and east to the spectacular form of Mount Popa, an extinct volcano with a deep caldera and a cloak of dense forest. Visitors who spend a night at the nearby Popa Mountain Resort will be treated to the vision of the temple's golden spires illuminated by the first rays of daylight.

The small *hti*-topped golden rock stupa at the shrine of Popa Taung Kalat

Main entrance to Popa Taung Kalat
The entrance to the *zaungdan* (covered stairway) that winds up the hill is crowned with a seven-tiered ceremonial *pyatthat* roof tower and flanked by a pair of large white elephants.

37 *Mahagiri Nats*
The elaborately decorated Mother Spirit shrine at the base of the hill holds life-sized statues of the 37 *Mahagiri Nats*, or Great Spirit Heroes. Dressed in golden crowns and vibrant silk, the deities are joined by various ogresses, wizards, and necromancers.

KEY

① **The Shrine of the Mother Spirit of Popa Nat**, opposite the main entrance, is visited by all pilgrims to Popa Taung Kalat. The shrine's doorway is flanked by a pair of tigers.

② **The bazaar** at the base of the hill contains souvenir stalls, shops selling flowers and religious paraphernalia, and teashops offering Burmese snacks and drinks.

③ **Taung Kalat (Pedestal Hill)** rises 2,400 ft (730 m) above sea level.

④ **The 777-step** *zaungdan* offers a 20-minute hike to the summit.

⑤ **Mount Popa** (4,981 ft/1,518 m) to the east is a national park. Trails wind up its forested slopes to the rim of the huge caldera at the summit.

Nat Worship in Myanmar

One of the most intriguing aspects of Burmese religious life is the worship of *nats*, nature spirits who represent human flaws, weaknesses, or vices, and who died unnatural and often violent deaths. Propitiated daily with flowers, fruit, and incense, *nats* may reside in trees, rocks, caves, or summits such as Popa Taung Kalat, the high altar of *nat* worship in Myanmar. *Nat* veneration in the country is known to predate Buddhism, which arrived in the 3rd century BC. King Anawrahta of Bagan wisely incorporated *nats* into Theravada ritual, which is why Burmese temples today nearly always also contain *nat* shrines. In addition, he fixed the official number of *nats* at 36, adding a 37th, Thagyamin, king of the *nats*, derived from the ancient Hindu deity Indra. In this way, he established the *nat* pantheon as subordinate to the Buddha, a position they retain to this day.

Tiger statue at the entrance to the Shrine of the Mother Spirit of Popa Nat

★ Taung Kalat Buddhist Monastery
The whitewashed and gilded monastery crowning the summit of Popa Taung Kalat is an important place of pilgrimage for Buddhist monks and nuns, as well as lay people from across the country.

VISITORS' CHECKLIST

Practical Information
Road Map C3. 32 miles (52 km) SE of Bagan (90-minute drive by car). **Open** 7am–10pm daily. 🛈 guides can be hired in Bagan and also at Popa Taung Kalat. 📷 🎭 May/Jun & Nov/Dec: *nat pwe*.

Transport
✈ Mandalay International.
✈ Nyaung U Airport. Taxis (individual and shared) & pick-up trucks are available from Bagan; truck passengers may have to change at Kyaukpadaung.

Hti-topped golden rock stupa

Macaques
Troops of pilfering macaques patrol the *zaungdan* up to the shrine and have become a well-known presence on Taung Kalat hill.

MANDALAY REGION

Scattered among the sand flats and low hills in and around the city of Mandalay are the remnants of four royal capitals spanning more than 500 years of Burmese history. They encompass some of the country's most iconic sights, from Mandalay's exquisite teak Shwenandaw Monastery and Amarapura's much-photographed U Bein's Bridge to Inwa's stucco monastery and the glittering, pagoda-encrusted ridges of Sagaing. Just upriver from Mandalay, the massive unfinished stupa at Mingun is another of the region's unmissable sights.

The first of the great centers built in the region was at Sagaing, on the west bank of the Ayeyarwady, where a huge concentration of religious monuments are a legacy of a kingdom that ruled over much of central Burma in the early 14th century. On the opposite bank, Inwa (Ava) was founded in 1364 on a man-made island protected by formidable walls. Today, its scant remains rise forlorn from an expanse of rice fields, best explored by horse cart via a tangle of sandy tracks.

Amarapura, spread around a lake on the southern fringes of Mandalay, became the next Konbaung capital in 1783 and retains some imposing monuments, among them the majestic Pahtodawgyi Pagoda and U Bein's Bridge. Much of the city was ruined by the massive earthquake of 1839, and it was finally deserted in the mid-1850s in favor of a site at the foot of Mandalay Hill.

Called Yadanabon – a Burmese corruption of the site's ancient Pali name, Ratanapura ("City of Gems") – Mandalay city was founded in 1857 as the Konbaung capital, a role it retained until the Third Anglo-Burmese War in 1885. Although shortlived, Yadanabon's golden era left in its wake an array of superb religious buildings, as well as the colossal royal palace – a forbidden city hidden behind walls and a wide moat.

Modern Mandalay has grown into a vast metropolis, whose heat and chaotic traffic are well worth braving for its wealth of historic sites, which include the Mahamuni Temple, Myanmar's second most venerated shrine, and the Shwenandaw Monastery, a remnant of the old palace. While most of the royal enclave was destroyed in World War II, many of the city's gilded and carved structures still survive, hinting at the splendor that must once have held sway here.

Statue of King Mindon outside the Kuthodaw Pagoda at the base of Mandalay Hill

◀ Yedanasini Pagoda, an atmospheric complex of crumbling brick stupas and stone Buddhas at Inwa (Ava), near Mandalay

Exploring Mandalay Region

Mandalay is the only practicable base from which to explore the sights in the city and its sandy environs. Foremost among these are the rebuilt royal palace and the finely carved teak Shwenandaw Monastery. Mandalay Hill and the bustling Mahamuni Temple warrant a detour, as does U Bein's teak bridge at Amarapura. Other essential stops in the area include the vestiges of the giant unfinished stupa at Mingun, reached by a memorable boat trip upriver; the elegant brick and stucco ruins of medieval Inwa (Ava); and the pagoda-covered hill at Sagaing. With two or three more days to spare, excursions can be made to a trio of lesser-visited sights around Monywa to the west, and to the colonial hill station of Pyin U Lwin to the east, which offers a leafy escape from the heat of the central plain.

▨ Area illustrated

Key

═══ Highway

─── Main road

═══ Other road

─── Railroad

═══ Regional border

Sights at a Glance

❶ *Mandalay City pp142–9*
❷ Amarapura
❸ The Ayeyarwady Bridges
❹ Sagaing
❺ *Inwa (Ava) pp154–5*
❻ *Mingun pp156–7*
❼ Monywa

❽ Thanboddhay Pagoda
❾ Bodhi Tataung
❿ Pho Win Taung Caves
⓫ A Myint
⓬ Pyin U Lwin (Maymyo)
⓭ Gokteik Bridge
⓮ Meiktila

The colorful exterior of the distinctive Thanboddhay Pagoda near Monywa

Getting Around

Mandalay's palace and hill can be covered on foot, but a taxi will be needed to get to the Mahamuni Temple and Amarapura on the city's southern edge, and for day trips to Inwa (Ava) and Sagaing. Mingun can be accessed by boat. Monywa is reachable by bus, and the sights around it are accessible using the Chindwin ferry and motorcycle taxis. There is a train service from Mandalay city to Pyin U Lwin and the Gokteik Bridge. Meiktila is on the Mandalay–Yangon bus route, and Thazi train station, east of the town, is on the Yangon, Mandalay, and Taunggyi lines.

The colonial-era Sacred Heart Catholic Church in Pyin U Lwin (Maymyo)

❶ Mandalay City

Spurred by massive Chinese investment in recent years, modern Mandalay is one of Southeast Asia's boom cities, and a far cry from the low-rise, slow-paced, bicycled-powered backwater it was after the great fires of the 1980s. Today, glass-sided malls and tower blocks loom over its main arteries, while the roads below are jammed with imported cars and motorcycles. Navigating the mayhem is easy, though, thanks to its regular grid plan. Streets running east–west are numbered 1–49, beginning in the far north, and those running north–south are numbered 50 onward, starting in the far east. Therefore the address 81st St (28/29) means on 81st Street between 28th and 29th Streets.

Cast bronze seated Buddha statue in the Setkyathiha Pagoda in Mandalay

Worshipper touching one of the Angkor statues in the hope of curing an ailment

🏛 Mahamuni Temple

82nd St, S of 45th St (Boba Htu Rd). **Open** 4am–11pm daily. 📷

The Mahamuni Temple is the country's second most revered shrine after the Shwedagon Pagoda in Yangon. Its stately bronze Buddha is said to be one of only five likenesses of the historical Buddha cast in his lifetime, although it was probably made 500 years later. More certain is that it came here in 1784 as plunder from Bodawpaya's raid on Arakan (see p115). While women are not allowed to enter the inner sanctum, men are permitted to press gold leaf on to the figure – so much has been added over the years that large lumps of solid gold formed. Only the face, polished daily, remains shiny and smooth.

In a hall off the main temple are six fine Hindu-Buddhist figures originally plundered from Angkor Wat, but subsequently looted from Arakan by Bodawpaya's army. Worshippers traditionally rub various body parts of the images in the hope of curing medical afflictions.

🏛 Jade Market

87th St (39/40). **Open** 8–11am & 2–4pm daily. 📷 entrance charge.

Myanmar is the source of the world's finest jade and nearly all of it passes through the huge jade market on 87th Street. It is a fascinating place, although only confirmed experts are advised to part with any cash – jade is notoriously difficult to price. All morning, buyers and traders meet to haggle around long Formica tables, shining lights through pieces of jade to assess their quality. Elsewhere, cutters and polishers can be seen transforming stones into finely worked pieces for export.

🏛 Shwe In Bin Kyaung

89th St (37/38). **Open** 7am–10pm daily.

Commissioned in the 1890s by two wealthy Chinese jade merchants, this elegant teak monastery was created in classic Konbaung style, with a slender central tower of seven receding tiers capped by a golden finial. The cornices and eaves retain splendid, intricately carved ox-horn embellishments, similar to those of Shwenandaw Monastery, although unlike its more famous cousin across town, Shwe In Bin receives only a trickle of visitors. An oasis of calm, it offers one of the most atmospheric retreats in the city.

🏛 Setkyathiha Pagoda

85th St (30/31). **Open** 7am–10pm daily.

This inconspicuous temple, seven blocks north of the Shwe In Bin Kyaung, houses a 16-ft (5-m) seated Buddha cast in bronze by King Bagyidaw in 1823, just before the outbreak of the First Anglo-Burmese War. Also housed in the complex is a sacred golden boulder and bodhi tree planted by the first prime minister of independent Burma, U Nu.

Gold Leaf

Mandalay is one of the few places in Myanmar where gold leaf, prized by the Burmese as a temple offering, is still made in the traditional way. At workshops concentrated around the intersection of 36th and 77th Streets, teams of pounders thump at booklets of bamboo pages between which tiny morsels of gold have been placed. The resulting foil is cut, replaced, and thumped again for hours until it is only a few molecules thick. Packets of these leaves make great souvenirs.

Teams of craftsmen pounding at gold morsels to make gold leaf

Eindawya Pagoda

Eindawya St (88/89). **Open** 8am–9pm daily.

Three blocks northwest of Setkyathiha stands the gilded Eindawya Pagoda. Resting on four square, receding terraces, the beautifully proportioned bell-shaped *zedi* (stupa) was built by Pagan Min (1811–80), ninth ruler of the Konbaung Dynasty, on the site of a royal palace where he lived while still a prince. In the popular imagination the pagoda is closely associated with rebellion: Pagan Min was the king whose non-compliance sparked the Second Anglo-Burmese War of 1852, and in 1919 a party of Europeans was expelled from the complex for not taking off their shoes (the monks responsible were subsequently sentenced to life imprisonment). One of Burma's best-loved singers of the 1930s, Myoma Nyein, later immortalized the shrine in his hit song, *Eindawya Paya Zay*, composed in support of Zegyo Market shopkeepers who occupied the temple precincts to protest against the British-imposed penal code.

The beautifully proportioned stupa of the golden Eindawya Pagoda, Mandalay

Zegyo Market

84th St (26/27). **Open** 9am–7pm daily.

Mandalay's main shopping area, Zegyo Market is centered on a couple of Chinese-style multistory malls and has a vast number of stalls where it is possible to buy everything from pickled tea to traditional felt slippers. The surrounding streets, where fresh produce is sold from vibrant stalls, also offer plenty of local flavor. The best time to visit is in the early morning before the crowds and heat build, and when local monks file through collecting alms. Between 5pm and 10pm in the evenings, a night market springs up in this area with barbecue stalls.

Mandalay Palace

See pp144–5.

Mandalay Hill

See pp146–9.

Sights at a Glance

① Mahamuni Temple
② Jade Market
③ Shwe In Bin Kyaung
④ Setkyathiha Pagoda
⑤ Eindawya Pagoda
⑥ Zegyo Market
⑦ Mandalay Palace
⑧ Mandalay Hill

0 meters   800
0 yards   800

Mandalay Palace

The seat of the last rulers of independent Burma, Mandalay Palace was built in the mid-19th century by King Mindon, but is most closely associated with his son, Thibaw, who was expelled from it by General Prendergast in 1885. The complex was commandeered by the British army for use as a barracks, before being destroyed by Allied bombs in 1945 while it was occupied by the Japanese during World War II. The present structures, built by the Tatmadaw in the 1990s, bear little more than a passing resemblance to the richly carved and gilded teak originals. To gain a sense of the architectural splendor of Mindon's time, visit the Shwenandaw Monastery nearby, a transplanted fragment of the original Glass Palace, and the only piece of the former palace to have survived.

★ **Nan Myin Watchtower**
This is one of the few original fort buildings to survive the Allied bombings of World War II.

Glass Palace
Decorated with mosaic and gilt iron trellis work, this sumptuous building contained the king's living chambers as well the Bee Throne Room.

KEY

① **Lion Throne (Sihasana) Room**

② **The Zetawunzaung**, containing the Goose Throne (Hamsasana), was where ambassadors were received. The Byedaik hall to its north held the Elephant Throne (Gajasana), which vanished after the British invasion.

③ **The Baungdawzaung** (Royal Crown Room), holding the Conch Throne (Sankhasana), was used for audiences with palace officials.

④ **The Lapetyezaung** (Tea Room) held the king's personal armory.

⑤ **The Bee Throne (Bhamarasana) Room** was where the Chief Queen's nomination and nuptials took place.

⑥ **The Peacock Throne (Mayurasana) Room** was used to review troops and watch races.

⑦ **Deer Throne (Mrigasana) Room**

⑧ **Chief Queen's Apartments**

⑨ **Central Queen's Apartments**

⑩ **The Queen's Audience Hall** held the Lotus Throne (Padmasana) and is now the palace museum.

West Gate

South Gate

Nan Myin
Watchtower

Mandalay Fort
North (Water) Gate
Palm Groves
Ornamental Gardens
King Mindon's Tomb
West Gate
Mandalay Palace
East (Main) Gate
Tooth Relic Tower
Barracks
Elephant Sheds
Water Palace
Moat
South Gate

Moat, walls, and bastions
Mindon's palace was encased by 1.2-mile (2-km) long walls on each side and a 210-ft (64-m) wide moat. Each of the walls had several bastions, and three gateways topped by tall, gold-tipped *pyatthat* roofs – 12 in total, corresponding to the signs of the zodiac.

VISITORS' CHECKLIST

Practical Information
Half a mile (1 km) N of the train station, east (main) entrance another 2 miles (3 km) NE; foreigners can enter only via this gate. **Open** 7:30am–4:30pm daily. all major sights in Mandalay, Inwa, and Amarapura covered by Archeology Department's combination ticket, valid for one week. hotels can arrange guides.

Transport
Taxis and motorcycle taxis easily available. Trishaws wait at the east gate for the half-mile (1 km) ride to the palace complex.

North Gate

Mandalay Hill

East Gate

★ Great Audience Hall
This gilded pillared hall, with north and south wings, was where the king held court while seated on the Lion Throne *(see p54)*. The seven-tiered *pyatthat* roof indicated the hall's symbolic importance as the epicenter of royal and cosmic power.

0 meters   50
0 yards   50

Entrance to the palace complex
Most of the area within Mandalay Fort is an army base, and the palace complex is a 15-minute walk in from the east gate. The entrance to the complex is flanked by a pair of 9.5-ft (3-m) British cannon, originally cast for the Royal Navy and stamped with the cipher of King George II (1727–60).

Mandalay Hill

According to Theravada lore, the Buddha visited Mandalay Hill, prophesizing that on the 2,400th anniversary of his death a great city would be founded at its foot. The vision was realized in 1857, when King Mindon moved his capital from Amarapura to carve out the foreseen "Golden City." Visitors continue to make the auspicious ascent in large numbers, both to pay their respects at the shrines punctuating the stepped pathway to the summit, and for the views of the distant Shan Hills. A perfect preamble to the climb is a tour of the structures at the base of the hill. Dating from Mindon's era, they include one of the last surviving fragments of the great teak palace of the Konbaungs.

Shweyattaw Buddha
The country's only pointing Buddha marks the convergence of the two main walkways up Mandalay Hill.

Main entrance with *chinthes*
The start of the main walkway up the hill is flanked by two huge *chinthes*, the grinning, luck-bringing leogryphs who gave their name to Orde Wingate's Chindits during World War II (*see p57*).

Atumashi Monastery
This handsome structure opposite the Shwenandaw is a copy of the one built by King Mindon in 1857. The original burned down in 1890, when its huge lacquered Buddha was lost.

Mandalay Palace

KEY

① **Sandamuni Pagoda**, companion to the nearby Kuthodaw Pagoda, houses a huge collection of stone slabs inscribed with Buddhist scriptures, plus a particularly splendid brass statue of the Buddha that dates from 1802.

② **Kyauktawgyi Temple**, built between 1853 and 1878 in Mindon's reign, stands near the start of the walkway and is worth a visit for its monolithic marble Buddha.

③ **Pedestrian walkway** up the hill.

Shwenandaw Monastery
Arguably the most beautiful Konbaung teak building to have survived, this masterpiece of classical Burmese architecture is famed above all for its carvings.

For hotels and restaurants in this region see p204 and pp212–14

Mwegyi Hnakaung
(Two Great Snakes)
Just over the summit are the statues of two great cobras and of the *nats* they transformed into after their death. The snakes were believed to visit the hill to worship the Buddha.

0 meters   200
0 yards   200

Sataungpyei Temple
At the summit, this gilded, brightly decorated shrine affords spellbinding views over the city and its surroundings. The site witnessed fierce fighting during World War II.

Kuthodaw Pagoda
Centered on a magnificent golden stupa, this complex was built in 1857 by King Mindon to house a vast assembly of stone tablets carved with the entire text of the sacred *Tipitaka* scripture.

Exploring Mandalay Hill

The fact that nearly all of Mandalay Palace was destroyed in 1943 lends great significance to the Konbaung-era monuments grouped northeast of the palace complex. The pick of the bunch is the transplanted Shwenandaw Monastery, the only part of Mindon's inner palace to have survived the Allied bombs. Nearby, a string of whitewashed and gilded temples holding tablets bearing the entire *Tipitaka* canon set the scene for the ascent of Mandalay Hill itself, best undertaken barefoot on the long, stepped *zaungdan* (walkway).

The entrance of the teak Shwenandaw Monastery, Mandalay

🔲 Shwenandaw Monastery

Golden Palace Monastery, off 62nd St near the NW corner of the moat. **Open** 8am–5pm daily. 🏛 combination ticket.

The sole remnant of the Konbaung Dynasty's magnificent Golden Palace is the Shwenandaw Monastery. Formerly part of the personal apartments of King Mindon, the building only survived the Allied bombing raids of World War II because in 1880, Mindon's son Thibaw had it dismantled and moved to its current site outside the palace walls. His father had passed away inside the hall in 1878 and Thibaw is said to have found the space too distressing to be in.

The rich exterior carving of the monastery and the gilded pillars and ceilings inside give visitors a vivid impression of how sumptuous the complex of which it formed a part must have looked in its prime.

🔲 Atumashi Monastery

63rd St. **Open** 8am–5pm daily. 🏛 combination ticket.

West of the Shwenandaw Monastery stands a modern reconstruction of a grand edifice originally built by Mindon

in 1857. Surmounted by five rectangular terraces, rather than the more usual Konbaung-style receding tiers, it formerly held a 30-ft (9-m) Buddha made from the king's own lacquered silk clothes. The enormous diamond that was once embedded in its forehead was looted during the British invasion of 1885, and five years later the Buddha itself was lost in a fire, along with the rest of the building. Although ornately decorated, the present structure, built by the Tatmadaw using convict labor in 1996, does not approach the refinement of its predecessor.

🔲 Kuthodaw Pagoda

62nd St. **Open** daily. 🏛 combination ticket.

King Mindon commissioned the sumptuously gilded Maha Lawka Marazein stupa, at the foot of Mandalay Hill, as the centerpiece of the walled Kuthodaw Pagoda in 1857. The 100-ft (30-m) *zedi*, or stupa, stands in a complex dominated by 729 slender, whitewashed ancillary pagodas, each containing carved alabaster slabs inscribed with a page of the *Tipitaka*, the Theravada Pali canon. The inscriptions were created to mark the Fifth Buddhist Synod of 1871 and, when they were completed, took 2,400 monks six months to recite. Local guides love to describe the collection as the "World's Largest Book."

In common with most of the Konbaung capital's sacred sites, this one fared badly at the hands of the British in 1885, losing precious stones off the stupa's *hti* or crowning finial, gold leaf from the *zedi* itself, and 6,370 bells from the miniature pagodas, which were melted down and used to cast ammunition. The original *Tipitaka* slabs were also looted for use by the British army in road construction.

🔲 Sandamuni Pagoda

Off East Moat. **Open** 6am–9pm daily. 🏛 combination ticket.

Adjacent to the Kuthodaw stands the lookalike Sandamuni Pagoda, where 1,774 more inscribed marble slabs are

The gilded iron Buddha commissioned by Bodawpaya, now in the Sandamuni Pagoda

housed in rows of neatly whitewashed shrines. Often dubbed "Volume II of the World's Largest Book," the inscriptions are commentaries on the *Tipitaka*. Before this pagoda was built, the site was where King Mindon and his family lived while waiting for work on their new palace to be completed. It is synonymous with the bloody coup of 1866 in which two of the king's sons mounted a bid for the throne, killing the incumbent crown prince and two others ahead of them in the line of succession. The victims were buried where they died, along with other members of the royal family who perished in the rebellion. A mausoleum in the complex is their final resting place. Pride of place in the Sandamuni Pagoda, however, goes to the large iron Buddha cast by the despotic, expansionist King Bodawpaya in 1802, which is now heavily encrusted in gold leaf.

The unusual Shweyattaw Buddha, the only pointing Buddha statue in Myanmar

Painting of King Mindon at Mandalay's Kyauktawgyi Temple

Kyauktawgyi Temple

10th St. **Open** 7:30am–9:30pm daily. combination ticket.

An even larger Buddha occupies the main shrine hall of the late-19th-century Kyauktawgyi Temple, diagonally opposite the southern entrance to the hill. It reportedly took between 10,000 and 12,000 men 13 days to drag the single piece of solid, pale-green marble 15 miles (25 km) from the quarry at Sangyin to Mandalay city. Several smaller statues of the *arahants*, or Great Disciples, attend the Buddha.

Mandalay Hill

Open 7am–10pm daily. through the elevator to the Sataungpyei Pagoda, reached via a surfaced road around the north side of the hill.

Four different *zaungdans*, or stepped, covered paths, wind up Mandalay Hill, each taking around 45 minutes to climb. A motorable road also zigzags up the north side to the summit.

The start of the southern stepway, the most popular, is flanked by a pair of huge leogryphs, or *chinthes*. First of the numerous landmarks along this route is the **U Khanti Tazaung**, a hall built as a memorial to the hermit-monk U Khanti who lived on the spot during the colonial era. The holy man was instrumental in the creation of Mandalay Hill as a pilgrimage site, raising funds to build numerous shrines and pagodas. The *tazaung* is also noteworthy for being the place where the Peshawar Relics were enshrined until World War II, when they were removed for safekeeping. Unearthed in 1905 inside the remains of a massive stupa on the outskirts of Peshawar, Pakistan, the three fragments of clavicles encased in crystal were brought to Burma by the British in 1924 as a gift. However, anticolonial sentiment was rife at the time and the Burmese never really accepted the relics as genuine. They are now in a pagoda near the base of the hill.

A short way farther up the steps, the unusual pose of the gilded **Shweyattaw Buddha**, sited where two paths meet, refers to Mandalay's foundation legend. The Buddha was said to have prophesized that a city would spring up at the foot of the hill 2,400 years after his death – hence the statue's outstretched arm and finger, which point directly to the palace where King Mindon fulfilled this prediction in 1857.

The penultimate shrine on the route centers on a statue of **Sanda Mukhi**, an ogress to whom the Buddha is said to have made the famous prophecy. On first meeting the great teacher, she entered a devotional frenzy of such force that she purportedly cut off her breasts and placed them at his feet as an offering. So impressed was the Buddha that he told her she would be reincarnated 2,400 years after his death as the king of the great city whose foundation he had foreseen.

The terrace encircling the **Sataungpyei Temple** at the summit offers stupendous views over Mandalay city. Surmounted by a forest of gilded spires and a central pyramidal pagoda covered in gold, the building is set amid colorful flame trees and magnolia bushes. Although a peaceful spot now, the slopes once witnessed ferocious hand-to-hand fighting during World War II, when Japanese forces dug into machine-gun posts mounted a desperate defense against battalions of Gurkha and British troops.

Girls cycling over beautiful U Bein's Bridge across Taungmyo Lake at Amarapura ▶

❷ Amarapura

Road Map C3. 8 miles (12 km) SW
of Mandalay city center. 🚉 56,000.
✈ Mandalay International. 🚌
Note: all major sights covered by
Archeology Department's combination ticket, valid for one week.

On the southwestern fringes of
Mandalay, Amarapura (literally
"City of Immortality") succeeded
Inwa (Ava) as the Burmese
capital in 1783. The move is said
to have been recommended
by the court astrologers of the
megalomaniac King Bodawpaya
to expiate the bad karma the
ruler had accrued by drowning
his grandnephew, King Maung
Maung (1763–82), in order to
seize the Konbaung throne.

The strip of lush, leafy land
between the east bank of the
Ayeyarwady and the shores of
Taungmyo Lake (also called
Taungthaman) provided the
perfect setting for the old Inwa
palace, which Bodawpaya dismantled and rebuilt near the
waterside, with four pagodas
protecting its corners. Of the
latter, the most impressive is
the soaring **Pahtodawgyi**,
which the king built in 1820.
With a spectacular bell-shaped
zedi raised on five terraces
decorated with beautifully
carved *Jataka* friezes showing
episodes from the Buddha's life,
the stupa still dominates the
town's skyline. Male visitors are

Stone carving of a mythical animal at the
early-19th-century Pahtodawgyi Pagoda

allowed up the steep steps to its
uppermost terrace, from where
a fine view extends over the
adjacent pagodas to the lake.

A low-rise town of sandy,
tree-lined lanes and wooden
houses, Amarapura has a very
different feel from the nearby
metropolis. Most of its residents
earn their living in workshops
that specialize in fine-quality
wedding *longyis* and *htameins*;
the distinctive sound of looms
at full tilt is a constant backdrop.
Amarapura's back roads all
seem to converge on the town's
most iconic sight, **U Bein's
Bridge**, built by Bodawpaya's

eponymous mayor using timber
from Inwa, the old capital.
Spanning a neck in the lake
0.7 miles (1.1 km) wide, this
impressive teak walkway –
the world's longest – rests on
wooden piles which stand at
least 20 ft (6 m) proud of the
waterline in the dry season,
but are almost completely sub-
merged during the monsoons.
Tourists descend in droves to
photograph the bridge in the
morning and evening light as
villagers, market gardeners in
traditional *kaukyoe* straw hats,
and red-robed monks stride
across it. Boatmen offer trips
over the water to the eastern
shore, where the **Kyauktawgyi
Pagoda** is the largest of a
scattering of mid-19th-century
monuments. Built by King
Pagan Min in 1847, the five-
tiered temple, gilded in high
Konbaung style, houses a giant
seated Buddha of jade-colored
Sangyin marble. Its entrance
porches contain wonderful
frescoes of traditional Burmese
monuments and scenes,
including one (in the northeast
entranceway) showing the
pagoda as it looked in its prime.

🏛 **Pahtodawgyi Pagoda**
Off Kanthitan Street.
Open 7am–11pm daily. ♿

🏛 **Kyauktawgyi Pagoda**
East bank, Taungmyo Lake.
Open daily.

U Bein's Bridge, supported by over 1,000 piles, spanning Amarapura's Taungmyo Lake

❸ The Ayeyarwady Bridges

Road Map C3. 11 miles (17 km) SW of Mandalay, via the expressway. 🚌

Connecting Amarapura with Sagaing, the **Old Inwa Bridge**, with 16 spans and two decks (one for road and another for rail traffic), used to be the only route across the Ayeyarwady from Mandalay when it was built by the British in 1934. They sabotaged it in 1942 by destroying two of the spans to forestall the Japanese advance. The bridge was repaired 14 years later and served as the main link between the two banks until 2008, when the three-span **Ayeyarwady Bridge**, carrying a four-lane highway, was built next to the old bridge.

The Old Inwa Bridge, one of the two bridges connecting Amarapura and Sagaing

❹ Sagaing

Road Map C3. 13 miles (21 km) SW of Mandalay. 🏙 80,000. ✈ Mandalay International. 🚌 **Note:** major sights covered by Archeology Department's Sagaing-Mingun joint ticket.

One of the great spectacles of Upper Burma is that of Sagaing Hill rising from the bleached west bank of the Ayeyarwady, its denuded ridges encrusted with whitewashed domes and shimmering golden spires. Thousands of Buddhist pagodas and monasteries cluster in and around this riverside market town southwest of Mandalay. They are the legacy of a brief period in the early 14th century when, as the country plunged

Buddha statues lining the crescent-shaped colonnade of Umin Thounzeh, Sagaing

into turmoil following the demise of the Bagan Empire, it served as the capital of a powerful regional dynasty led by the young King Sawyun (1300–27). After only 50 years, however, one of Sawyun's descendants, Thadominbya (1345–67), decided to move the royal palace across the river to a new, more easily defensible site at Inwa (Ava). Sagaing has since devoted itself largely to spiritual rather than political matters. Today around 6,000 monks reside in the numerous *kyaungs* (monasteries) dotted around the town, and buses loaded with pilgrims are very much part of the local scene.

Crowning the southern extremity of a long ridge rippling north all the way to Mingun, the gilded **Soon U Ponya Shin** is the most prominent of the many temples scattered across Sagaing Hill. It can be reached on foot, by following one of several covered walkways leading to the summit via a constellation of ancillary shrines, or on a bumpy metaled road that ends at the temple gates. Either way, visitors first pass through a hall lined with dazzling turquoise glass mosaic where a huge, golden-robed Buddha smiles down beneficently. Beyond, the east terrace affords a spellbinding view over the Ayeyarwady and the myriad temples that overlook it.

Just below the Soon U Ponya Shin, a northern spur of the main Sagaing Hill approach

road winds up to the **Umin Thounzeh**, a cave temple housing 45 Buddha images arrayed in a grand semicircular shrine. Decorated with a backdrop of sparkling glasswork, the richly gilded statues offer one of Sagaing Hill's most distinctive photo opportunities.

From the terrace of Umin Thounzeh another great view extends west over a patchwork of millet and sesame fields toward Monywa, a landscape dominated by the huge golden dome of the **Kaunghmudaw Pagoda**, on the outskirts of Sagaing. Rising to a height of 150 ft (46 m), the gigantic *zedi* dates from 1636 and was built to celebrate the foundation of Inwa (Ava) as the royal capital. Local legend claims its unusual shape was inspired by that of the breast of Thadominbya's queen, although the Abhayagiri Dagoba in Anuradhapura, Sri Lanka, was more probably the model. Interred inside the stupa is the fake tooth relic with which the Ceylonese famously hoodwinked King Bayinnaung of Bago (Pegu) *(see p95)*, and which was brought here as plunder by the Taungoo ruler Anaukpetlun in 1599.

🧍 **Soon U Ponya Shin**
Sagaing Hill. **Open** 7am–10pm daily.

🧍 **Umin Thounzeh**
Sagaing Hill. **Open** 7am–10pm daily.

🛕 **Kaunghmudaw Pagoda**
5 miles (8 km) NW of Sagaing city center. **Open** 7am–11pm daily.

❺ Inwa (Ava)

Called Ava by the British, Inwa served as the Burmese capital for longer than any other city – over six centuries in all – and retains evocative temples, stupas, and monasteries, the finest of them being Konbaung structures of the early 1800s. The crumbling edifices occupy a spit of land protected by fortified walls, moats, and earthworks in the south and west, by the Myitnge River in the east, and by the Ayeyarwady in the north – this gave rise to the site's name, which means "Mouth of the Lake." A massive earthquake in 1839 left the city and its structures in ruins, after which King Tharrawaddy shifted the court to Amarapura. While it is possible to travel to Inwa by road, most visitors arrive by ferry, transferring to a horse cart for a tour of the monuments.

Horse carts driving down a tree-lined road on a tour of the ruins of Inwa

Yedanasini Pagoda
Just off the route to the Bagaya Kyaung is this complex of brick stupas, roofless pillars, and meditating stone Buddhas surrounded by palmyra palms and flame trees.

Sagaing

Ayeyarwady River

KEY

① **Ferry point**

② **Horse cart waiting area**

③ **Htilangshin Pagoda**, next to the Maha Aungmye Bonzan Kyaung, consists of a group of gilded stupas with elegantly tapering spires. They date from the Bagan era, but were substantially renovated during the Konbaung period.

④ **Ticket point**

⑤ **Shwedigon Pagoda**, Inwa's largest stupa, presides over the southwest corner of the site, overlooking the old moat.

⑥ **Nogatataphu Pagoda**, whose golden spire towers high above the surrounding rice fields, is the largest stupa at Inwa after the Shwedigon Pagoda.

Key
— Suggested route

| 0 meters | 500 |
| 0 yards | 500 |

Inwa
Bridge

★ **Maha Aungmye Bonzan Kyaung**
Designed in the style of a teak monastery, this brick and
stucco structure is among the few survivors from the Ava
era. It dates from the reign of King Bagyidaw (r. 1819–37),
who moved the capital back here from Amarapura in 1824.

Mandalay City ↑

Myitnge River

Nan Myin Tower
Inwa's own "leaning tower,"
damaged during the 1839 earthquake, was part of Bagyidaw's
now vanished palace complex.

★ **Bagaya Kyaung**
One of Myanmar's finest
surviving teak monasteries, the
Bagaya Kyaung retains some
superb carving. Particularly
noteworthy are its ornate door
surrounds. Young novices attend
school here in the mornings.

⑥ Mingun

Bodawpaya (1745–1819) was one of the most expansionist and militarily daring rulers in Burmese history, and the mighty stupa he raised on the banks of the Ayeyarwady at Mingun was intended to match in scale his prowess as an empire builder. Commissioned in 1790 to house a tooth of the Buddha, Pahtodawgyi (also called the Mingun Pagoda) was constructed by slaves, whom the king supervised personally while living on an island nearby. However, the upheavals of the early 19th century caused a shortage of funds and labor, and the project was never completed. Had it been, the stupa would have risen even higher than the Great Pyramid of Giza in Egypt. A massive earthquake in 1839 reduced its upper portions to rubble, and left huge cracks in the facades. Even so, King Bodawpaya's folly remains an imposing sight, particularly when first glimpsed from the Ayeyarwady River.

The eastern entrance
Facing the river and rising sun, the eastern doorway leads to a shrine containing a Buddha image that is much venerated by the Burmese.

Settawya Pagoda
This whitewashed shrine was built in 1811 to house a footprint of the Buddha. Although somewhat extravagant in its design, the temple provides a splendid backdrop for passengers alighting at the nearby boat jetty.

KEY

① **Settawya's five-level terrace**, with rows of statues of *nats*, leads down to the river.

② **The south and north facades**, badly damaged in the 1839 earthquake, receive the least interest from visitors, although both have beautifully ornamented Konbaung-style door arches and surrounds.

③ **The proportions of the stupa** are impressive, even in its unfinished state. Each of its sides is about 230 ft (70 m) in length, and its walls rise 164-ft (50-m) high, only one third of their intended height. To see what it was meant to look like when complete, visitors can stop off at its scale model, Pondaw Pagoda, sited 600 ft (182 m) to the south.

④ **The eastern entrance**

★ Hsinbyume Pagoda
To the north stands this extraordinary pagoda, built in 1816 by Bagyidaw, Bodawpaya's grandson. It depicts the mythical Mount Meru, the wavy concentric terraces below the stupa representing the seven ranges that encircle the sacred peak.

Magnificent views
Pahtodawgyi was designed to make an impact when viewed from the river, and to provide sweeping vistas of it. An earthquake in 2012 further damaged the stupa and has prevented access to the top, but even from river level, the unfinished structure remains a striking sight.

VISITORS' CHECKLIST

Practical Information
Road Map C3. 14 miles (24 km) N of Sagaing; 29 miles (47 km) from Mandalay Hill by road, one hr upriver from Mandalay.
Open daily. 🔲 covered by the Archeology Department's Sagaing-Mingun joint ticket. 🔲 guides available at the bell. 🔲 Feb/Mar: brother and sister teak tree *nat* festival, 5–10th waxing moon days of Tabaung.

Transport
✈ Mandalay International. 🚢 9am, west end of 26th St; private boats at 8am, Gawain Jetty, 35th St, Mandalay.

The western entrance
The more peaceful western entry is the place to sidestep the crowds, especially in the evening when its cracked facade looks dramatic in the warm light.

Giant ruined *chinthes*
Only the ruined haunches remain of the pair of colossal stone *chinthes* (leogryphs) that originally flanked the stupa's landing stage and main approach.

★ **The great bell of Mingun**
Cast on a vast scale and weighing 200,000 lb (90,700 kg), the stupa's bell had to be floated into position via a specially built canal.

The multicolored spires of the unique Thanboddhay Pagoda

❼ Monywa

Road Map C3. 84 miles (136 km) W of Mandalay. 190,000. Mandalay International. direct from Mandalay & Bagan; also from Pakokku on the Ayeyarwady River, where some cruisers may pause on the Bagan–Mandalay trip.

Monywa is the main port on the Chindwin, Myanmar's second most important river, whose headwaters rise just across the Patkai Range in Assam. The town has long been a hub for trade with northeast India, although with the northern border currently closed, its principal role is as a clearing house for produce grown in the fertile Sagaing plains. While the town's two pagodas are worth a look, the few foreigners who travel here tend to do so en route to or from Bodhi Tataung, the Thanboddhay Pagoda, and the Pho Win Taung Caves, which are more comfortably explored using Monywa as a base than as day trips from Mandalay.

Novice monks shopping at one of Monywa's open-air produce markets

❽ Thanboddhay Pagoda

Road Map C3. 6 miles (10 km) SE of Monywa via Highway 71. **Open** 6am–5pm daily.

The riotously colorful Thanboddhay Pagoda is a temple unlike any other in Myanmar. The brainchild of a local abbott named Moe-hnyin Sayadaw, it was built in the 1930s as a monument to the 512,028 souls who are believed to have achieved Buddhahood in the era of Gautama – a concept artistically expressed in a multitude of Buddha figures, both large and small. Every inch of the building's exterior is festooned with statues, along with the pillars, niches, walls, and ceilings inside, which are smothered in vibrantly painted and gilded stucco. The pagoda's distinctive roof is layered with rows of small gilded stupas, and the temple itself is flanked by 30-ft (9-m) high obelisks covered in tiny Buddha statues.

The somewhat kitsch theme park effect is further enhanced by the pastel-colored monks' cells, the large masonry fruits seen around the complex, the pair of large white concrete elephants standing guard at the main entrance, and the Arlin Nga Sint, a lofty watchtower built in the form of a snake. Men (but not women) may climb this tower via a spiral staircase for a bird's-eye view over the complex.

❾ Bodhi Tataung

Road Map C3. 5.5 miles (8 km) E of Thanboddhay. **Open** 7am–9pm daily.

An astonishing apparition rises from a hilltop to the east of Thanboddhay at Bodhi Tataung, where two colossal gilded Buddhas – one standing, one reclining – gaze serenely across the Chindwin Valley. The giant figures form part of a modern complex founded by a globe-trotting Burmese monk named Sayadaw Bhaddanta Narada, who traveled the Buddhist world to raise funds for the project, but died before seeing it completed.

Bodhi Tataung's spectacular centerpiece, on the summit of the hill, is the **Laykyun Setkyar**, a 424-ft (116-m) standing Buddha depicted with arms held stiffly at his side. A staircase winds halfway up the hollow interior, via a series of galleries featuring gaudy moral murals, to a viewing platform that is not for the fainthearted.

Immediately below the standing figure, his neighbor measures 312 ft (95 m) from head to toe and is the second largest reclining Buddha in Myanmar after the one at Win Sein Taw Ya near Mawlamyine (see p193). Finally, on level ground at the foot of the hill stands a gleaming golden pagoda, the 430-ft (131-m) **Aung Setkyar**, which, like the Laykyun Setkyar, can be scaled via an inner passageway. The stupa is set in a park featuring thousands of parasol-wielding Buddhas placed in perfect rows.

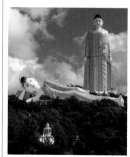

The massive reclining and standing Buddhas of Bodhi Tataung

The Pho Win Taung cave complex, with hundreds of caves containing wood and stucco Buddha statues

⑩ Pho Win Taung Caves

Road Map C3. Pho Win Taung village, 4 miles (6 km) S of the Yinmarbin Rd; 15 miles (25 km) SW of Monywa via the Chindwin ferry, or 26 miles (43 km) SW via the Chindwin Bridge. ✈ Mandalay International. 🚌 🚲 **Open** 8am–6pm daily. 📷 📱

Buried deep in the rural hinterland west of the Chindwin River is one of Upper Burma's less-visited gems, a complex of Buddhist cave temples hollowed from an oddly shaped outcrop of sandstone near the village of Pho Win Taung (also known as Hpo Win Daung). The name translates as "Mountain of Solitary Meditation" and the site, which holds more than 520 rock-cut chambers, has about it an aura of great sanctity, despite being in generally poor condition, with no visitor facilities beyond a ticket office and a handful of basic local food stalls.

Carved between the 14th and 18th centuries, the first group of caves, close to the village, contain numerous wood and stucco Buddhas, and a few retain some vibrant murals of geometric patterns and episodes from the *Jatakas*. Local guides are on hand to show visitors around – worth employing to help fend off the aggressive macaques who patrol the stone steps connecting the various sites. A smaller, more recent complex of 46 rock-cut monuments lies about half a mile (1 km) beyond the village at **Shwebataung**, where the entrances to the cave chambers are approached via a series of steep stone staircases hewn from an impressive limestone cliff face.

⑪ A Myint

Road Map C3. 15 miles (25 km) S of Monywa on the Chindwin River. By road, reachable via Chaung U village on Highway 71. ✈ 1,500. ✈ Mandalay International. 🚌 🚲

On the banks of the Chindwin River amid the flat riverine countryside south of Monywa is the unspoiled backwater village of A Myint, where luxury cruisers occasionally pause for passengers to explore a complex of **ancient stupas**. Smothered in weeds and mildew, the crumbling *zedis* are scattered around a plot of slender palm trees on the edge of the village. Some retain superb murals on their walls and ceilings. Near the stupas, a picturesque **teak monastery** sports a traditional seven-tiered tower, beneath which a cavernous interior holds antique Buddhas and some fine wood carving. The young novices of the *kyaung* (monastery) obligingly pose for photographs beneath the building's delicately carved window surrounds.

The only other structure of note in A Myint is the home of the former village headman. The grand double-storied mansion, built in Neo-Classical style and painted terra-cotta and ocher, dates from the British colonial era. The family who own the house, like the building itself, have seemingly fallen on hard times and retain only one vestige of their ancestral prosperity: an old wind-up gramophone that is still in perfect working order.

Crumbling *zedis* in the ancient stupa complex of A Myint

⓬ Pyin U Lwin (Maymyo)

Road Map D3. 43 miles (73 km) E of Mandalay. 66,000. ✈ Mandalay International. 🚉 🚌

Located on the western edge of the Shan Plateau, Pyin U Lwin (formerly known as Maymyo or Maytown after its first governor, Colonel May) was founded in the 1890s by the British as a military post. When the rail line to Lashio was completed, the town became the official summer capital of the colonial administration. At an elevation of 3,510 ft (1,070 m), the town enjoys a much cooler climate than that of Mandalay on the central plains, which appealed to the homesick British. Mock-Tudor and Scottish Baronial mansions with turrets and ample verandas duly sprang up under the pine trees, along with a whites-only club, a golf course, and botanical gardens. After Burma gained its independence, the sizable Anglo-Burmese community gradually dwindled, but the Sikh and Nepali minorities whose forebears were brought here to work on the railroads

Tower made of flowers at Pyin U Lwin's botanical gardens

are still very much in evidence. Although Pyin U Lwin is often described as a hill station, the term is a misnomer, as the town is set on a plateau rather than a mountain. Its role as a hot-season retreat from the plains, however, has seen a new lease of life in recent years with the rise of an affluent Burmese middle class. Several of the old hotels have been renovated, among them Candacraig (now dubbed Thiri Myaing), a former bolthole of the Bombay-Burmah Timber Company. Dozens of new establishments have also opened since the NLD-led tourist boycott was relaxed in 2010. Most visitors pass time in the town by shopping for soft fruit and flowers grown in the local nurseries, and taking sightseeing rides around the pleasant tree-lined roads in horse-drawn carriages (locally called "wagons"), along with an obligatory visit to the **National Kandawgyi Botanical Gardens**. Created in 1915 and modeled on London's Kew Gardens, the 150-acre (60-ha) site holds nearly 600 species of trees, over 500 of them endemics, and 480

kinds of flowers, including 25 types of roses, all displayed around rolling lawns and ornamental lakes spanned by pretty wood bridges. The rock gardens, fountains, playgrounds, and a small zoo are popular with local children. There is also a delightful Orchid Garden featuring more than 300 species of indigenous blooms, and a well-stocked Butterfly Museum, with beetles and butterflies displayed in cases.

🌳 **National Kandawgyi Botanical Gardens**
Nandan Rd (southern edge of town).
Open 8am–5:30pm daily. 🚫 ♿ 🖥

⓭ Gokteik Bridge

Road Map D3. 47 miles (76 km) NE of Pyin U Lwin. 🚉

The linchpin of the railroad line connecting Mandalay and Lashio is the dizzying Gokteik Bridge, a gravity-defying construction that the travel writer Paul Theroux aptly described as "a monster of silver geometry in all the ragged rock and jungle." Commissioned at the end of the 19th century, it spans a precipitous gorge between two sheer limestone bluffs, above a carpet of dense forest. The challenge of spanning this wild terrain fell to the Pennsylvania and Maryland

Pyin U Lwin's Mock-Tudor Candacraig, a colonial mansion now operating as a hotel

For hotels and restaurants in this region see p204 and pp212–14

The gilded *karaweik*-shaped Phaung Daw U Pagoda at Meiktila

Bridge Company, which shipped all of the steel used in the construction from New York, transporting it to the site on a specially constructed trackway. Meauring 2,260 ft (689 m) across and 335 ft (102 m) in height, the bridge is supported by 15 lattice-work trestles and was the largest structure of its kind in the world when it was completed. Catching a first glimpse of the giant, with its silvery steel girders soaring above the trees and red-tinged cliffs, is an experience few passengers on the rattling ride to Lashio forget.

⑭ Meiktila

Road Map C3. 106 miles (171 km) S of Mandalay. 🚐 280,000. 🛫 Mandalay International. 🚏 🚌

Travelers following the inland route between Bagan and Mandalay, rather than the slower journey by river, generally pass through the lakeside town of Meiktila, at the head of the Sittaung Valley. Its strategic position as the gateway to Upper Burma made it the scene of an epic battle in 1944, when the Allies took it from the Japanese, and were then promptly surrounded by the enemy. Two months of bitter fighting ensued before the siege could be broken. A legacy of the conflict is the large air base on the city's outskirts, which ensures a high-profile military presence. Tatmadaw

troops have taken to the streets several times in recent years to quell outbreaks of communal violence, including in March 2013, when dozens of people were killed and around 12,000 displaced in mob attacks by Buddhists on Muslims.

The city itself holds no sights worthy of a special detour. With time to kill, however, the path around the lake makes for a pleasant cycle ride, passing the picturesque **Phaung Daw U Pagoda**, a floating shrine made in the shape of a gilded *karaweik* bird. Among the old British-era mansions on its western shore is the one where NLD leader Aung San Suu Kyi and her husband Michael Aris spent their honeymoon.

🏛 **Phaung Daw U Pagoda**
Meiktila Lake, near Main Bridge. **Open** 6am–9pm daily. ♿

The Abode of Kings

Rare are the first-time visitors to Myanmar who can correctly name the country's capital, and rarer still those who actually travel there. But since 2005, the seat of the government has been Naypyitaw (literally "Abode of Kings") 200 miles (320 km) north of Yangon. Why the military junta saw fit to lavish an estimated US$4 billion on constructing a brand new city in the middle of nowhere remains a subject of much speculation.

Rumors circulated at the time

Ministers' villas and workers' apartments in the capital, Naypyitaw

that it was in response to astrological predictions that a foreign power was about to invade – located in the center of the country, the site is more easily defensible than its predecessor Yangon. Whatever the reason, Naypyitaw now serves as the permanent home of the Myanmar parliament, as well as the army and civil service. Around a million soldiers and bureaucrats had to be relocated to the new site, leaving their families behind until schools, hospitals, and other essential facilities could be built. While the low-ranking office workers live in color-coded blocks, the ruling elite inhabit luxury villas in the surrounding hills. Sprawling over the dusty plains of the upper Sittaung Valley, the new capital is a city of vast proportions, a concrete metropolis of empty multilane highways and huge civic structures, mostly unused and expensive to maintain. As such, it holds little of interest to foreign travelers, but does reveal a great deal about the priorities of Myanmar's former military rulers.

EASTERN MYANMAR

Much of Eastern Myanmar falls within Shan State, a vast upland of remote valleys divided by bare ridges and tracts of scrub forest, with the mighty Thanlwin River slicing through its heart. Although now largely denuded of their original forest cover, the grand river valleys and rippling mountains of the Shan Plateau include some of the country's signature landscapes, foremost among them Inle Lake, with its backdrop of misty hills and soaring ridgetops. The east also boasts an exceptional cultural diversity and is home to several ethnic groups.

Arriving in Shan from other parts of the country, the differences between this hill region and lowland Myanmar are immediately apparent. The climate is noticeably cooler, and the stupas are more slender and tapered than in the rest of the country. The population is mostly ethnic Shan – Thai-speaking descendants of the tribes who accompanied Kublai Khan on his 13th-century invasion of the Bagan Empire. However, there are several other ethnic minority groups from the hills – including the Pa-O, Padaung, and Danu – who, with their distinctive head-gear, clothes, and jewelry, are also among the defining features of the region.

On the western edge of the plateau, beautiful Inle Lake is the area's undisputed highlight. Every year, thousands of visitors come to experience the unique way of life of the Intha people, symbolized by the distinctive leg rowers standing on the back of their long-tailed canoes. Boat trips to Shan stupa sites, monasteries, and stilt villages provide the focus for lakeside stays, while in the surrounding hills a network of trails offers outstanding treks.

For more adventurous travelers, Hsipaw in the north and Kengtung in the far east are springboards for long-distance treks to still more remote hill-tribe villages. However, in the past few decades, the Golden Triangle – where the borders of Thailand, Laos, and Myanmar meet – was a no-go zone for foreign tourists. The drug cartels who control the opium trade for which this area has long been notorious had been waging war against the state. With the signing of various accords in recent years, though, the region is slowly moving toward peace, allowing visitors to again travel to most parts of the region.

Long-tailed Intha boat moored in one of the quieter reaches of Inle Lake, surrounded by the distant hills of the Shan Plateau

◀ Young novice monks standing at the distinctive wooden oval windows of Shwe Yaunghwe Kyaung monastery, Nyaungshwe, Inle Lake

Exploring Eastern Myanmar

Most of this region lies within Shan State, the largest administrative division in Myanmar, extending from China's Yunnan province in the northeast to the borders of Thailand and Laos in the southeast. Inle Lake is easily accessible to visitors, and the busy market town of Nyaungshwe on its northern fringes makes an ideal base for boat trips. To the west, the former colonial hill station of Kalaw is the recommended departure point for treks through the surrounding minority villages. Farther north, Hsipaw is a much less frequented trekking hub, with trails leading through a variety of different terrains and ethnic zones, as is Kengtung in the east, from where day trips can be made on foot to Golden Triangle villages. Local markets across the region provide opportunities to meet minority people, who travel down from the hills dressed in their traditional finery on market days.

Detail of wood carving, Hsin Khaung Taung Kyaung, Pindaya

A patchwork of fields in the countryside around Kalaw

Getting Around

As most of the roads in the region are in a dismal state, flying is the best way to reach the principal hubs – for example, the journey from Mandalay to Inle Lake is a grueling nine hours by bus, but only 40 minutes by air. For Kengtung, visitors already within Myanmar have to fly as the road from Mandalay is still closed to foreigners, but those entering from Mae Sai, Thailand, may cross into the country by road at Tachileik (although onward travel is restricted to Kengtung). Bicycles are usually available for rent in the major towns, and provide an enjoyable means of getting around. On Inle Lake, a fleet of long-tailed boats is on hand to transport visitors to otherwise inaccessible sites.

For hotels and restaurants in this region see p205 and pp214–15

A long-tailed boat on Inle Lake moving past the floating gardens of the Intha

Sights at a Glance

Detail of a carving at the remote Buddhist site of Kakku

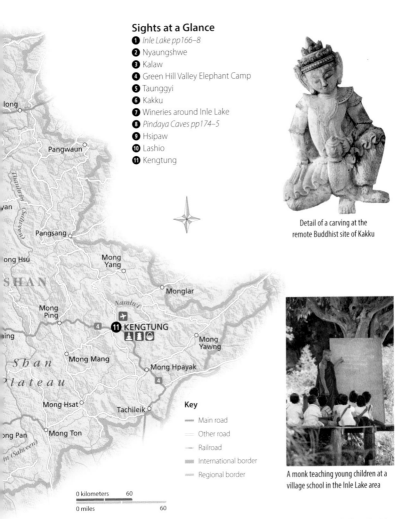

Key

— Main road
— Other road
— Railroad
— International border
— Regional border

0 kilometers   60
0 miles   60

A monk teaching young children at a village school in the Inle Lake area

For additional map symbols see back flap

❶ Inle Lake

Enfolded by the rippling Shan Hills, Inle Lake forms a world apart from the rest of Myanmar. The Intha people *(see p168)* who live in stilt villages along its fringes have evolved a unique way of life, beautifully adapted to the seasonal ebb and flow of the shoreline, where slender-topped stupas overlook a mosaic of rice paddies and floating vegetable gardens. Each morning, a fleet of long-tailed motorboats skim across Inle's glassy surface, ferrying visitors to monasteries and temples, and workshops where silk is handwoven from lotus fiber. The idyll is only slightly marred by the hordes who descend on the lake in the tourist season. Plenty of quiet corners remain, however, where it is possible to experience the essential tranquillity of wood-and-thatch villages far removed from the road network.

Ywama, a key tourist hub with a rotating market and silver jewelry workshops

Floating gardens of the Intha
The Intha of Inle Lake are famous for their amazingly productive vegetable beds, made by piling weeds and compost on long poles fixed to the lake floor.

KEY

① **Khaung Daing** is the site of famous hot springs where trekkers ease their aching limbs. It also has some of Inle's oldest resort hotels.

② **Inle Bo Teh**, marooned in the middle of the lake, is a British-era government guesthouse, now deserted and derelict.

③ **Nampan** is the largest village actually on the lake, with whole streets of stilt houses. Cheroots are handmade here by rolling a mixture of tobacco and aromatic herbs into Indian cherry leaves.

④ **Alodaw Pauk Pagoda**

⑤ **Inpawkhon** is a major silk weaving center where fine textiles are woven with fiber drawn from lotus stems.

⑥ **Inthein** is one of the largest settlements around Inle, and the venue of one of the region's busiest five-day rotating markets.

⑦ **Nyaung Ohak** is a small, weed-choked collection of Shan stupas at the base of the hill on which stands the Shwe Inthein stupa complex.

Phaung Daw U Pagoda
Inle Lake's main shrine holds five Buddhas that are now unrecognizable under innumerable layers of lumpy gold leaf.

Paramount Resort

Ywama

0 kilometers 2
0 miles 2

Nyaunghshwe

1 Inle Lake View

2

Inle Lake

Inle Princess

Inle Resort

Myanmar Treasure Resort

Aureum Resort and Spa

Villa Inle

VISITORS' CHECKLIST

Practical Information
Road Map D4. 170 miles (275 km) SE of Mandalay. hotels can arrange guides. five-day markets in Ywama, Phaung Daw U, Inthein, Nampan, Nyaungshwe. Sep/Oct: Golden Bird Festival, Phaung Daw U Pagoda (waxing moon of Thadingyut month).

Transport
Mandalay International. Heho Airport (23 miles/38 km N of Inle). Nyaungshwe & resorts have long-tailed boats for excursions. Bicycles for rent at hotels.

★ **Shwe Yaunghwe Kyaung, Nyaungshwe**
One of the area's finest sights is the traditional teak monastery of Shwe Yaunghwe north of Nyaungshwe *(see p169)*, where red-robed novices pose for pictures in the large oval windows.

Resorts on Inle Lake
Around the lake are a host of luxury resorts *(see p205)*, most of them featuring stilt chalets with teak decks from which to admire the sublime effect of the changing light on the water.

★ **Shwe Inthein stupa complex**
A total of 1,054 slender-spired Shan *zedis* (stupas) are packed into this enclosure above Inthein. Most date from the 17th and 18th centuries. The site is reached via a long *zaungdan* (covered stairway).

The Intha of Inle Lake

The glassy waters of Inle Lake support a population of between 70,000 and 100,000 people, most of whom are members of an ethnic minority group called the Intha. Originally from Dawei (Tenasserim), in the far southeast of Myanmar, the Intha settled in the region in the 18th century, fleeing invasions by their Thai neighbors across the border. It is said that the local Shan chief refused to grant them rights to land around Inle, which is allegedly why the Intha built their stilt houses on the fluctuating waterline of the lake itself. Brilliantly adapted to the climate and ecosystem, the way of life they have since evolved – from their distinctive one-legged rowing style to their impressively fertile floating gardens – is unique in Southeast Asia.

Handmade cheroots produced by the Intha

Traditional Intha stilt houses on Inle Lake

The unusual floating gardens in which the Intha grow their fruit and vegetables are anchored to the lake bed by bamboo poles.

Leg-rowing position, used only by men

Traditional Intha conical net

Inle Lake fisherman standing on a long-tailed boat in the distinctive leg-rowing stance used by the Intha people

Leg-rowing races are part of the Phaung Daw U Pagoda's Golden Bird Festival, Inle's biggest religious celebration.

Fried red tree ants and crickets are among the local delicacies available at markets around the lake.

Exquisitely fine silk spun from lotus stalks is woven in local workshops into vibrant *longyis* and *htameins*.

The unique octagonal stepped stupa of the Yadana Mon Aung Pagoda

❷ Nyaungshwe

Road Map D4. 296 miles (477 km) SW of Mandalay, to the north of Inle Lake. 🏔 12,000. ✈ Mandalay International. ✈ Heho Airport, 19 miles (31 km) west. 🚉 Shwenyaung, 7 miles (12 km) north. 🚌 🛥 five-day market. **Note:** a fee must be paid on entering the town and lake area.

Nyaungshwe is the principal hub for Inle Lake, to whose northern shore it is joined by a 3.5-mile (5.5-km) feeder canal. Fleets of motorized long-tailed boats leave on sightseeing trips throughout the day from the jetties lining the waterway's banks, and the sound of their engines churning through the green-blue water has become characteristic of the town.

Set on an orderly grid plan, Nyaungshwe is bisected by Yone Gyi Road, a broad main street running east-west, lined by open-fronted hardware shops, restaurants, and cafés. Northeast of the point where it crosses Main Road, the principal north-south axis, is **Mingalar Market**, the town's main source of fresh produce, sold by Pa-O and other ethnic minority villagers from the surrounding hills. Every five days, their ranks swell when the covered bazaar plays host to the area's rotating market, worth catching in the early morning, when the air is filled with the aroma of cooking as stallholders prepare Shan-noodle breakfasts for shoppers.

The sandy streets south of Yone Gyi Road are dotted with numerous stupa complexes and Buddhist monasteries, best explored by bicycle. The largest is the **Yadana Mon Aung Pagoda** on Phaung Daw Seiq Road, whose centerpiece is a gilded stupa of unusual octagonal stepped design, set in a white-walled compound. A couple of blocks east, along the banks of the Mong Li Canal, the adjacent **Hlaing Gu** and **Shwe Gu** monasteries are home to the 200 or so novices and monks who file through the town with their alms bowls each morning at dawn.

Prettiest of all the monasteries in the area, though, is the **Shwe Yaunghwe Kyaung**, about 1.5 miles (2.5 km) north of town. Retaining its splendid carved teak eaves and whitewashed staircases, the traditional *thein*, or ordination hall, is lined with unique oval windows, creating frames in which the young novices happily pose for photographs when foreign tourists visit the monastery.

View of the hill town of Kalaw, located on the edge of the Shan Plateau

❸ Kalaw

Road Map D4. 37 miles (61 km) W of Nyaungshwe. 🏔 11,000. ✈ Mandalay International. ✈ Heho Airport, 20 miles (33 km) east. 🚉 🚌 🛥 five-day market.

Situated in the green hills on the western edge of the Shan Plateau, Kalaw was originally developed by the British as a summer retreat. Swathed in pine forest, groves of orange trees, and stands of bamboo, it remains a pleasant, if somewhat disheveled, hill town. Its Raj-era roots are underlined by a scattering of colonial houses and its cosmopolitan population of Tamils, Sikhs, and other Indians descended from workers brought here in the 19th century. The main reason to visit Kalaw, however, is for the chance to trek in the hills separating it from Inle Lake *(see pp222–3)*. Wrapped in terraced fields and forest, picturesque wooden villages nestle on the slopes, most of them hours away from the nearest road, and inhabited by ethnic minorities such as the Pa-O and Danu.

Young monks walking through Nyaungshwe to collect alms

Slender, graceful Shan stupas in the Buddhist shrine at Ywama near Inle Lake ▶

The resident elephants of the Green Hill Valley Elephant Camp

❹ Green Hill Valley Elephant Camp

Road Map D4. 14 miles (24 km) out of Kalaw; 17 (5A) Kyaung St, Ahlone, Yangon (bookings). **Tel** (0) 973107278, (0) 95145838. ✈ Mandalay Intl. ✈ Heho Airport. 🚍 Kalaw. **Open** 8am–7pm daily. 🅿 ♿ partial. 🎫 📷 🕙 ghvelephant.com

Myanmar may hold the world's largest population of domesticated elephants, but visitors rarely catch sight of one unless they travel to remote timber camps *(see p96)*. A more easily accessible alternative is the Green Hill Valley Elephant Camp, a sustainable tourism initiative set up to care for retired pachyderms by a vet who used to work for the government timber company in the hills around Kalaw. Among them are a few young, fit animals who take visitors on short rides through the orchid, bamboo, and teak jungle. As well as providing a humane home for its charges, the camp promotes education in local villages and oversees a forest recovery program – visitors are encouraged to help by planting a tree in the camp.

❺ Taunggyi

Road Map D3. 175 miles (283 km) SE of Mandalay. 👥 210,000. ✈ Mandalay International. ✈ Heho Airport, 22 miles (37 km) west. 🚍 🚐 ℹ Pa-O National Organization (PNO) office, West Circular Rd, four blocks W of Myoma Market (10am–4pm Mon–Sat). 🍴 📷 May: Pa-O Rocket Festival; Oct/Nov: Balloon Festival.

The capital of Shan, Taunggyi sits on a plateau surrounded by sheer cliffs, crags, and high ridges. It was founded by the British in 1894 when the former administrative offices at Fort Stedman, on Inle Lake's eastern shore, were moved to this more elevated spot 4,712 ft (1,436 m) above sea level to take advantage of its cooler climate, widely regarded as the most pleasant in Myanmar. Taunggyi is today the fifth largest urban area in the country and has the feel of a big city. Pa-O and Intha people account for the majority of its inhabitants, although there has been a deluge of illegal immigrants from southwest China in recent years, many of them importing cheap manufactured goods overland from Yunnan. This merchandise can be seen at **Myoma Market**, in the center of town, which is Shan State's largest bazaar and a great place to experience local life.

Although few visitors choose to stay in the city, a couple of monuments warrant detours. Crowning a ridge to the east, the **Shwe Phone Pwint Pagoda** affords a fine panoramic view of Taunggyi. Just off National Highway 4 on the city's southeast edge, the **Sulamani Pagoda** is a huge white structure surmounted by a gilded corncob stupa inspired by the design of the stately Ananda Temple in Bagan; the Sulamani pagoda was built in 1994 to commemorate the centenary of Taunggyi's founding.

Taunggyi Balloon Festival

The most famous, colorful, and potentially lethal celebration in Shan State is Taunggyi's Balloon Festival, held annually over the full moon of Tazaungmon (October/November). Legend says the festival originated 1,000 years ago, although the balloons are probably a more recent addition. Seen as offerings to the Sulamani *cetiya* (memorial) in one of the heavens of Buddhist cosmology, extravagantly decorated giant hot-air balloons made of rice paper are lit and released over a period of three nights, watched by crowds of 10,000 or more. The loudest cheers are reserved for the massive explosions that occur when the fireworks in the balloons ignite, sending rockets spiraling and showering cascades of sparks and fire on onlookers below.

Launching lit paper lanterns into the night sky, Taunggyi Balloon Festival

❻ Kakku

Road Map D4. 28 miles (45 km) SE of Taunggyi. ✈ Mandalay International. ✈ Heho Airport. ℹ PNO office, West Circular Rd, four blocks west of Myoma Market, Taunggyi (10am–4pm Mon–Sat). **Open** 7am–7pm daily. 📷 fee per person plus separate fee per group for a guide; pay at Taunggyi's PNO office. 🎫 🚫 📷 🕙 📷 Mar: Kakku annual pagoda festival.

A recommended day trip from Taunggyi or Inle is the drive south to Kakku, a remote Buddhist site near the village of Mway Taw where thousands of medieval stupas stand in a walled compound above a bend in the river. There are said

The elongated, slender stupas of the Shan people at the sacred Buddhist site of Kakku

to be 2,548 monuments in total. Most of the pagodas date from the Bagan period (11th–13th centuries), but the largest, in slender Shan style, is believed to have been built by Ashoka, the Mauryan emperor of India, in the 3rd century BC. A permit to visit Kakku has to be obtained in advance from the PNO office in Taunggyi. The cost covers the services of a guide, in traditional Pa-O dress, who will explain the cultural significance of the site.

The vineyards of the Red Mountain Estate near the town of Nyaungshwe

❼ Wineries around Inle Lake

Road Map D4. 🛪 Mandalay Intl. ➡ Heho Airport. Taxi from Inle/Taunggyi.

While Myanmar may not be internationally renowned for its viticulture, a couple of wineries around Inle Lake do a brisk trade supplying the country's top hotels and tourist resorts. Both lie an easy day trip away from Inle and offer tours and tastings. On the outskirts of Nyaungshwe, **Red Mountain** was set up in 2003 and comprises two separate estates where a team led by a French winemaker produces New

World-style vintages, from Shiraz-Tempranillo and Pinot Noir to Sauvignon Blanc and Chardonnay. The estate has a delightful restaurant where visitors can enjoy fine local cuisine after a tasting tour.

Closer to Taunggyi, **Aythaya** was set up in 1999 by a German entrepreneur. The site, at an altitude of 4,000 ft (1,200 m), was chosen for its climate and soil, which provide perfect growing conditions for Shiraz and Cabernet Sauvignon, as well as Sauvignon Blanc and Chenin Blanc. Visitors can tour

the site, dine in a pretty garden restaurant, and stay overnight in teak lodges that offer views over the estate and Aythaya Valley.

🏠 **Red Mountain Estate**
Mya Thein Tan, Taung Chay village, 3 miles (5 km) south of Nyaungshwe. **Tel** (81) 209366. **Open** 9am–6pm daily. 🍴 🏪 🏠 W redmountain-estate.com

🏠 **Aythaya Vineyard**
Off NH 4, Aythaya, west of Taunggyi. **Tel** (01) 651141 (Yangon). **Open** tours: 8:30am–6pm daily; restaurant: 8:30am–11pm daily. 🍴 🏪 🏠 W myanmar-vineyard.com

Trekking in the Inle Region

The hill tracts between Kalaw (see p169) and Inle Lake (see pp166–8) are interlaced with footpaths connecting the area's many villages, which are home to several ethnic minorities, including the Pa-O, Danu, Padaung, and Intha. Local travel agents and hotels arrange trekking trips through the region, offering foreign visitors the chance to witness life in these remote subsistence farming communities, most of which have changed little in decades. Winding across forest, orchards, terraced hillsides, and field borders, the trails pass through varied, and often bucolic landscapes, although it is the local scene rather than scenery that tends to be the main incentive to visit here. Routes range from three- to five-hour walks to ridgetop settlements around Kalaw to multistage, multiday treks (including a well-liked three-day route from Inle Lake to Kalaw), where walkers stay overnight in village houses and share meals with local families.

Trekkers walking on the popular route between Inle Lake and Kalaw

❽ Pindaya Caves

A popular day trip from Inle, Pindaya is a complex of three caverns honeycombing the flanks of a steep hillside. The largest of them, extending 490 ft (150 m) into the rock, has become a major Buddhist pilgrimage site due to the 8,000 gilded Konbaung-era Buddhas inside. Dating to the late 1700s, they come in a variety of sizes and styles, but it is the ensemble that makes the real impact. After a stiff walk up the 200-step pathway, or via the road and elevator, the sight of the golden statues vividly illuminated against the stalactite-encrusted ceiling and rock walls is one few visitors forget. After a tour of the caves, the restaurants along the breezy shores of nearby Pone Ta Lote Lake offer a welcome break.

Elevator to the cave entrance
Pilgrims' donations paid for an elevator that bypasses 130 of the steepest steps of the *zaungdan*.

Diorama showing Prince Kummabhaya shooting the spider

The Archer and the Spider

The diorama at the head of the path to the caves recalls the legend of the giant spider that captured seven princesses who were bathing in Pone Ta Lote Lake and imprisoned them in the Shwe Umin cave. Prince Kummabhaya of Inle Lake bravely battled the outsized arachnid, shooting it with a single deadly arrow. The name of the site, derived from *pinguya*, literally "taken the spider," was inspired by this event.

Main road up to the caves

Shwe Umin Cave

KEY

① **Hsin Khaung Taung Kyaung**, at the foot of Pindaya Hill, is an elegant 200-year-old teak monastery built in traditional Shan style. Inside are bronze and bamboo Buddhas.

② **Archer and spider diorama**

③ **Zaungdan to the lake**

④ **Pone Ta Lote Lake**, lined with banyan trees, *zedis* (stupas), and temples, separates the cave complex from the main part of Pindaya village and the market area.

⑤ **Pindaya village**, spread around the lake, is a typical Shan market hub where locally made Shan paper parasols, pottery, and conical bamboo hats can be found.

***Zaungdan* to the caves**
Chinthes, or leogryphs, flank the entrance to the main *zaungdan* (covered, stepped path) up to the Shwe Umin cave, a steep 30-minute ascent punctuated by small pavilions with traditional, multi-tiered *pyatthat* roofs.

★ **Shwe Umin Cave**
About 8,000 gilded Buddha images fill the interior of Shwe Umin (literally "Golden Cave"), the oldest of them dating from 1773. The cave's entrance has a spectacular wall of seated Buddhas, and the main cavern beyond is a labyrinth of statues and stupas.

Giant seated Buddha
In the cave north of Shwe Umin is a seated Buddha depicted in *bhumisparsha* mudra with a halo of flashing lights.

0 meters 100
0 yards 100

Nget Pyaw Taw Pagoda
This large complex of gleaming white and gold Shan stupas close to the start of the main eastern walkway to the caves is an impressive sight. *Nat* statues and monumental *taguntaing* towers crowned by gilded *hamsa* birds complete the ensemble.

The gilded bamboo Buddha of the Maha Nanda Kantha, Hsipaw

⑨ Hsipaw

Road Map D3. 124 miles (200 km) NE of Mandalay. 🚉 22,000. 🚗 🚌

A busy market hub on the Dokhtawady River, Hsipaw is the obvious place to break the long journey on National Highway 3 or the rail trip between Pyin U Lwin and Lashio. The town is the setting for *Twilight Over Burma*, the best-selling autobiography of Austrian-born Inge Sargent, who in 1953 married Sao Kya Seng, the hereditary Shan prince or *saopha* (literally "sky lord"). She lived with him in a glamorous European-style mansion until his disappearance during the military coup a decade later. He never returned,

and is believed to have been killed by the Tatmadaw. Sao Kya Seng's nephew, Mr. Donald, was arrested a few years ago, allegedly for fraternizing with foreigners. His wife, Mrs. Fern, still lives in the old **Shan Palace (East Haw)** and shows visitors around, talking about the history of the family and the building.

Most people who overnight in Hsipaw do so in order to trek in the surrounding hills, where numerous ethnic minorities live in traditional villages. Single and multiday trekking circuits are offered by local guesthouses and hotels, and are much less frequented than routes around Kalaw and Inle Lake. An ideal way to prepare for hiking in the

high country is to climb Five Buddha Hill, an ascent rewarded with a spectacular view over the town and valley. The **Thein Daung Pagoda** on the hill is popular for evening walks. In the old quarter of Myauk Myo, on Hsipaw's northern fringes, it is worth visiting the **Madahya Kyaung** monastery and the **Maha Nanda Kantha** opposite, whose bamboo Buddha is covered in gold leaf.

🏛 **Shan Palace (East Haw)**
Open 9am–noon, 3–6pm daily.
🎟 donation.

🛕 **Thein Daung Pagoda**
Open 7am–10pm daily.

🛕 **Madahya Kyaung and Maha Nanda Kantha**
Open daily.

Environs
Hsipaw's most important Buddhist shrine is the **Bawgyo Pagoda**. Thousands of Palaung minority people come for its annual festival, when the temple's four Buddhas are processed around the complex in decorated palanquins. A lively fair and market are held at the same time, where local handicrafts can be purchased.

🛕 **Bawgyo Pagoda**
5 miles (8 km) W of town. **Open** 7am–9pm daily. 🎉 Mar: annual festival over the full moon period.

The ornately decorated Bawgyo Pagoda, Hsipaw's main Buddhist shrine

❿ Lashio

Road Map D3. 45 miles (73 km) NE of Hsipaw. 123,000. Lashio Airport.

The extent of the recent surge in Chinese migration to eastern Myanmar can most keenly be felt in Lashio, terminus of the railroad line from Mandalay. Only 66 miles (100 km) south-west of the Ruili–Muse border crossing point into Yunnan, the large market town now has a significant Chinese majority. During World War II, it played a crucial role in the engagement against the Japanese by form-ing a waystage on the famous Burma Road, by means of which the Allies were able to resupply Chiang Kai-Shek's Kuomintang nationalist forces. Today, contra-band electronic goods, rather than the Chinese tea, walnuts, silk, and Yunnanese camphor of former times, pack the convoys of trucks lumbering to and from the frontier.

Little remains of the former Shan princely capital that stood here in the British era. The old, mainly wooden town burned to the ground in a massive fire in 1988. However, on a forested hill overlooking the southern flank of Lashio, stands a photo-genic modern Chinese temple, the **Quin Yin Shang**, complete with upswept eaves and cor-pulent Buddha.

🏯 Quin Yin Shang
Open 7:30am–9pm daily.

Buddhist monk outside the painted exterior of the Wat Jong Kham stupa in Kengtung

⓫ Kengtung

Road Map E3. 262 miles (422 km) E of Taunggyi. 23,000. Kengtung Airport. May: Wat Jong Kham festival; Aug: Swing Festival (Women's New Year); Dec: New Year.

Off-limits for decades due to the long-running conflict between the Burmese Tatmadaw, Shan insurgents, and local opium barons, Kengtung (pronounced cheng-*dong*) is the capital of the Golden Triangle region and a springboard for exploring one of the most fascinating regions in Southeast Asia. While Tai minorities (mostly Tai Lü, Tai Nuea, and Tai Khün) dominate the town itself, the surrounding hill villages are divided between Ann, Akha, Wa, and Palaung, all of whom retain their traditional ways of life. The best introduc-tion to the various groups, who are distinguished by their elab-orate costumes, is the daily **Gard Luang Central Market**, for which shoppers from the hill tracts don their finest clothes and jewelry. For a more intimate experience of life in the villages, local agencies arrange guided treks that take in a cross-section of the area's minorities. Permits may be required, and overnight stays are not allowed, although this may change.

Kengtung itself makes a pleasant base for day trips. The road around Naung Tung Lake, in the center of town, affords great views of the somewhat ramshackle skyline, dominated by the graceful profile of the **Wat Jong Kham** (Zom Kham), a gilded stupa crowned by a golden *hti* (finial). The wat is said to date from a 13th-century migration from Chiang Mai's Lanna kingdom. At an intersec-tion nearby stands the **Maha Myat Muni** (Wat Mahamuni), whose interior is richly deco-rated with traditional gold-leaf Tai murals on burgundy back-grounds. The Buddha here is a replica of Mandalay's shiny-faced Mahamuni. Near the lake's southwest corner, the **Yet Taw Mu**, an impressive 60-ft (18-m) standing Buddha swathed in gold leaf, is among the town's more distinctive landmarks.

Myanmar's Golden Triangle

After Afghanistan, Myanmar is the second largest producer of opium in the world, and the center of this lucrative trade is in the hill tracts of eastern Shan, the notorious Golden Triangle region where the borders of Myanmar, Laos, and Thailand intersect. Remnants of the defeated Kuomintang army ran the drugs trade in the 1950s and 1960s, but local warlords later took control in order to finance insurgencies against the state, often with the collusion of Myanmar gov-ernment officials. Despite the concerted US-led crackdown of the 1990s and 2000s, opium is again flowing freely from these hills. Peasants earn five times as much by growing poppies rather than tea, rubber, or fruit. A 50 percent rise in the price of raw opium in recent years has seen a surge in the land given over to its cultivation. Illicit opium money, laundered via Yangon banks and state-owned oil and gas companies, is said to percolate through almost every part of Myanmar's economy, including the tourism industry.

Opium poppies, grown widely in the hills of eastern Shan

NORTHERN MYANMAR

From the sun-scorched plains of the Ayeyarwady Valley to the eternal snows of the eastern Himalayas, Northern Myanmar encompasses a spectacular gamut of landscapes. Red pandas and tigers roam the dense jungles along the border with India, while endangered freshwater dolphins arc through the wakes of the ferries that remain this remote region's main form of long-distance transport. Over the past decade, however, few foreign travelers have experienced these natural wonders at close quarters due to the long-running armed conflict between Kachin insurgents and the Myanmar army.

Myanmar's far north has long been the prime source of the country's legendary teak, and although much of the forest cover disappeared during the 20th century, huge tracts survive. Carpeting the hills that hug the main river valleys of the Chindwin and Ayeyarwady, these jungles remain some of the most inhospitable, unexplored territory in the world, particularly the regions lining the border with India, which form the traditional homeland of the Naga tribes. Although for the most part evangelized by Christian missionaries, the Nagas have retained many aspects of their traditional way of life. Prior to the closure of the region to visitors, a handful of river cruise operators ran luxury steamer trips up the Chindwin River and included visits to the Naga New Year festivities in their itineraries.

Farther north, the Hukawng Valley forms the heart of a vast wildlife sanctuary that may, in time, become a major visitor attraction, along with the pristine valleys of the Hkakabo Razi National Park, site of Myanmar's highest mountains.

However, due to sporadic outbreaks of fighting between the army and Kachin insurgents, overland and river travel is often restricted. Until recently, foreigners were only permitted to reach Myitkyina and Putao by air, but backpackers are once again starting to take Ayeyarwady ferries between Mandalay and Myitkyina. However, with the peace accord between the Myanmar government and the Kachin Independence Army (KIA) still relatively untested, it remains to be seen whether travel along Myanmar's great northern artery will remain open to all.

The Ayeyarwady flowing past the red-roofed Nondo Zedi stupa on its banks at Kyaukmyaung

◄ A Tangkhul Naga in ceremonial finery celebrating the Naga New Year festival at Leshi village in the Naga Hills

Exploring Northern Myanmar

The great travel experience of the north is without doubt the journey along the Ayeyarwady from Myitkyina to Mandalay. Passing remote settlements, supply jetties, and gold panners' encampments, the trip can take upwards of a week on the old two- and three-story ferries of the Inland Water Transport (IWT) company. This route is rarely attempted by foreigners, which makes it a uniquely intense way of experiencing local life at close quarters. Ferries and privately owned motorboats also depart regularly from Bhamo. Kachin State's other main attractions, at least potentially, are two protected areas in the far north – the Hukawng Valley Tiger Reserve and Hkakabo Razi, Southeast Asia's highest peak. With the former off-limits due to the ongoing insurgency, only the latter is currently accessible.

Area illustrated

Iconic green-and-white IWT ferry at Kyaukmyaung on its way north to Bhamo

Getting Around

At the time of writing, some uncertainty surrounded the status of travel restrictions in Kachin State. While the river journey between Mandalay and Myitkyina is technically open, some travelers have not been allowed to continue farther north along the Ayeyarwady than Kyaukmyaung. Road travel remains subject to controls, meaning that the only way to reach Putao in the far north is by air from Myitkyina. Daily flights connect Myitkyina with Mandalay and Yangon. Hkakabo Razi is accessible via expensive tailor-made tours and trekking trips organized through a couple of hotels in Putao; access to the Naga Hills above the Chindwin River is also only granted via Burmese tour operators who set up bespoke transport and accommodations *(see p229)*.

Key

— Main road

═ Other road

⊶ Railroad

▬ International border

▬ Regional border

△ Peak

9 **HKAKABO RAZI**
Dazungdam

Nam Tamai

10 **HPONKAN RAZI WILDLIFE SANCTUARY**

8 **PUTAO**
Rabawt
Machanbaw

0 **HUKAWNG VALLEY TIGER RESERVE**

Bumba Bum
14,190 ft (3,411 m)
Sumprabum
Hipzaw

Tawang

K A C H I N

Tanai

Mali Hka

Mankye

Shangaw Taungdan

Nmaihka

Chipwi

Kumon Taungdan

Myit Sone

Kamaing
Namti
1 **MYITKYINA**

Sanghpe

Mogaung
Kazu

Mogaung

Simbo
Nalon

Myothit

SHWEGU
5
4 **SECOND DEFILE**
3 **BHAMO**
Mansi

Muse

Si U

31

abein

ong Mit

0 kilometers   50
0 miles   50

Artisan painting pots in a workshop, Kyaukmyaung

Sights at a Glance

1 Myitkyina
2 Indawgyi Lake
3 Bhamo
4 Second Defile
5 Shwegu
6 Katha
7 Kyaukmyaung
8 Putao
9 Hkakabo Razi
10 Hukawng Valley Tiger Reserve and Hponkan Razi Wildlife Sanctuary

Vendors selling fresh produce at a riverside market in the town of Bhamo

For additional map symbols *see back flap*

The delicate gilded spires of the Hsu Taung Pyi Pagoda in Myitkyina

❶ Myitkyina

Road Map D2. 345 miles (555 km) N of Mandalay. 🏔 63,000. ✈ Mandalay International. 🚉 Myitkyina Airport, 5 miles (8 km) W of the center. 🚌 🚤 🚆 Jan: Manau festival.

Capital of Kachin State and the main market town in the north of the country, Myitkyina has, since ancient times, been a center for trade between China and Myanmar. Lying on the west bank of the Ayeyarwady, it became the terminus of the British-built railroad line in the 1890s, and stands at the nexus of several major routes across the Himalayas to the north, including the Ledo Road to Assam (see p185), constructed during World War II. This strategic importance explains why the town was the scene of a fierce battle in 1944 between a combined force of Chinese and Allied troops and Lieutenant General Honda's 33rd Imperial Japanese Army, during which it was virtually destroyed.

As a consequence, modern Myitkyina holds no sights of great note beyond the small but beautifully gilded **Hsu Taung Pyi Pagoda** overlooking the river, which has been restored by Japanese veterans.

A two-minute walk north of the stupa, the Sheduna Stadium is the venue for the nationally significant, annual **Manau Festival** (see p43), held in mid-January, when teams of elaborately costumed dancers from all of Kachin's seven tribal subgroups perform around tall totem poles, or *manautaing*. Although almost all of the Kachin population are Christian these days, the minority's animist roots are clearly discernible in styles of dress and dance. The Manau Festival is derived from a pre-Christian *nat* (nature spirit) worship ritual traditionally performed before the annual harvest, or for other important occasions such as weddings.

🛕 Hsu Taung Pyi Pagoda
Hsu Taung Pyi Pagoda Road, two-minute walk S of Sheduna Stadium. **Open** 7am–10pm daily.

❷ Indawgyi Lake

Road Map C2. 105 miles (170 km) southwest of Myitkyina. ✈ Mandalay International. 🚉 Myitkyina Airport. 🚗 Hired cars available from Myitkyina.

One of the few stand-out attractions in Kachin State still accessible to foreign visitors is beautiful Indawgyi Lake, a long day's journey by rail and road west of Myitkyina. Despite being marginally larger than Inle, the lake sees hardly any tourists and supports only a scattering of poor Kachin and Shan villages along its shores – a consequence of an old superstition stating that the waters were the home of a demon. Not until a Buddhist pagoda was built on an islet in the middle of the lake during the Konbaung era did people start to settle in the area. Connected to land by a narrow causeway that is only accessible during the dry season, the gilded **Shwe Myintzu Pagoda** has become a revered pilgrimage destination. Worshippers from all over the country travel here during Tabaung (February/March) for the ten-day pagoda festival.

🛕 Shwe Myintzu Pagoda
1 mile (2 km) SE of Nampade village. **Open** daily. 🚤 🚆 Feb/Mar: annual pagoda festival.

Fisherman drawing in his nets on Indawgyi Lake

The Four Faces Pagoda, one of the modern Buddhist shrines in Bhamo

❸ Bhamo

Road Map D2. 119 miles (193 km south of Myitkyina. 🏔 32,000. ✈ Mandalay International. ✈ Bhamo Airport, 2 miles (3.5 km) to the east. 🚌 🛥

The largest town on the Ayeyarwady between Myitkyina and Mandalay, Bhamo is also the one closest to the Chinese border, 40 miles (60 km) east. Traders, merchants, emissaries, and holy men have for hundreds of years traveled here along the Daying Jiang Valley to reach the mighty river. Among the visitors in medieval times was Marco Polo, who penned an account of the route in the 13th century. Then, as now, jade mined in the surrounding hills dominated the region's trade.

Evidence of the site's ancient commercial importance lies 3 miles (5 km) north at **Old Bhamo** (Bhamo Myo Haung), where the ruins of a lost city are scattered around two gold-tipped stupas, the Eikkhawtaw and Shwekyaynei Pagodas, believed to date from the Pyu era (1st century BC–9th century AD). Modern Bhamo was gutted by fire in the 1990s and holds little to detain visitors, although its daily market, attended by ethnic minority people from the nearby hills, is worth a browse early in the morning. On the riverfront, a large open-air pottery bazaar provides the town's best photo opportunity.

❹ Second Defile

Road Map D2. 37 miles (61 km) SW of Bhamo. ✈ Mandalay International. ✈ Bhamo Airport. 🛥

One of the most beautiful stretches on the Ayeyarwady River lies a couple of hours downstream from Bhamo, where the river narrows to just 330 ft (100 m) as it flows through a belt of thickly wooded mountains. Water levels along this scenic 7.5-mile (13.5-km) segment, known as the Second Defile (the First Defile lies north of Bhamo), can reach nearly 200 ft (60 m) in the rainy season, when boatmen have to keep a close eye on the famous green and red Parrot's Beak warning marker painted on a rock – if the bird is not visible, the flood is dangerously high and vessels are obliged to turn back.

Equally emblematic of the Second Defile is the impressive 985-ft (300-m) high **Nat Myet Hna Taung** or Welatha Cliff, a soaring limestone escarpment reminiscent of those that line parts of the Mekong River in neighboring Laos.

❺ Shwegu

Road Map D2. 63 miles (102 km) W of Bhamo. 🏔 16,500. ✈ Mandalay International. ✈ Bhamo Airport. 🚌 🛥

Just west of the Second Defile, Shwegu is a remote agricultural town on the Ayeyarwady's south bank where IWT ferries make an obligatory stop. Much of the fruit and rice sold in the local market is grown on the sandy soil of the two islands visible in the river opposite. The smaller, **Kyundaw**, holds the remnants of between 6,000 and 7,000 old stupas from the Bagan era of the 11th–13th centuries. While some have recently been renovated and sport coats of whitewash, most remain in a state of charismatic dereliction.

Stacks of decorated pottery for sale in the open-air market in Shwegu

Irrawaddy Dolphins

The Upper Ayeyarwady is among the last places in the world to support a breeding population of Irrawaddy dolphins (Orcaella brevirostris). Only 60–70 of these rare cetaceans survive along this stretch of the river, where they have evolved a unique bond with local fishermen. When summoned by a knocking of an oar on the side of the boat, the dolphins drive shoals of fish into the waiting nets, a service for which the animals receive a share of the spoils. Sightings are most common along a 46-mile (74-km) stretch of the Ayeyarwady between Kyaukmyaung and Mingun, officially designated as a sanctuary for this group, which has been listed as Critically Endangered on the IUCN Red List of Threatened Species.

Irrawaddy dolphin swimming alongside a fishing boat

A view of Katha, once home to George Orwell, from the Ayeyarwady River

❻ Katha

Road Map C2. 196 miles (317 km) southwest of Bhamo. 🚶 29,000. ✈ Mandalay Intl. ✈ Bhamo Airport. 🚌 Mandalay to Naba, then bus. ⛴

One of the more appealing stops on the Upper Ayeyarwady river journey, Katha surveys the river from its high bank, over-shadowed by the densely wooded hills of the Gangaw Taung to the west. This quiet, tree-lined administrative town is perhaps best known for being the place to which the British writer George Orwell was posted in 1926–7 as a District Superintendent in the Imperial Indian Police. His short sojourn here inspired his 1934 autobiographical novel, *Burmese Days*. A few buildings mentioned in the book still stand, including the half-timbered British Club, the double-storied police commissioner's house, and the Anglican church.

Stonework logo of the British Club, Katha

❼ Kyaukmyaung

Road Map C3. 28 miles (46 km) N of Mandalay. 🚶 11,000. ✈ Mandalay International. 🚉 Shwebo. ⛴ 🚌 ⛴

About an hour's drive north of Mandalay, Kyaukmyaung is a small river port renowned for its ceramics, especially the huge, kiln-fired pots which were used to transport oil, fish paste, and other foodstuffs for export. Known as Martaban jars, these distinctive containers are characterized by their glossy brown glaze and sweeping floral designs. Hundreds of newly turned specimens lie drying on the riverbank and outside the potteries in the Ngwe Nyein area, where visitors are welcome to watch the manufacturing process. It is thought that these giant receptacles were first made here in the 18th century, after King Alaungpaya brought families of potters back from his conquest of Bago (Pegu).

❽ Putao

Road Map D1. 520 miles (837 km) N of Mandalay. 🚶 10,000. ✈ Mandalay International. ✈ Putao Airport. ℹ Putao Trekking House, No. 424/425 Htwe San Lane, Kaung Kahtaung, Putao, (0) 98400138. 🌐 **putaotrekkinghouse.com**

In the far north of Kachin State, 220 miles (345 km) beyond Myitkyina, Putao is a distant outpost reached by very few foreign travelers. Thanks to its proximity to the snow-clad mountains of the Myanmar–Chinese border, the town holds great potential as a hub for trekking trips.

In British times, Putao was known as Fort Hertz, after William Axel Hertz, the intrepid District Commissioner who first mapped the area in 1888. Not much has changed here since then, beyond the addition of an airstrip – famous in the annals of World War II for being the only one in Burma not taken by the Japanese, and playing a role in the legendary Allied airlift over the "Hump" of the eastern Himalayas to resupply Kuomintang forces.

Weather permitting, flights from Mandalay land here twice a week – the only sanctioned route into the region for foreign nationals. Trekking tours have to be pre-arranged through one of the few hotels operating in the town *(see pp222–3)*; their fees generally include permits, excursions, and food. The hotels also organize trips to waterfalls, local beauty spots, minority villages, and timber camps.

Large Martaban jars drying on the banks of the Ayeyarwady in Kyaukmyaung

The icy summit of Hkakabo Razi, thought to be the highest mountain in Southeast Asia

❾ Hkakabo Razi

Road Map D1. Hkakabo Razi base camp is about 200 miles (320 km) N of Putao. *i* Putao Trekking House, Htwe San Lane, Kaung Kahtaung, Putao. **W** **putaotrekkinghouse.com**

Putao's northern horizon is dominated by the con-voluted, ice-encrusted summit of Hkakabo Razi, Myanmar's highest mountain at 19,294 ft (5,881m). The first ascent of the peak was made by a Japanese expedition as recently as 1996. In the same year, American conser-vationist Alan Rabinowitz surveyed the area's wildlife and discovered herds of

Leaf deer found in Northern Myanmar

Himalayan blue sheep, takin, red panda, stone martens, and an endemic species of leaf deer *(Muntiacus putaoensis)* hitherto unknown to science. His find-ings led to the creation of a national park, which now nominally protects a 1,500-sq-mile (2,424-sq-km) tract of rain forest and Alpine valleys around the mountain. A ten-day round trip is required to reach Hkakabo Razi's base camp, and access to the park is permitted only to those foreign travelers who are on pre-arranged tours, either via government-approved agents or through the two hotels cur-rently operating in Putao.

❿ Hukawng Valley Tiger Reserve and Hponkan Razi Wildlife Sanctuary

Road Map D1. 124 miles (200 km) NW of Myitkyina.

Dubbed the "Indiana Jones of Wildlife Protection" by *Time* magazine, Alan Rabinowitz was also the driving force behind the Hukawng Valley Tiger Reserve and Hponkan Razi Wildlife Sanctuary, a vast, contiguous 8,452-sq-mile (13,602-sq-km) tract of swampy rain forest and jungle-covered mountains that forms the world's largest tiger reserve. When it was set up by the Myanmar government in 1999, it was estimated that around 100 tigers inhabited the area. However, since then, a combi-nation of poaching and habitat erosion through logging and mining has resulted in a sharp fall in numbers. Some Myanmar experts have even suggested that the creation of the sanctu-ary was merely a ruse by the Tatmadaw military regime to wrest control of the area – and its lucrative uranium, oil, and teak reserves – from the Kachin Independence Army (KIA).

Visits to the Hukawng Valley are currently not allowed, although following the recent reduction in hostilities between the KIA and the Myanmar government, restrictions may well be relaxed in the future.

The Ledo Road

The great wilderness of jungle, roadless valleys, and peaks in the far north of Myanmar was a region notorious among US airmen during World War II as the "Hump." In 1942, dozens of cargo planes vanished while flying missions across it to resupply troops in northern Burma and China. The Allies, under the command of General "Vinegar Joe" Stilwell, were keen to replace the airlift with an all-weather overland route from India. A new road through the 3,727-ft (1,136-m) Pangsau "Hell" Pass over the Patkai Range dividing Assam and the Hukawng Valley was key to the project's success. In December 1942 work began on the Ledo Road, named after the Assamese town where it began. Conditions in the jungle were appalling. By the time the first bulldozers reached Shwingbyiang in Burma a year later, 1,100 US servicemen and many more local laborers had died from malaria and Japanese sniper bullets. Eventually, the Ledo Road reached Myitkyina to link with the old Burma Road from Bhamo to Kunming in China, a total distance of 1,079 miles (1,736 km), which the first convoy completed in 1945. As a result of the insurgencies on both sides of the Myanmar-India border, the route has been closed for decades.

A 1945 US military booklet by S/Sgt C.M. Buchanan and Sgt J. R. McDowell

SOUTHEASTERN MYANMAR

Extending from the mouth of the Sittaung River to the Isthmus of Kra, Southeastern Myanmar encompasses three states. Mon State is home to the sublime Kyaiktiyo Pagoda, the region's main pilgrimage spot. Kayin offers visitors the otherworldly sight of karst outcrops rising from lush paddy, while Tanintharyi's magnificent landscape includes the myriad coral-fringed islands and islets of the unspoiled Myeik Archipelago.

Facing Yangon across the Gulf of Mottama (Martaban) is the heartland of the Mon, who until the rise of Bagan had been Burma's most powerful ethnic group, but were thereafter confined to an ever-shrinking enclave around Thaton port. Today, Mawlamyine, known as Moulmein in colonial times, is the Mon capital, while the state itself occupies a mere sliver of lowland tapering down the Andaman coast. During World War II, the hills lining the Thai border inland became notorious as the site of the "Death Railway," built by the Japanese in the 1940s using a slave labor force of Allied PoWs. Overgrown for most of its length, the rail route sees far fewer visitors today than the one leading to the top of Kyaiktiyo Hill north of Mawlamyine, where a golden boulder perched precariously above a cliff is the region's principal pilgrimage destination.

Buttressed between Mon State and the Dawna Hills along the Thai frontier, Kayin is the stronghold of the Karen, who, since Independence, have been engaged in a war with the Myanmar army that has forced thousands of them into refugee camps. While a 2012 ceasefire promises a long-awaited opening up of this beautiful region, currently Kayin's only officially accessible area is the karst landscape around Hpa-an, an area of extraordinary limestone rock formations and caves spreading from the banks of the Thanlwin.

Farther south, Tanintharyi extends to Thailand, its pristine coastline of sand and coral tracked by forested hills. Offshore, the Myeik (Mergui) Archipelago, where Moken sea gypsies still lead a nomadic lifestyle, is regarded by many as the area of Myanmar most likely to be transformed by tourism over the coming years.

The spectacular Myeik Archipelago, offering opportunities for diving, snorkeling, and kayaking

◀ The delicately balanced golden rock on Kyaiktiyo Hill, one of Myanmar's most revered sites

Exploring Southeastern Myanmar

The undisputed highlight of Southeastern Myanmar is Kyaiktiyo, site of the fabled Golden Rock Pagoda. To see the shrine at its most ethereal, it is essential to be there at dawn or dusk, which means a night in one of the pricey hotels near the summit. A half-day drive away is Mawlamyine (Moulmein), a coastal city with great Burmese character and a string of hilltop pagodas with spectacular views over the mouth of the Thanlwin River. From there, a short detour inland leads over the Kayin State border to Hpa-an, springboard for forays into spellbinding karst country to the southeast. The unspoiled Myeik Archipelago is currently off-limits to all but keen divers on cruises and tours run out of Ranong or Phuket in Thailand, for which special permits issued in Yangon are required.

☐ Area illustrated

Getting Around

Foreigners may travel freely in Mon State, and from Mawlamyine to Hpa-an (in Kayin State) on local buses and ferries. Travelers to Kyaiktiyo can choose between regular buses and a dedicated air-conditioned express train that leaves Yangon on Saturday and returns on Sunday. Tickets are cheap but must be bought in advance at Yangon's Myanmar Railways booking office (see p239). In Tanintharyi foreigners are only allowed to visit the towns on National Highway 8, and can take a bus or train from Mawlamyine to Dawei, then a bus to Myeik (Mergui), and then a boat to Kawthaung. However, the easiest way is to take one of the daily flights from Yangon. The Myeik Archipelago can only be explored on pre-arranged cruises or expensive live-aboard diving tours (see p223).

Sights at a Glance

1. *Kyaiktiyo Golden Rock Pagoda pp190–91*
2. Mawlamyine (Moulmein)
3. Thanbyuzayat
4. Hpa-an
5. Mount Zwegabin
6. Saddar Cave
7. Kyauk Kalap Pagoda
8. Myeik (Mergui)
9. Kawthaung

Bago

KYAIKTIYO GOLDEN ROCK PAGODA

Sittaung

8

K

Kyaikto

Taunkz

Zokt

Gulf of Mottama (Martaban)

Buddhist shrine located in the Saddar Cave, a vast limestone cavern near the town of Hpa-an

Buddha statues at the start of the trail up Mount Zwegabin

The gilded rocks of Nwa-la-bon Taung Pagoda

Key

▬▬	Highway
▬	Main road
▭	Other road
─	Railroad
▬▬	International border
▬	Regional border

For additional map symbols *see back flap*

① Kyaiktiyo Golden Rock Pagoda

One of the most iconic sights Southeast Asia has to offer is that of the gravity-defying Golden Rock Pagoda, perched on its ledge above a jungle-cloaked valley, seemingly about to plunge into the void. From the roadhead at Kinpun, an arduous six- to seven-hour hike takes visitors up the Paung Laung ridge to the rock; less devout pilgrims are carried up on litters or take one of the pick-up trucks that grind up a bumpy, potholed track for an hour to the mountaintop. Visitors who spend the night in or near the pagoda will be well placed to see the ethereal sight of the setting or rising sun illuminating the richly gilded boulder, which is the third most revered site in Myanmar after the Shwedagon Pagoda in Yangon and the Mahamuni Temple in Mandalay.

The gilded balancing boulder, revered by Burmese Buddhists

Lower terrace
A paved walkway has been built around the base rock from which female visitors, prohibited from touching the boulder, may admire the pagoda at close quarters, as well as the amazing views of the forested valley below.

KEY

① **Pilgrims' bazaars**, both in the main approach and adjacent village, are crammed with restaurants and shops selling fruit, flower, and incense offerings to pilgrims.

② **The Mountain Top Hotel** is the most comfortable place to spend the night within easy reach of the boulder; foreigners are not allowed to join the Burmese pilgrims who sleep on the main terrace.

③ **Viewing pavilion** on the upper terrace.

④ **Polished bells** strung with red ribbons are a popular pilgrim offering, and are tied to spikes on the railings of the upper terrace.

⑤ **A narrow causeway** flanked by low railings leads to the boulder. Only men are permitted to cross it.

⑥ **The famous golden boulder**, measuring 50 ft (15 m) around, is balanced on a rock decorated with a lotus pattern.

⑦ **The 24-ft (7-m) tall pagoda on top of the boulder** enshrines a hair of the Buddha and is, contrary to appearances, the main object of veneration rather than the boulder.

The route
Devout pilgrims walk all the way to the top from Kinpun, a few hire sedan chairs to carry them up, and the majority squeeze into trucks with slat benches that run through the day to bus stops just below and at the summit.

For hotels and restaurants in this region see p205 and p215

★ The gilded boulder
The culmination of any visit to Kyaiktiyo for men is the chance to apply gold leaf to the rock. Large protruberances of solid gold have, as a result, built up around the base of the boulder.

VISITORS' CHECKLIST

Practical Information
Road Map D5. 100 miles (160 km) SE of Yangon; 7 miles (4 km) from Kinpun. **Open** daily. 🎟 paid at the top. 🎫 guides available. 📅 Mar: Festival of 9,000 Lamps (over full moon of Tabaung).

Transport
✈ Yangon International. 🚆 three daily trains plus special weekly Pilgrims' Express from Yangon to Kyaikto, the nearest town on the main highway. 🚌 to Kyaikto & Kinpun. Trucks run between Kinpun and the summit, 6am to 5pm (cheaper ones stop a mile/1.5 km short, at the bazaar, leaving a 45-minute walk up).

The *taguntaing*
With images of Thagyamin, king of the *nats*, around its base, and a *hamsa* bird crowning its tip, this monumental column reaffirms the subordination of animist *nat* spirits to Theravada Buddhism.

★ Festival of 9,000 Lamps
The number of pilgrims visiting Kyaiktiyo soars during the annual pagoda festival (held over the full moon of Tabaung in March), when the upper terrace is illuminated by 9,000 candles.

The Legend of Kyaiktiyo

The hair of the Buddha now secreted inside the Golden Rock Pagoda is said to have been given as a gift to King Tissa in the 11th century by a hermit, who had kept it for 100 years in his top knot. The holy man asked the king to find a boulder in the shape of a head upon which the hair could be enshrined. Tissa, who was blessed with magical powers, dived to the bottom of the ocean where he found a suitable rock and magically transported it to its present position. The weight of the sacred hair is believed to prevent the boulder from toppling into the ravine below.

❷ Mawlamyine (Moulmein)

Road Map D5. 195 miles (314 km) E of Yangon on National Highway 8. 🏙 208,000. ✈ Yangon Mingaladon; Mawlamyine Airport, SE edge of town. 🚌 ⛴ from Hpa-an. 🚐

Known as Moulmein in colonial times, Mawlamyine became the capital of British Lower Burma when it was ceded by the Konbaungs as part of the Treaty of Yandabo, following the First Anglo-Burmese War of 1824–6. Strategically sited at the mouth of the Thanlwin (Salween) River, the town provided a convenient harbor for steamers traveling between the cities of Calcutta (India) and Singapore, and on to the Straits Settlements and the Pacific. Among the legions of linen-suited passengers to have admired its gilded hilltop pagodas en route to more distant corners of the empire was Rudyard Kipling, who immortalized it in his popular 1892 poem "Mandalay." George Orwell was also briefly a resident of the town in 1926, while he was serving as a police officer in Burma. It is believed that he drew on an experience he had here for his famous 1936 essay "Shooting an Elephant."

The great bridge spanning the estuary at Mawlamyine, carrying road and rail traffic

Since Independence, the town has become the capital of Mon State, and is one of the largest cities of Myanmar. The sizable Anglo-Burmese community for which Mawlamyine was once known dispersed long ago, but the old quarter overlooking the riverfront retains plenty of faded charm. Dominating its low-rise, tin-roofed skyline from atop Pagoda Hill inland is the huge **Kyaikthanlan Pagoda**, a classic Mon-style stupa founded in the 9th century, but enlarged several times since. A fancily decorated elevator leads to its terrace, a popular spot for a sunset stroll from where the views across the Thanlwin are glorious.

Farther north along the hill stands the equally grand **Mahamuni Temple**, whose glittering central shrine houses a much revered replica of Mandalay's Mahamuni, donated by Mibayagyi, one of Mindon's queens. During the British annexation of Upper Burma, after Thibaw was deposed and the court exiled in 1885, she is said to have pined for her beloved Mahamuni statue, and commissioned this replica image in 1904.

🏛 Kyaikthanlan Pagoda
Pagoda Hill, just off NH 8.
Open 7am–10pm daily. 🚹 via the elevator. 💻 📷

🏛 Mahamuni Temple
Pagoda Hill, just off NH 8.
Open 7am–10pm daily. 💻 📷

Environs
Flowing 1,749 miles (2,825 km) from the Tibetan Plateau to its mouth in the Gulf of Mottama (Martaban), the **Thanlwin (Salween)** is one of the world's longest free-flowing rivers – as

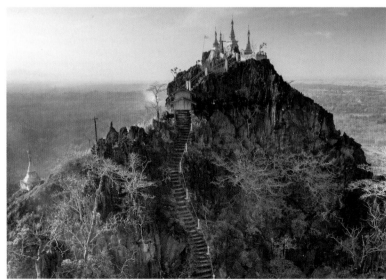

Dramatic limestone outcrop housing the Kyauktalon Kyaung pagoda, offering superb views of the surrounding countryside

yet, not a single dam blocks its route to the sea. Appropriately enough, the great bridge spanning the estuary at Mawlamyine, where the river meets the Andaman Sea, is the longest in Myanmar and carries both the highway and main rail line north.

Overlooking the coastal transport artery from a hilltop inland is the **Nwa-la-bon Taung Pagoda**, a golden boulder temple much less well known than the one at Kyaiktiyo. It consists of three gilded rocks balanced on top of each other. A fleet of 4WD trucks, with wooden slats in the rear for passengers, waits to shuttle pilgrims to the summit, which offers fabulous views of the coastal plain and river-mouth.

On a scrub-covered hillside south of Mawlamyine, just off the main highway at Yadana Taung, reclines a huge, red-robed Buddha, **Win Sein Taw Ya**, depicted at the moment of *parinirvana*, or attaining freedom from the cycle of rebirth. Measuring 600 ft (180 m) in length, it is the largest statue of its kind anywhere in the world and, like the one at Bodhi Tataung near the town of Monywa *(see p158)*, is hollow. Pilgrims may venture inside to see dioramas depicting scenes from moral tales and the life of the Buddha.

Rising sheer from the rice paddies across the National Highway from Win Sein Taw Ya, a dramatic outcrop of limestone is the site of a small but

Old locomotive marking the starting point of the "Death Railway" at Thanbyuzayat

spectacularly located pagoda called the **Kyauktalon Kyaung**. A flight of whitewashed steps leads to the summit of the rock, from where the views across the surrounding fields to the river are superb.

🏯 Nwa-la-bon Taung Pagoda
17 miles (28 km) NW of Mawlamyine, via a cement road branching off National Highway 8 (NH 8) between Kawpamagon and Mutkyi.
Open 7:30am–9:30pm daily.
Closed during the monsoons. 📷

🗿 Win Sein Taw Ya
Yadana Taung, 12 miles (20 km) S of Mawlamyine on NH 8.
Open 7am–9pm daily. 📷 📷

🏯 Kyauktalon Kyaung
12 miles (20 km) S of Mawlamyine on NH 8. **Open** 7am–10pm daily.

Burma's "Death Railway"

One of the most notorious human rights atrocities committed during World War II was the use of slave labor by the Japanese to carve a rail link between Bangkok and Rangoon in 1942–3. The line was later called the "Death Railway" because so many lives were lost during its construction.

Allied submarines off Malaysia made it difficult for the Japanese to resupply troops in Burma, so it was decided that Allied PoWs and Asian workers would be used to cut a rail track through 258 miles (415 km) of jungle and mountains. Begun in late 1942, the work was carried out at great speed in appalling conditions. The men worked 24-hour shifts,

❸ Thanbyuzayat

Road Map D5. 40 miles (65 km) S of Mawlamyine on NH 8. 🚌 **Open** cemetery: 7am–5pm daily. ♿

The infamous "Death Railway," connected with the Burmese rail network at Thanbyuzayat. The large **War Cemetery** on the northwest side of town is the final resting place of 3,617 of the estimated 16,000 Allied PoWs who died working on the line. Memorials on the site also feature dog tags taken from some of those who were buried where they fell beside the tracks. Maintained by the Commonwealth War Graves Commission, the immaculate headstones are set amid lawns around a single white cross.

Gravestones and memorials at the Thanbyuzayat War Cemetery

used shovels and pickaxes instead of mechanical equipment, and were fed meager rations of rotten meat and rice. Disease, exhaustion, starvation, and torture killed 16,000 PoWs and around 90,000 Malaysian and Burmese laborers over the 15 months it took to finish the job. The most severe loss of life occurred when 69 men were beaten to death and hundreds more died from disease during the construction of a cutting called the "Hell Fire Pass" through the watershed ridge of the Tenasserim Hills. Shortly after it was finished, the Allies bombed the line and it is no longer in use.

Giant reclining Buddha statue at Win Sein Taw Ya, the largest of its kind in the world

The Thanlwin flowing through Hpa-an, with Mount Zwegabin in the background, the tallest of the hills around the town

❹ Hpa-an

Road Map D5. 186 miles (300 km) SE of Yangon. 🚏 52,000. ✈ Yangon Mingaladon; Mawlamyine. 🚌 🚤 from Mawlamyine. 🚢

A peaceful, predominantly Karen market town on the banks of the Thanlwin (Salween) River, Hpa-an features on the southeastern tourist circuit due to its proximity to the spectacular karst terrain of the surrounding countryside. Apart from the unremarkable Shweyinhmyaw Pagoda, whose terrace juts out over the river, sights are thin on the ground. The most enticing option for a late-afternoon stroll is the trip across the river to **Hpa-pu Mountain**, a prominent peak on the far side of the Thanlwin whose summit may be reached via a stepped path in a little under half an hour. The views from here over the river and beyond to Mount Zwegabin are magnificent.

❺ Mount Zwegabin

Road Map D5. The trailhead begins 5 miles (9.5 km) south of Hpa-an at Zwegabin Junction. **Note:** carry sufficient food and water for the climb.

The definitive landform among the many outlandish limestone outcrops and massifs blistering the otherwise flat terrain beyond Hpa-an is Mount Zwegabin (2,373 ft/732 m), whose forested flanks surge upward from the vivid green

rice fields. Legend has it that the hill is the home of local spirits and souls.

Reached via a steep flight of stone and cement steps, Zwegabin's summit holds a small, lonely monastery, staffed by a couple of young monks who welcome visits from the odd party of pilgrims willing to brave the heat and the voracious troops of macaques that patrol the approach path. After a stiff hike of around two hours, the effort is repaid with an astounding view that is at its most sublime around sunrise. To reach the top in time, however, visitors will have to set out in the middle of the night, as foreigners are no longer permitted to spend the night in the monastery.

❻ Saddar Cave

Road Map D5. 17 miles (27 km) SE of Hpa-an via Naung Lon village. **Open** daily.

Southwest of Hpa-an, just off the main road to Eindu, is the Saddar Cave, the largest grotto in the area. A pair of monumental white elephants flank the entrance to the cavern, a reference to the local legend that an elephant king once took shelter inside it. Narrow, winding staircases lead from there through a series of immense chambers encrusted with Buddha statues and impressive rock formations and populated by bats, until the passage emerges on the far side of the mountain at a small lake – a magical experience.

The passage through the Saddar Cave emerging at the lake on the far side of the mountain

Kyauk Kalap Pagoda perched on an outcrop of limestone outside Hpa-an

❼ Kyauk Kalap Pagoda

Road Map D5. 7 miles (12 km) south of Hpa-an. **Open** 8am–noon and 1–5pm daily.

Rising from the glassy waters of an artificial lake, the golden Kyauk Kalap Pagoda caps a thin, knobbly finger of limestone draped in vegetation, a spectacle all the more amazing for its backdrop of beautiful karst outcrops. Visitors are permitted to visit the small monastery at its base and climb to the top of the rock for a wonderful view of Mount Zwegabin. The resident monks are staunch vegetarians and animal lovers, which explains the colony of rabbits hopping around the grounds.

❽ Myeik (Mergui)

Road Map D7. 569 miles (916 km) SE of Yangon. 127,000. Yangon Mingaladon; Mawlamyine. Myeik Airport. from Kawthaung.

The largest town in southern Tanintharyi, Myeik (formerly known as Mergui) juts into the mouth of the Tanintharyi River – a strategic location from which it dominated the area's maritime trade for many centuries. To avoid the pirates and tropical storms that plagued the sea route into the Gulf of Thailand via the Malacca Straits, the kings of Siam used Myeik as the main port for Ayutthaya, transferring goods by road through the jungles of the peninsula.

A building boom on the back of soaring seafood prices in the 1990s obliterated many of the old colonial-era buildings that formerly characterized the town. Today the **Theindawgyi Pagoda**, a slender, gilded stupa on a low rise above the covered riverfront market, is the only noteworthy sight in Myeik.

Boats leave at regular intervals from Myeik's harbor, on the south side of town, for the short crossing to Kadan, a twin-peaked barrier island opposite the mouth of the river. The port also serves as the main embarkation point for the 800 or more islands of the stunning **Myeik Archipelago** to the southwest, one of the last pristine marine wilderness

zones in Southeast Asia. The region, which is the homeland of the Moken sea gypsies, is strictly off-limits to all land-based tourists, although some cruises and live-aboard diving tours travel there from Ranong and Phuket, Thailand *(see p223)*.

❾ Kawthaung

Road Map D7. 500 miles (804 km) by air from Yangon. 56,000. Yangon Mingaladon; Mawlamyine. Kawthaung Airport. from Myeik & Ranong (Thailand).

At the southern extremity of Tanintharyi, Kawthaung is the main border crossing point between Myanmar and Thailand, and the town has a distinctly hybrid feel, with a population fluent in both languages and a reputation for producing the country's top kick boxers. The numerous tourists milling around are nearly all on visa runs from Ranong, Thailand, on the opposite side of the Kra Buri River. For those who stop off for a couple of days, it is worth visiting the **Pyi Taw Aye Pagoda**. Standing on a low rise immediately west of the harbor, this pretty Mon-style stupa is set in a compound with gleaming ceramic floors. The interior features some dazzling glass mosaics.

The Moken Sea Gypsies

In the far southeast of Myanmar, the beautiful Myeik (Mergui) Archipelago is the last bastion of an indigenous minority whose nomadic lifestyle has earned them the nickname "sea gypsies." Somewhere between 2,000 and 3,000 Moken, as they refer to themselves, live amid the turquoise waters and coral reefs of the islands, traveling between fishing sites and sheltered mooring places in long-tailed houseboats. Their ability to free-dive to astonishing depths and

Moken sea gypsies diving in the Myeik Archipelago

hold their breath underwater while spear fishing is the stuff of legend. Many Moken children do not set foot on dry land for years, unless accompanying their parents to trade seafood for rice in markets on the mainland. Widespread resettlement programs initiated by the Myanmar government in recent years have led to the creation of dedicated Moken villages on the archipelago, an attempt to clear the sea gypsies from areas rich in oil and gas. Despite this, many continue to roam as they have for centuries.

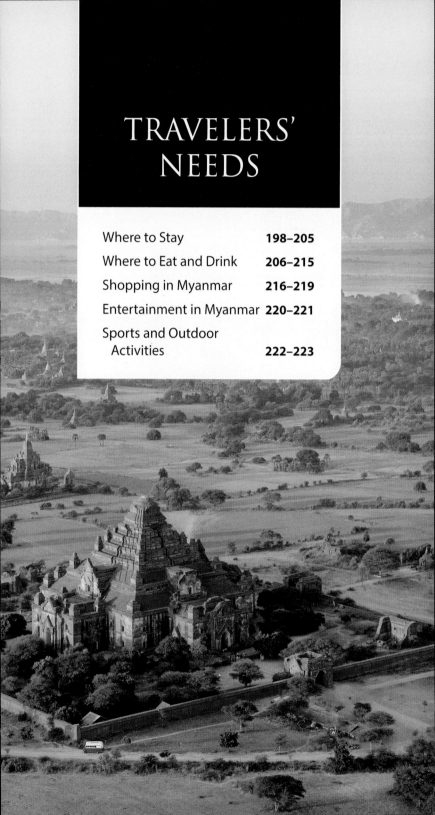

TRAVELERS' NEEDS

WHERE TO STAY

Accommodation options in Myanmar cover the full spectrum, from boutique luxury to run-down guesthouses. While the big city hotels tend to be characterless, international-style blocks, the more appealing places are those with a Burmese atmosphere, where local handicrafts, art, and building materials enliven the interiors. Hotels of all grades are expensive by Southeast Asian standards. Reluctance on the part of the government to grant new trading licenses, coupled with the sudden spike in demand when the tourism boycott ended in 2010, has ensured a chronic shortage of rooms across the country, particularly in the more popular visitor destinations such as Bagan and Inle Lake. Numerous new hotels are being built, and licenses for extensions to existing guesthouses fast-tracked by the government, but there remains a dearth of accommodations in all categories.

Hotel Grading

Accommodation licenses in Myanmar are issued by the Ministry of Tourism, which grades hotels in the country according to a star-rating system of one to five stars. Every establishment is obliged to display its grade plaque in reception. Only a handful of ultra-luxurious places in Yangon make the five-star category, whereas, at the other end of the scale, there are numerous one-star hotels.

The ministry does not publish its grading criteria, but the stars give a fair reflection of a hotel's standard. Not all hotels and guesthouses achieve star status, however. And just because an establishment does not display a plaque, it does not mean that it is not licensed.

Luxury and Business Hotels

The recent rise in foreign investment in Myanmar, in particular from Singaporean chains, means that the coming years are likely to see a sharp rise in the number of luxury hotels in the country. For the time being, however, capacity barely keeps pace with demand, and falls well below it at the height of the tourist season between November and March, when rates soar.

Myanmar's top five-star hotels are nearly all in Yangon. Places such as the Strand and the Chatrium (see p202) are on a par with other Asian counterparts, with international-grade facilities, standards of service,

The gracious lobby of the luxury Chatrium Hotel Royal Lake in midtown Yangon

and comfort. Popular with both visiting business clients and foreign tourists, the five-star hotels all occupy landmark properties downtown. Rooms are spacious, richly furnished, and centrally air-conditioned. Flatscreen TVs and in-room Wi-Fi are the norm, and the complexes include state-of-the-art leisure facilities such as large outdoor pools, gym, and spa, as well as a choice of restaurants, cafés, bars, and, in a few cases, glamorous clubs attracting the rich and famous of Yangon.

Only slightly less luxurious are business hotels, which are to all intents and purposes five-stars, but with fewer frills and lower tariffs. Some business hotels lack a pool, but the rooms are always very comfortable.

If you are making your own reservation (rather than staying as part of a package tour) it is worth knowing that the best rates for high-end hotels are always posted online; booking in person or over the phone invariably means being offered the far higher "rack rate." As with high-end hotels in other countries, extras such as mini-bar purchases and in-room phone calls can add significantly to the final bill.

Note that payments made by card will incur an additional charge of 5 percent or more, so it is better to settle in cash (usually in US dollars).

Yangon's Kandawgyi Palace Hotel, with the Karaweik Palace in the background

◀ Visitors floating over the ancient temples and pagodas of Bagan in a hot-air balloon

The Governor's Residence in Yangon, a boutique hotel housed in an exquisite teak mansion from the 1920s

Boutique Hotels

In recent years, a handful of small-scale luxury hotels have started to appear in Myanmar, where the emphasis is as much on bespoke designer style as comfort. As well as being more compact, boutique places tend to favor Burmese aesthetics, fusing traditional wood carving, stone sculpture, art, and crafts with contemporary chic. The effect can be memorable, but so can the prices: places such as Bagan's Hotel @ Tharabar Gate *(see p204)*, Mandalay's Hotel by the Red Canal *(see p204)*, and Yangon's Governor's Residence *(see p202)* are in particularly high demand in peak season from November through February and their tariffs reflect this.

Resort Hotels

Large self-contained hotels that are a destination in themseves are few and far between in Myanmar, although this is bound to change over the coming decade as areas such as the Myeik (Mergui) Archipelago *(see p195)* are developed for tourism. Boasting pools, stylish accommodations, smart restaurants, and sports and games facilities, Myanmar's few bona fide resort hotels tend to be situated on the shores of Inle Lake. Places such as the Aureum Resort and Spa and Inle Lake View *(see p205)* make the most of their spectacular situation, with chalets on stilts or facing

the waterfront. Ngapali beach, in the northwest state of Rakhine, is the other place where resort hotels tend to dominate. Set in the shade of mature palms, the likes of Amazing Ngapali, Sandoway, and Bayview *(see p203)* offer beautiful swimming pools and sea views from their luxurious designer chalets, only a few steps away from the surf of the Andaman Sea.

The dividing line between a boutique hotel and a resort is often a fine one, depending on the amount of effort that has been put into the decor, and many places categorize themselves as "boutique resorts." This is the preferred option among foreign tour operators, which is why these places tend to be full of tour groups. Bookings are usually made through agents, or via email or telephone, rather than online reservation systems. Payment is in cash (US dollars).

Conventional Hotels

The "conventional" category used in the listings on pp202–5 refers to a class of upper- and mid-range hotels that are lacking the kind of glitz that may appeal to foreign tourists. Sometimes dubbed "Chinese-style," they are often intentionally bland to appeal in the main to visiting Chinese business people, with rooms in simple, motel-style chalets or multi-storied blocks. The furniture and

fixtures are usually worn and smell of cigarette smoke, but the tariffs are more affordable.

Guesthouses, B&Bs, and Budget Hotels

Small, family-run hotels, guesthouses, and what might be classed as B&Bs or homestays (allowed in a few places where no other accommodations are available, such as in the hill tracts and ethnic minority villages of the north) are in short supply across the country. While standards of cleanliness tend to be high and the welcome warm, prices are, as a consequence, prone to inflation. When booking a room on spec, always check the quality of the plumbing, the thickness of the mattresses, and the air-conditioning, which can vary greatly. Many mid-range hotels also offer different categories of rooms and it is always worth comparing these if vacancies are available.

Budget hotels generally offer the poorest value for money, especially those popular with foreign backpackers. Often with small or no windows, old-style air-coolers rather than modern air-conditioning, and blighted by unpleasant odors from their tiny bathrooms (if they have one), the rooms may be stuffy and cramped. When traveling on a tight budget, always ask to see the rooms before parting with any money.

Villas arranged like an Intha stilt village at the Myanmar Treasure Resort, Inle Lake

Homestays

It is against the law in Myanmar for foreign visitors to stay in the homes of local people. Exceptions, however, are made in some parts of the country such as Shan State – notably between Kalaw and Inle Lake, and around Hsipaw – where trekking is a popular activity, but where no other accommodations are available. Trekkers wishing to undertake two- or three-stage routes are allowed to stay overnight in the villages of ethnic minority people along the way *(see p173)*. All the necessary arrangements will be made by your guesthouse or by the travel agent hired to organize the trek.

Staying in Monasteries

Many monasteries accept guests for a night or two in exchange for a small donation. In the rural hinterland of Inle Lake, this enables tourists to undertake multistage hikes, an arrangement formally ratified by the Ministry of Tourism in March 2013 to ease pressure on beds in the area. Elsewhere, monasteries may serve as a last resort when the only other lodgings in the region are occupied. Monastery visitors should not expect much in the way of creature comforts beyond shared bathrooms and a thin cotton mattress or straw mat to sleep on.

Booking

Given the shortage of rooms, it is essential to book as far ahead as possible – at least a month, or more, in advance. Reservations may be made verbally by telephone (although the English spoken may not always be fluent, and the cost of calls extremely high), or directly by email or through the hotel's website. Either way, it is wise to ask for confirmation via email, and to reconfirm the reservation a couple of days before the intended date of arrival. Always check the rate in advance. Most upscale hotels expect full payment at the time of booking. Some of the less expensive places require payment at check-in, while others waive payment until check-out.

Travel agents in Myanmar *(see p229)* will be happy to make all the necessary arrangements on behalf of travelers. Charges for this service vary: larger agents

Staff at the reception desk of one of Mandalay's mid-range hotels

have access to discounted rates that they may hand on in part to clients, which can work out cheaper even after their mark-up. In addition, many hotels in Myanmar accept bookings via the website agoda.com, and some smaller guesthouses even insist that guests make reservations this way.

Prices

Tariffs are high compared with other countries in Southeast Asia as a result of the shortage of accommodations. A very basic budget room in downtown Yangon can cost upward of US$25–30 per night, and a threadbare mid-range one more than double that. At the high end, rates are even more inflated: a room in one of the landmark five-star hotels in the November–February peak season can cost US$500–900, excluding government taxes.

Bargaining

It was once easy in Myanmar to haggle down the cost of accommodations – vacancies were plentiful and alternatives close to hand. Far from being able to negotiate a reduction, visitors are now more likely to find the rate has increased since the time of booking. If demand is high, many hotels, particularly those in tourist areas, will adjust their tariffs accordingly.

Taxes

Service charges of between 5 and 10 percent are routinely collected on rooms in luxury hotels and resorts, in addition to the flat-rate 10 percent government tax. These amounts tend not to be included in the price quoted at the time of booking. These taxes do not, however, apply to cheaper places.

Tipping

Although tipping didn't used to be customary, the practice has gradually become more widespread over the past few years. If a staff member has been particularly helpful, a gratuity of a few US dollars will be welcomed. Bear in mind that upscale hotels already levy a service charge of 10 percent on top of the bill.

Checking In

When checking in, foreign visitors are required to fill in government forms listing their passport and visa details, date of arrival in Myanmar, and onward itinerary. Some places also insist that you hand over your passport for the duration of your stay, although they can usually be dissuaded from doing this if you are firm enough. Ask to have a look at the room you have been allocated before any money is handed over, as it will be easier to change at this stage than later. Some hotels require payment in full and in cash at check-in; the balance for any extras will need to be paid when checking out.

The stylish Arakan-style villas of the Amazing Ngapali resort complex

Facilities for Disabled Travelers

Visitors with mobility problems will find high-end hotels more straightforward than budget ones. Luxury places tend to have wheelchair-friendly luggage runways to their lobbies, spacious elevators, and help for any heavy lifting. Beyond that, however, disabled travelers can expect no dedicated facilities. Staying in cheaper hotels can mean endless stairs, cramped lifts, and small bathrooms with only squat toilets and no tubs.

Facilities for Children

Very few hotels in Myanmar offer dedicated facilities for kids; those that do tend to be the most expensive five-stars, where "kid's clubs" are sometimes featured on weekends. Nearly all hotels, however, allow under-12s to share a bed with their parents for free, or charge a small amount for an extra bed or cot. Babysitter services are available in some hotels. Upscale places are likely to have extensive grounds and gardens with areas where youngsters can let off steam, as well as swimming pools with special shallow sections for children.

Recommended Hotels

The hotels in this guide have been selected across a wide price range and represent the most commendable options in their location and category. Value for money, quality of furnishings, facilities, the overall setting and atmosphere, and the warmth of the welcome have been taken into consideration. The best of these are highlighted as DK Choice. The prices listed are those charged by the hotel during the high season from November to February for a double room, inclusive of all taxes. Hotels are listed by region (further divided into towns) and by price range.

The swimming pool at The Hotel @ Tharabar Gate, a luxury boutique hotel in Old Bagan

Where to Stay

Yangon

Wai Wai's Place $
B&B
26C, Thiri Mingalar Rd, Kamayut Tsp
Tel *(0) 9421150524*
W waiwaisplace.wordpress.com
Quiet, friendly B&B near the
university and Inya Lake offering
unusually restrained rates and
genuine hospitality.

Bike World $$
B&B
10F, Khabaung Road, 6 Miles Pyay Rd
Tel *(01) 527636*
W cyclingmyanmar.com
Quirky, cycling-themed B&B run
by an Australian-Burmese couple.
Immaculate, comfortable rooms,
a relaxing terrace, sound travel
advice, and guided cycle tours.

Garden Home $$
B&B   **City Map** E2
*10, Bogyoke Museum Lane,
Bahan Township*
Tel *(01) 541917*
W gardenhomebnb.asia
Located down a side road in the
embassy enclave, this is one of
the cozier, more welcoming B&Bs
in the city, with a relaxing garden
and terrace. Walking distance
from the Shwedagon Pagoda.

Hotel Alamanda $$
Boutique   **City Map** C1
*60B, Shwe Taung Gyar St (Golden
Valley Rd), Bahan Township*
Tel *(01) 534513*
W hotel-alamanda.com
This French-run boutique B&B
offers stylish rooms in an old
house that has plenty of character, with varnished wood floors,
wicker chairs, and deep verandas.

Central Hotel $$
Conventional   **City Map** D4
335–357, Bogyoke Aung San Rd
Tel *(01) 241001*
W centralhotelyangon.com
A bit frayed around the edges,
but in a great location. Ask for a
top-floor room as traffic noise
can be loud on the lower floors.

Classique Inn $$
B&B   **City Map** C1
*53B, Shwe Taung Gyar St (Golden
Valley Rd), Bahan Township*
Tel *(01) 525557*
W classique-inn.com
Smart, professionally run
guesthouse in a residential
suburb. The staff are friendly,
and there is a relaxing pebble
and brick terrace to lounge on.

The Chatrium's huge, palm-lined pool, one
of the hotel's main selling points

Clover City Center $$
Conventional   **City Map** D4
217, 32nd St (Upper Block)
Tel *(01) 377720*
W cloverhotelsgroup.com
Clean and modern, with so-so
service and small rooms for the
price, but it is well maintained
and its location opposite the
Traders Hotel is hard to beat.

Yuzana Garden $$
Conventional   **City Map** D4
*44, Signal Pagoda Rd, Mingalar
Taung Nyunt Township*
Tel *(01) 248944*
W yuzanahotels.com
Dependable mid-range hotel
within easy reach of downtown.
In need of a facelift, but fine for
a short stay and the rates are
low for Yangon.

Chatrium Hotel Royal Lake
Yangon $$$
Conventional   **City Map** E2
40, Nat Mauk St
Tel *(01) 544500*
W chatrium.com
Extensive grounds, a huge pool,
an excellent location next to the
historic royal Kandawgyi Lake,
and spectacular views of the
Shwedagon Pagoda over the
waters are this grand, five-star
hotel's greatest assets.

Inya Lake Hotel $$$
Business
37, Kaba Aye Pagoda Rd
Tel *(01) 9662866*
W inyalakehotel.com
Set amid wonderful lakeside
gardens, this Soviet-built five-star
hotel has a faded 1960s feel, but
comfortable furnishings. It is
owned by the government.

Kandawgyi Palace Hotel $$$
Business   **City Map** E3
*Kan Yeik Tha Road, Mingalar Taung
Nyunt Township*
Tel *(01) 394837/8/9*
W kandawgyipalace-hotel.com
Occupying a great lakeside spot,
this government-owned, five-star
hotel is run to high standards.
Well placed for sightseeing.

DK Choice

The Governor's
Residence $$$
Boutique   **City Map** B3
35, Taw Win Road, Dagon
Tel *(01) 229860*
W governorsresidence.com
This British-owned hotel in the
leafy embassy quarter occupies
a beautifully renovated 1920s
mansion. The paddle fans, split-
cane blinds, and liveried staff
re-create the colonial-era ambience to perfection. Lotus ponds
and a well-shaded pool in the
grounds add to the charm.

The Savoy $$$
Boutique   **City Map** C1
129, Dhammazedi Rd
Tel *(01) 526289*
W savoy-myanmar.com
Gorgeous boutique hotel in a
colonial mansion, with in-period
fixtures, furniture, and decor,
down to the claw-foot bathtubs.
Walking distance from the
Shwedagon Pagoda.

The Strand $$$
Boutique   **City Map** E5
92, Strand Rd
Tel *(01) 243377*
W hotelthestrand.com
The grandfather of Yangon's
colonial-era hotels, the Strand
dates from 1903 and is still
replete with old-world elegance.
High tea here is a must.

Traders $$$
Business   **City Map** D4
223, Sule Pagoda Rd
Tel *(01) 242828*
W shangri-la.com/yangon/traders/
Myanmar's top business hotel,
and a landmark to rival the
nearby Sule Pagoda, of which its
best rooms have superb views.

Bago Region

BAGO: Bago Star $
Conventional   Road Map D5
11–21, Kyaik Pun Pagoda Rd, Oatha Myothit
Tel *(052) 23766*
Few people stay in Bago, due to the lack of decent accommodations. While overpriced, this place is the best of the bunch, with wooden chalets in a garden plot.

PYAY: Lucky Dragon $$
Resort   Road Map C4
772, Strand Rd, Sandaw Quarter
luckydragonhotel.com
Well-maintained, comfortable, modern bungalows set around leafy gardens in the heart of town. Facilities include a Jacuzzi and pool. Good value.

DK Choice

TAUNGOO: Royal Kaytumadi $$
Resort   Road Map D4
Royal Kaytumadi St
Tel *(054) 24761*
kmahotels.com
This beautiful lakeside five-star hotel offers generous-sized air-conditioned rooms and an outdoor pool looking across the lake to the Shwesandaw Pagoda. As befits the location, the architecture, decor, and fixtures are in regal Burmese style.

Western Myanmar

CHAUNGTHA: Belle Resort $$
Boutique   Road Map C5
Chaungtha
belleresorts.com
Chalets and bungalows with Thai gabled roofs sit right behind the beach. The suites are huge.

MRAUK U: Shwe Thazin $$
Boutique   Road Map B3
Sun Sha Seik Quarter
shwethazinhotel.com
An attractive two-star hotel close to the ruins. The air-conditioned bungalows have rooms decorated with local art.

MRAUK U: Mrauk Oo Princess $$$
Boutique   Road Map B3
Aungdat Creek
Tel *(043) 50232*
mraukooprincessresort.net
Luxurious Arakan-style villas scattered around leafy tropical gardens. They have their own boat for transfers from Sittwe.

DK Choice

NGAPALI: Amazing Ngapali $$$
Resort   Road Map C4
27, Inya Myaing Road, Zee Phyu Gone village
amazingngapaliresort.com
Set well away from the bustle of the main beach area, this complex of Arakan-style mini villas is flawlessly stylish. The rooms are huge and most face the ocean.

NGAPALI: Bayview $$$
Resort   Road Map C4
205, Hgnet Pyaw Khaung Kwin
Tel *(01) 504471*
bayview-myanmar.com
A small-scale resort hotel with a perfect location; large, cool, wood-floored rooms; lovely pool; and pretty restaurant.

NGAPALI: Sandoway $$$
Resort   Road Map C4
Mya Pyin village
Tel *(043) 42244*
sandowayresort.com
Glamorous, Italian-owned boutique resort. Palm trees frame the poolside and cottages; the villas have beach views.

NGWE SAUNG: Bay of Bengal $$$
Resort   Road Map C5
North side, Ngwe Saung
bayofbengalresort.com
Ultra-stylish resort hotel arranged around a central pool, with gorgeous teak and stone chalets facing the beach.

PATHEIN: La Pyae Wun $
Conventional   Road Map C5
30, Mingyi St
Tel *(042) 25151*
The most comfortable option in town and well situated for the market area and riverfront. The rooms – all twin – have tiled floors and are generous-sized and air-conditioned.

Bagan Archeological Zone

NEW BAGAN: Kumudara $$
Resort   Road Map C3
Corner of 5th St and Daw Na St, Pyu Saw Htee Quarter
Tel *(061) 65142*
kumudara-bagan.com
One of the few budget hotels where you can admire the ruins while lounging in a pool. Furnishings show signs of wear, but are acceptable for the price.

NEW BAGAN: Ruby True $$
Conventional   Road Map C3
Myat Lay Rd
Tel *(061) 65043*
rubytrue.com
Clean and comfortable chalets in a peaceful spot on the edge of the village. The hotel's remote location explains the low tariffs – a bargain for Bagan.

DK Choice

NEW BAGAN: Bluebird $$$
Boutique   Road Map C3
Myatlay St, Bagan Myothit (East), Naratheinkha 10
Tel *(01) 398030, (061) 65051*
bluebirdbagan.com
This boutique hotel has been exquisitely designed by its French owner, who has used local arts and crafts to create a romantic, stylish hideaway near the ruins. The rooms are minimalist and cool, and there is a small, gorgeous pool in a walled spice garden to lounge beside.

OLD BAGAN: Aye Yar River View Resort $$$
Resort   Road Map C3
Near Bupaya Pagoda
Tel *(0) 92042135*
baganayeyarhotel.com
Set in vast river-facing gardens, this resort has had an expensive makeover and offers smartly furnished rooms with great views.

The cottages of the glamorous Sandoway Resort, located on the beachfront

For more information on types of hotels *see pages 198–201*

OLD BAGAN: Thande $$
Conventional   Road Map C3
Near Gawdawpalin Temple
Tel *(061) 60025*
W baganthandehotel.net
Bagan's oldest hotel was built
in 1922 for a visit by the Prince
of Wales. It is arguably the best
situated, on a raised plot over-
looking the river. The refurbished,
spacious, teak-paneled rooms
offer good value.

**OLD BAGAN: The Hotel @
Tharabar Gate** $$$
Boutique   Road Map C3
Tharabar Gate
Tel *(061) 60037*
W tharabargate.com
Five-star, boutique luxury on a
small scale, set in an oasis of
dense greenery. In a prime loca-
tion near the river and ruins.

**OLD BAGAN: Thiripitsaya
Sanctuary** $$$
Resort   Road Map C3
Old Bagan
Tel *(061) 60048*
W thiripyitsaya-resort.com
Large riverside resort boasting
spectacular sunset views and
a good-sized swimming pool.
Popular with tour groups.

**POPA TAUNG KALAT: Popa
Mountain Resort** $$$
Resort   Road Map C3
Mount Popa
W myanmartreasureresorts.com
Dreamy views from the poolside
terrace of this boutique resort
extend over the spectacular Popa
Taung Kalat monastery – one of
the country's most exotic sights.

Mandalay Region

**MANDALAY CITY: Peacock
Lodge** $
B&B   Road Map C3
5, 61st St
W peacocklodge.com
Peaceful, clean, and cool, with
quality Myanmar meals served
on a sociable garden terrace.
This is by far the best budget
option in Mandalay, but book
well ahead.

**MANDALAY CITY: Hotel
Yadanarbon** $$
Conventional   Road Map C3
125, 31st St (76/77)
Tel *(02) 71999*
W hotelyadanarbon.com
Large, modern hotel in the heart
of Mandalay's downtown shop-
ping district. It offers clean,
generous-sized rooms and
courteous service.

**MANDALAY CITY: Mandalay
City Hotel** $$
Conventional   Road Map C3
26th St (82/83)
Tel *(02) 61700*
W mandalaycityhotel.com
With its fish ponds and pool, this
place is a relaxing retreat from
the heat and dust.

MANDALAY CITY: Smart $$
Conventional   Road Map C3
167, 28th St (76/77)
Tel *(02) 32682*
W smarthotelmandalay.com
A top mid-range choice for its
spotless rooms, central location,
and efficient, smiling staff.

DK Choice

**MANDALAY CITY: Hotel by
the Red Canal** $$$
Boutique   Road Map C3
417, corner of 63rd St & 22nd St
Tel *(02) 68543*
W hotelredcanal.com
Resembling a Burmese palace,
with carved wooden eaves and
rattan blinds on the windows,
this 26-room bolthole is the
city's most alluring place to stay.
It is hidden in the northeast
corner, away from the bustle,
but close to the main sights.

**MANDALAY CITY: Mandalay
Hill Resort** $$$
Resort   Road Map C3
9, Kwin (416B), 10th St
Tel *(02) 35638*
W mandalayhillresorthotel.com
This lavish resort in landscaped
grounds at the foot of the hill is
among Myanmar's top hotels.

**MANDALAY CITY: Rupar
Mandalar** $$$
Boutique   Road Map C3
A15, corner of 53rd St & 30th St
Tel *(02) 61555*
W ruparmandalar.com
Beautifully designed boutique
hotel on the eastern outskirts of
Mandalay. Made mostly of

varnished teak, the place has all
the facilities of a five-star but a
lot more style.

**MANDALAY CITY: Sedona
Mandalay** $$$
Conventional   Road Map C3
1, corner of 26th St and 66th St
W sedonahotels.com.sg
Grand five-star hotel in a choice
location opposite the palace
complex. It has great views, a
large pool, and cheerful service.

MONYWA: Monywa Hotel $$
Resort   Road Map C3
Yone Kyi Or, Bogyoke Rd
Tel *(071) 21581*
Motel-style place offering red-
tiled bungalows with hardwood
decks facing the lake and pool.
A relaxing, secure, and peaceful
base for visits to nearby sights.

PYIN U LWIN: Pyin Oo Lwin $$
Conventional   Road Map D3
9, Nandar Rd, Kandawgyi Lakeside
Tel *(085) 21226*
W hotelpyinoolwin.com
Built in 2011, this is the newest
and best value option in town,
with teak-lined chalets in land-
scaped grounds above the lake.

**PYIN U LWIN: Aureum Palace
Governor's House** $$$
Boutique   Road Map D3
*Ward 6, Governor's Hill, Mandalay–
Lashio Highway*
W aureumpalacehotel.com
Luxury reconstruction of a grand,
colonial-era mansion, with rooms
in the main building and bunga-
lows in the grounds. Polished,
but a bit short on atmosphere.

**PYIN U LWIN: Kandawgyi Hill
Resort** $$$
Resort   Road Map D3
Kandawgyi Lakeside
W myanmartreasureresorts.com
Converted from an old British
colonial rest house, the resort
offers accommodations in spa-
cious bungalows amid well-
tended grounds with lake views.

The colonial-style buildings of Pyin U Lwin's Kandawgyi Hill Resort

Eastern Myanmar

HSIPAW: Lily The Home $
B&B   Road Map D3
108, Aung Tha Pyae Rd
Tel *(082) 80077, 80318, 80408*
W facebook.com/pages/Hotel-Lily-The-Home/239557689447449
This popular Hsipaw guesthouse is comfortable, friendly, and good value. They also arrange treks and guides for keen hikers.

INLE LAKE: Paramount $$
Resort   Road Map D4
Nga Hpe Chaung
W paramountinleresort.com
Wood-lined rooms, the best ones with decks jutting out over the water. Not ideal for longer stays as it is on the southwest shore, an hour's boat ride from town.

DK Choice

INLE LAKE: Aureum Resort and Spa $$$
Resort   Road Map D4
Mine Thauk
Tel *(081) 209866*
W aureumpalacehotel.com
Luxurious stilt chalets in a spectacular location facing the lake. Private decks offer perfect sunset views. The interiors contrast warm-toned hardwoods with luminous local silks in fiery colors. Currently the benchmark among Inle's high-end resorts.

INLE LAKE: Inle Lake View $$$
Resort   Road Map D4
Khaung Daing
Tel *(081) 23656*
W inlelakeview.com
Set just 650 ft (200 m) from the shore in delightful, butterfly-filled gardens, the hotel has beautiful teak rooms with high ceilings, canopied beds, and big windows.

INLE LAKE: Inle Princess $$$
Resort   Road Map D4
Magyizin
Tel *(081) 209055*
W inleprincessresort.net
Gloriously peaceful setting down a private water channel. The huge chalets are mountain- or lake-facing, and have kitsch boat-shaped bath tubs.

INLE LAKE: Inle Resort $$$
Resort   Road Map D4
Nyaungshwe
Tel *(0) 95154444*
W inleresort.com
This spectacular lakeside resort is accessed via a stilt bridge across beautiful lotus ponds, with chalets on the water boasting

The spacious wood-panelled bedrooms of the Paramount Resort at Inle Lake

traditional Burmese roofs. Guests are offered high standards of service and cuisine.

INLE LAKE: Myanmar Treasure Resort $$$
Resort   Road Map D4
Maing Thauk, Nyaungshwe
W myanmartreasureresorts.com
There are dreamy sunset views from the front-row villas of this resort on the northeast shore, set up like an Intha stilt village.

INLE LAKE: Villa Inle $$$
Boutique   Road Map D4
Mine Thauk
Tel *(01) 242259*
W hotelinline.com
Particularly beautiful teak villas, swathed in banana plants, with floor-to-ceiling windows and king-sized beds suspended from high-vaulted ceilings.

KENGTUNG: Princess $
Conventional   Road Map E3
Zay Dan Kalay St
Tel *(084) 21319*
The best base for exploring the surrounding minority villages. Unprepossessing looks, but very clean. Central location in town.

NYAUNGSHWE: Aquarius $
B&B   Road Map D4
2, Phaung Daw Pyan Rd, Nam Pan Quarter
Tel *(081) 209352*
W agoda.com
Cozy little budget guesthouse down a quiet street within walking distance of the bus station and market. Friendly and clean, with a leafy garden terrace.

NYAUNGSHWE: Amazing $$$
Boutique   Road Map D4
Yone Gyi Rd
Tel *(081) 209477*
W hotelamazingnyaungshwe.com
Attractive boutique hotel close to the boat jetty. Spacious rooms, artful decor, and a great location close to the local market.

Northern Myanmar

BHAMO: Friendship Hotel $
Conventional   Road Map D2
Letwet Thondaya Rd
Tel *(074) 50095*
Large, well-maintained rooms in a modern block within easy reach of the market and river. Free transfers to the boat jetty.

MYITKINA: United $
Conventional   Road Map D2
38, Thitsat St
Tel *(074) 22085*
The town's cleanest option, this is a basic, Chinese-style hotel popular with foreign aid workers.

DK Choice

PUTAO: Malikha Lodge $$$
Boutique   Road Map D1
Mulashidi village
W malikhalodge.net
A beautiful boutique hideaway, nestled between forest and rice terraces south of Putao, this is the only international-standard hotel in the far north, and an atmospheric springboard for adventures in the nearby hills. Each spacious bungalow is centered on a handmade teak bathtub with a fireplace next to it.

Southeastern Myanmar

HPA-AN: Golden Sky $
Conventional   Road Map D5
2, Thida St, West Thida Ward
Tel *(058) 21510*
Basic hotel facing the river on the north side of town. Its institutional decor is redeemed by the views from the upper floor. Not very well maintained, though.

KYAIKTIYO: Mountaintop Hotel $$
Conventional   Road Map D5
Kyaiktiyo
Tel *(01) 502479*
The most comfortable rooms on the summit of Kyaiktiyo, only five minutes from the shrine. The hotel is overpriced, but worth it to be in position for sunrise.

MAWLAMYINE: Mawlamyaing Strand $$
Conventional   Road Map D5
Strand Rd, Phat Than Quarter
W mawlamyaingstrand.com
Mawlamyine's smartest hotel surveys the riverfront. The rooms are large and bright with comfortable beds, but lack views.

For more information on types of hotels *see pages 198–201*

WHERE TO EAT AND DRINK

The Burmese are deservedly proud of their cuisine which, while borrowing heavily from those of its neighbors, manages to remain totally distinctive. A wealth of spices and pungent seafood pastes combine to create curries with intense flavors, while dry-roasted nuts, pulses, and seeds sprinkled over the top add surprising textures. Noodles and tofu feature prominently in the cooking of the Shan Plateau, just one of several regional styles represented throughout the country. International food, such as pizza, pasta, and burgers, is also widely available in the big cities and tourist resorts, which offer a variety of dining options. The range extends from swish air-conditioned restaurants to relatively basic Burmese places where you can order a feast for a few dollars, and street stalls selling piping hot, tasty snacks for even less than that. Cafés range from American-style coffee houses in the cities to traditional hole-in-the-wall teashops, while Chinese-style beer stations offer lively venues for watching soccer matches in the evenings.

Burmese Restaurants

The most authentic Burmese food is served in busy, no-frills restaurants around shopping districts and local neighborhoods, where the emphasis is definitely more on the cooking than the decor. It is best to ignore the strip lighting and plastic furniture, and head for the glass-topped buffet cabinet where dozens of different stews, curries, salads, and side dishes will be on display. Having selected one or two main courses, diners wait for them to be brought to their table, along with a host of accompaniments, clear soup, and side dishes, ranging from bowls of steaming white rice to nose-tingling *balachaung* (dried shrimp relish), fermented tea-leaf salad, roughly chopped crudités, and green leaves.

Chinese influence is apparent in the open-air barbecue stalls, where customers pick a skewer of pork, chicken, mutton, or fish and wait for it to be flame-grilled and served up with delicious sauces. Restaurants in Shan also reveal Chinese inspiration in the different noodles they serve up in meaty broths, along with tofu made from chickpeas (garbanzo beans).

Tourist Restaurants

Until recently, foreign food was the exclusive preserve of restaurants in Myanmar's few five-star hotels, but since the revival of tourism, scores of places have opened in major

Muffins, cakes, and cookies at downtown Yangon's trendy Coffee Club bakery café

visitor destinations such as Nyaungshwe (Inle Lake), Bagan, and Ngapali (Western Myanmar) where visitors can enjoy pizza, burgers, and sushi.

In metropolitan cities such as Yangon and Mandalay, the appetite of the affluent elite for culinary novelties means that it is now possible to enjoy French patisserie and designer ice creams, and surf the web over a muffin and a cappuccino.

Street Food

Some of the tastiest meals and snacks on offer in Myanmar are sold from street outlets. In larger cities, food stalls often cater for dozens of diners who sit at low tables on undersized plastic chairs while they eat. *Mohinga* or noodle soup *(see p208)* is a favorite breakfast meal among local workers. In the evenings, Indian chapati and curry vendors spring up in downtown areas. Contrary to appearances, the food served in such places is usually safe and hygienic because turnover is brisk and everything freshly prepared each day. The same applies to fried snacks, such as the Indian *pakora*, cooked on hot griddles in the street, and the delicious *mont linmayar* (literally "husband and wife") – mini rice flour pancakes filled with quail eggs, yellow split peas, tomatoes, and spring onions. When crispy on the outside, two pancakes are flipped on top of each other to form a ball, said to resemble a loving couple, from where their Burmese name is derived. They are served in bags of ten pairs with a tablespoon of sesame powder.

Vegetarian Options

Myanmar presents no particular problems for vegetarians, and although the choice of dishes

A bowl of Shan-style noodles served with vegetables in a broth, Eastern Myanmar

will inevitably be more limited, most restaurants, whether Burmese or tourist-oriented, offer plenty of options. Stews made from chickpeas and other beans or pulses, which go well with rice and noodles, as well as Myanmar's delicious tomato salads are popular with vegetarians. Shan State is a region where vegetarians are particularly well served, thanks to the predominance of tofu, vegetable and noodle soups, and filling clay pot meals.

Feel Myanmar Food, a popular Burmese self-serve restaurant in Yangon

Teashops and Beer Stations

Traditional Burmese teashops are very much part of the culinary scene, particularly in Yangon, where a brew of strong, sweet tea (usually made with condensed milk) provides the accompaniment to a bowl of hot *mohinga*, steamed bun, *samosa*, or semolina cake. Teashops are where workers and senior citizens go to relax, chat, and read the newspaper.

Younger Burmese, however, tend to congregate more in Chinese-style beer stations, where soccer matches are shown on widescreen TVs and karaoke or other live entertainment is often laid on.

Alcohol

Beer is fast overtaking tea as the country's national drink. By far the most popular brand is Myanmar Beer, produced by a company jointly owned by the military and a conglomerate backed by Wa drug barons. Dagon and Mandalay, both refreshing lagers, are also owned either by the government or by military-linked conglomerates. In more high-end bars, Singaporean Tiger Beer may be on offer, along with boutique beers such as Spirulina (made with the eponymous algae) and ABC (a strong, dark beer rated at 8 percent ABV).

Demand in tourist centers for wine has spawned two Burmese vineyards (*see p173*), Aythaya on the outskirts of Taunggyi, and Red Mountain on the shores of nearby Inle Lake. Both produce reds and whites, from mostly European vinestocks such as Shiraz, Cabernet Sauvignon, Tempranillo, and Dornfelder. Quality, while improving each year, is roughly comparable with mid-price New World wines.

Prices

As in any country, prices for meals vary greatly in Myanmar. While you can expect to pay no more than US$4 for an elaborate, filling meal in a traditional Burmese restaurant, a simple bowl of pasta with pesto could cost double that in a tourist café. Only in smart hotels and the odd gourmet restaurant are you likely to pay more than US$20 per head for a meal. Wine can dramatically increase your bill, with local bottles and New World imports costing US$15-25, or double that in upscale hotels.

Tipping

Service is nearly always included in the cost of your meal and tipping is not customary in ordinary Burmese places. In tourist restaurants, it is commonplace to leave the small change from the bill – up to 1,000–1,500 kyat – as a tip.

Tourists relaxing on the patio of a small Burmese teashop

Recommended Restaurants

The restaurants on the following pages have been carefully chosen from across the country to cover a range of possibilities, from fine-dining and traditional to modern Burmese fusion cuisine and gourmet Thai. The more high-end places are often located in smart hotels, where the price you pay is as much for the ambience and showy service as the cooking. The DK Choice category draws attention to establishments that are exceptional in some way – either because they offer great value for money or because the food they serve stands out from the crowd.

The Flavors of Myanmar

Myanmar's cuisine is as varied and distinctive as the country itself. While sharing many of the culinary traditions of neighboring Thailand, it encompasses a wealth of dishes and flavors found nowhere else – a legacy of Myanmar's position at the cultural crossroads of Southeast Asia. Chinese influence is seen in the ubiquity of noodles and clear, sour soups, while the popularity of Indian curries, breads, and fried snacks dates from the period of British rule. Myanmar offers a veritable feast of flavors for the adventurous palate.

Balachaung shrimp and chili paste

Fresh produce being sold at one of the five-day markets around Inle Lake

Burmese Cuisine

The keynote flavors of Burmese cooking derive primarily from the extensive use of *ngapi* sauces, which are made using fermented seafood (shrimp, prawns, and fish) pounded with salt and fiery spices. Condiments and pastes, such as the ubiquitous *balachaung*, are based on *ngapi*. They are

the meal's *apu za* or "heating" component, which is always counterbalanced by *a-aye za* or "cooling" foods, including eggplant, cucumber, and dairy produce. The basic staples are rice or noodles, with protein provided by meat, poultry, or fish, but dozens of pulses, vegetables, fruits, spices, herbs, and pungent condiments are deployed to concoct even a

simple, everyday meal across Myanmar, many of them completely unfamiliar to Western taste buds.

A Typical Burmese Meal

Burmese meals are traditionally eaten on low tables, with diners seated cross-legged on straw mats, although small chairs are more common these

Garlic   Kaffir limes   Turmeric root   Banana stems
Cumin seeds   Dried shrimp   Preserved ginger   Peanuts   Chillies   Cilantro

Selection of the many aromatics and flavorings found in Burmese cuisine

Regional Dishes and Specialties

The quintessential dish of Yangon and the Ayeyarwady Delta is *mohinga*. This reviving stew has a base of fish broth flavored with onions, garlic, ginger, and lemongrass. Rice vermicelli noodles and sliced banana stem give substance, and it is served with boiled eggs, *nga hpe* (fried fish cakes), and *akyaw* (chickpea fritters). It is most often eaten before work at street stalls, with diners seated on low plastic chairs. The equivalent in the Mandalay and Shan regions is *Shan kauk swe* (hot Shan noodles), prepared in a

Burmese tofu

broth with chunks of chicken, pork, or mutton, and steamed greens. Early morning markets are the best places to find authentic versions. A vegetarian variety uses tofu, in Myanmar made not with soy beans but with chickpeas and turmeric. These combine to give the tofu a rich yellow color and a firm, creamy consistency.

Mohinga, the national dish, is packed with definitively Burmese aromas and ingredients, such as tender banana stem core.

A typical Myanmar meal, consisting of dozens of different dishes and condiments

days. Among families, the first spoon of rice is always reserved for the elders, whether present or absent – a tradition known as *u cha*. While rice, curries, meat, and fish are eaten with the hands, chopsticks are used for noodles and spoons for salads. More than a dozen different preparations are served simultaneously, typically in small bowls, along with a pile of vegetables and raw salad, mint, radishes, watercress, and cucumber.

Salads and Street Foods

The Burmese are great lovers of *a-thoq*, or salads, which involve a wide range of ingredients blended with spices, oils, and a sprinkle of dry-roasted nuts. Perhaps the most distinctive of all is *lahpet thoq*, fermented

tea-leaf salad, a pungent, slimy tangle of pickled tea leaves with many aromatic additions. On formal occasions it is served in special lacquerware boxes, divided into sections, and few meals are eaten without a taste-tingling portion on the side. The equally popular

Yangon street food vendor making *mohinga*, a substantial noodle soup

karyanchintheet thoq (tomato salad) is more likely to appeal to the Western palate. In Shan State, Burmese tofu is often used to make nourishing, filling salads featuring bean sprouts and raw green leaves.

Snacks and even full meals are served from street stalls. Workers frequently breakfast on *mohinga*, served from steaming cauldrons, while Indian deep-fried samosas and *pakoras* provide a boost before the commute home.

ON THE MENU

Myae oh myi shae Clay pot meals, consisting of Chinese-inspired clear soups with vegetables and pork or chicken pieces.

Nangyi thoq A salad of thick rice noodles with spicy chicken, toasted chickpea flour, onions, chillies, lime, and sliced egg.

Htamin jin Dumplings from the Shan highlands, made with fermented rice, boiled fish, tomato paste, and mashed potato.

Mont lone ye bawn A typical Burmese dessert using coconut, jaggery (palm sap sugar), and rice, rolled into balls and steamed.

Shwe yin aye A dessert of agar jelly, tapioca, and sago, steeped in sweetened coconut milk.

Mont let saung Balls of sticky rice, tapioca, toasted sesame seeds, coconut milk, shredded coconut, and sugarcane syrup.

Shan noodles are wide and flat, and feature in the very popular spicy, tomato-based stew that takes their name.

Fermented tea-leaf salad also includes fried peas, garlic, chilies, tomatoes, crushed shrimp, lime, ginger, and peanut oil.

Burmese tomato salad is a deliciously refreshing amalgam of tomato and onion in a sweet and spicy peanut sauce.

Where to Eat and Drink

Yangon

999 Shan Noodle House $
Shan **City Map** D4
130B, 34th St, Kyauktada Township
One of the best and most
conveniently located places in
the city to sample big bowls of
Shan noodles (rice, yellow, and
traditional) and crispy fried tofu.

Aung Thukha $
Burmese **City Map** C1
17A, Dhammazedi Rd
Within walking distance of the
Shwedagon Pagoda, and among
the city's most popular budget
Burmese restaurants, this dowdy
but clean canteen serves a range
of salads and meaty curries.

Coffee Club $
Bakery Café **City Map** C5
*Level 1, corner of Mahabandula Rd &
11th St, Lanmadaw Township*
Tel *(0) 943207764*
In the heart of downtown, this
trendy air-conditioned café has
free Wi-Fi, pleasant music, beautiful teak tables, and welcoming,
English-speaking staff. Great for
a light meal, sandwich, or latte.

Feel Myanmar Food $
Burmese **City Map** C3
124, Pyidaungzu Yeiktha St
Busy and crowded but a good
place to experiment with a wide
range of Burmese dishes from a
covered buffet. They are served
with a range of sides and sauces.

Khaing Khaing Kyaw $
Burmese
*671A, off 5.5 Miles Pyay Rd, Near Thu
Kha Kabar Clinic*
There is no better place in the
city than Khaing Khaing Kyaw to
initiate yourself into the joys of

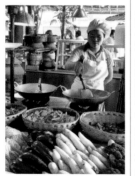

A range of fresh vegetables ready to be
cooked at Khaing Khaing Kyaw

traditional Burmese cuisine, with
dozens of dishes prepared daily.
The restaurant offers great value
and is always scrupulously clean.

Kosan $
Burmese/Chinese **City Map** C4
108, 19th St, Latha Township
Tel *(0) 9420061869*
"Beer Bar Street," as the brightly lit
19th St is known, is lined with
lively, Chinese-style barbecues
after dark, and this tiny, open-
fronted restaurant is a tourist-
friendly place to soak up the
atmosphere. Serves cocktails.

Min Lan Rakhine $
Rakhine
*Min Lan St, Sayar San (South),
Sanpya Quarter, Bahan Township*
Succulent lobster, crab, squid,
and tiger prawns are sold to
customers by weight and
prepared Rakhine-style on an
open-flame grill. Although it
looks a bit down-at-heel from
the outside, the food is amazing.

Nilar Biryani $
Indian **City Map** D4
*216, Anawrahta Rd, between
29 St & 30 St*
Yangon's best biryani restaurant,
where the rice is spooned from
huge vats on the terrace. Dishes
are full of flavor and the service is
brisk. Try banana lassi for dessert.

Sai's Tacos $
Mexican
*32A, Inya Myaing Rd, Bahan
Township*
Tel *(01) 514950*
For a break from Asian cooking,
try this down-to-earth Tex-Mex
joint offering tasty chicken bur-
ritos, black bean and vegetable
quesadilla, corn chips with gua-
camole, and great tortillas.

Green Elephant $$
Burmese
*33, Thiri Mingalar Road (Attia Road),
Kamayut Township*
Tel *(01) 537706, (0) 973152300*
Quality Burmese home cooking
served in a large, open-sided
garden pavilion. Popular with
tour groups, with a range of
dishes tailored to Western tastes.
Attached crafts store.

House of Memories $$
Burmese **City Map** B1
290, U Wisara Road, Kamayut Tsp
Tel *(01) 525195*
Proper Burmese food served in
a half-timbered, colonial-era
house with linen tablecloths,

Price Guide
Prices are based on an evening meal
for one person, including service tax
but no alcohol.

$	up to $7
$$	$7 to 20
$$$	above $20

historic photographs, and family
heirlooms as décor. Ask for a
seat on the upstairs veranda.
Service is brisk.

Padonmar $$
Southeast Asian **City Map** B3
105–107, Kha Yay Pin St, Dagon
Tel *(0) 973029973*
Delicious Burmese and Thai
curries and a tempting array of
fresh salads (including wonderful
grilled eggplant) served in the
garden or the loudly decorated
interior. Popular with tour groups.

Yangon Bakehouse $$
Bakery Café **City Map** D1
*Pearl Condominium, Block C,
Kaba Aye Pagoda Rd*
Tel *(0) 9250178879*
Divine pastries, cookies, and
muffins freshly baked by female
workers trained as part of a
scheme to help disadvantaged
women. They also whip up great
salads and sandwiches, and the
best coffee in Myanmar.

L'Alchimiste $$$
French/Fusion
5, U Htun Nyein St
Tel *(01) 660612*
No one comes to Yangon to eat
gourmet French food but it is
hard to resist the romantic set-
ting and sumptuous cooking of
this fabulous restaurant sited in
an old colonial-era mansion on
the shores of Inya Lake. Reserve
ahead as it is popular with the
local elite and affluent expats.

DK Choice

Le Planteur $$$
Fusion **City Map** D1
22, Kaba Aye Pagoda Rd
Tel *(01) 541997*
Gourmet modern European
and Indo-Chinese fusion cuisine
from Michelin-starred Swiss-
French chef Felix Epissier.
Lobster bouillabaisse with
lemongrass and ginger is the
signature dish. The service is
snappy to the point of osten-
tation. For the full five-star
experience, however, choose
from the à la carte menu, as the
set ones are not great value.

L'Opera $$$
Italian
62D, U Htun Nyein St, Mayangone Township
Tel *(01) 665516*
Set in a garden on the leafy shores of Inya Lake, this top-notch Italian has a setting to match its wonderfully authentic food, although the service can be a bit pretentious. Advance booking is recommended.

Mandalay $$$
International **City Map** B3
Governor's Residence Hotel, 35, Taw Win Rd
Tel *(01) 229860*
One of Myanmar's finest restaurants, where you can dine on fragrant Burmese or Western cuisine seated on a veranda overlooking lotus ponds. Snappy service from liveried staff.

Sharky's $$$
European **City Map** C1
117, Dhammazedi Rd
Tel *(01) 524677*
This trendy deli-diner is hugely popular for pizza, artisan breads, cold meats, locally made cheeses, and delicious homemade ice cream. The restaurant upstairs is fancier, using state-of-the-art sous-vide cooking to ensure the Norwegian salmon, fresh Ngapali fish, and succulent local steaks are cooked to perfection. Imported wines are served.

Strand Café $$$
Continental **City Map** E5
Strand Hotel, 92, Strand Rd, Dagon Township
Tel *(01) 243377*
A high tea of light sandwiches, scones, and pastries at the Strand Café has been de rigeur for visitors to the city since colonial times – although many now consider the experience to be a little overpriced.

Strand Grill $$$
International **City Map** E5
Strand Hotel, 92, Strand Rd
Tel *(01) 243377*
Lobster thermidor at the Strand Grill has been a Yangon institution for decades, and the menu remains as unashamedly gourmet as ever, with truffle and foie gras donuts for starters.

Thiripyitsaya Sky Bistro $$$
International **City Map** D4
Sakura Tower, 339, Bogyoke Aung San Rd, Kyauktada Township
Tel *(01) 255277*
The famous 360° view over the city and the nearby Sule Pagoda from the top of Yangon's highest

Htay Htay's Kitchen on Ngapali beach, one of the area's many seafood restaurants

skyscraper is a must-see, and the food is commendable if a little pricey. Come for coffee and cake if you're on a budget.

Traders Café $$$
International **City Map** D4
Traders Hotel, 223, Sule Pagoda Rd
Tel *(01) 242828*
Tasty sushi and sashimi, tender roast lamb, fabulous curries, a smorgasbord, and a chocolate fountain for Sunday brunch are just some of the reasons to dine at this swanky hotel restaurant. In addition, the café also offers fast Internet access to guests.

Bago Region

BAGO: Hanthawaddy $$
Burmese/Chinese **Road Map** D5
192, Hintha St, Shin Sawpu Quarter
By far the best of a generally poor bunch of restaurants in town, serving Burmese and Chinese dishes to visiting tour groups. Try the tasty grilled river prawns.

TAUNGOO: Mother's House $
International **Road Map** D4
501–502, Yangon–Mandalay Hwy
Tel *(054) 24240*
A dependable hotel restaurant that is popular with tour groups as it serves delicious curries, rice, and noodle dishes in a large, clean dining room on the side of the main road. A handy stop on the journey north from Yangon.

Western Myanmar

MRAUK U: Moe Cherry $
International **Road Map** B3
East of the palace walls
Tel *(043) 24200*
Tourist-oriented restaurant near the royal palace and museum that is the most popular place in town thanks to its eclectic menu and welcoming hosts.

DK Choice

NGAPALI: Htay Htay's Kitchen $$
Seafood **Road Map** C4
North end of beach, just past the Bayview Hotel
Htay Htay's Kitchen makes more effort than most to vary their menu, offering garlic butter tiger prawns, squid salad, and stuffed crab tempura in addition to the usual range of grilled fish steaks and curries – all melt-in-the-mouth fresh and served by cheerful staff. The friendly couple who run this restaurant also have a little souvenir store on site.

NGAPALI: Ngapali Kitchen $$
Seafood **Road Map** C4
Main Rd, behind the Aureum Palace hotel
Run by a fishing family from the village, this cafe offers a bit more variety than other places around, including Burmese, Chinese, and Thai food. They serve seared tuna fish, snapper, crab, and lobster fresh off the boat, beautifully cooked and presented.

NGAPALI: The Green Umbrella $$
Seafood **Road Map** C4
Ngapali
One of many virtually identical seafood places on the beach, but with especially delightful owners. The fish steaks are fabulous, as are the cocktails and sunset views from the restaurant's sandy terrace.

NGWE SAUNG: The Royal Flower $$
Seafood **Road Map** C5
Ngwe Saung village
Market-fresh local fish, prawns, crab, octopus, and lobster are all expertly grilled and served with spicy sauces. Fun atmosphere, cordial service, and only a short trishaw ride from the beach.

For more information on types of restaurants *see pages 206–7*

SITTWE: River Valley $$
Seafood   Road Map B4
5, Main St
Succulent Rakhine seafood at good prices is on offer at River Valley. The menu is extensive, the service cordial, and the dining room immaculate. The restaurant is popular mainly with foreign visitors and aid workers.

Bagan Archeological Zone

MYINKABA: San Thi Dar $
Pan-Asian   Road Map C3
Myinkaba village, on New Bagan–Old Bagan Rd
Copious portions of fresh, honest, tasty cooking from a warm local family whose curries and salads are the stuff of legend in this tourist enclave. The food is mostly vegetarian, but the menu does have a page of chicken and beef alternatives.

NEW BAGAN: Green Elephant $$$
Pan-Asian   Road Map C3
Yamonar, Thiripyitsaya Quarter
Tel *(061) 65182*
The food served at this chain restaurant is so-so and a bit overpriced, but it is worth dining here at sunset for the superb riverside location and romantic decor of antiques and candles.

NEW BAGAN: Si Thu $$$
Pan-Asian   Road Map C3
Yamonar, Thiripyitsaya Quarter
With a fabulous location looking on to the river and views of the distant Rakhine-Yoma Hills, this café is perfect for sunset. The Thai, Chinese, and Burmese food is of consistently high quality.

NEW BAGAN: Sunset Garden $$$
Chinese/Burmese Road Map C3
Yamonar, Thiripyitsaya Quarter
Tel *(061) 65037*
Spellbinding views of the Lawkananda Pagoda reflected in the Ayeyarwady extend from the terrace of this smart restaurant on the riverfront. It is usually busy with large tour groups during the day, but is recommended for sunset.

NYAUNG U: Aroma 2 $
Indian   Road Map C3
Thiripyitsaya 4 St (Yarkin Thar Hotel Rd)
Tel *(0) 92042630*
"No Good, No Pay" is the motto of this enduringly popular Indian restaurant on Nyaung U's main

road. The vegetarian curries, dals, butter chicken, rice, and chapatis are more Burmese than Indian, but they are tasty enough.

NYAUNG U: Queen $
International   Road Map C3
Near Bagan-Umbra Hotel, Bagan–Nyaung U Rd
Tel *(061) 60176*
This popular roadside restaurant on the outskirts of Nyaung U is renowned for its superb river prawn and butterfish curries, served in traditional lacquerware or clay pots, with local chicken-soya bean paste and the full range of condiments. They also do tasty burgers, milkshakes, and lassis throughout the day. A great place to break a temple tour, or for supper.

DK Choice

NYAUNG U: Black Bamboo $$
International   Road Map C3
Off Thiripyitsaya 4 St
Tucked away off Nyaung U's main strip, this pretty, French-run garden restaurant is a relaxing haven. The menu of international and Burmese dishes is well thought-out, and includes delicious tofu curry, eggplant salad, and spaghetti carbonara. The service is slow or serene, depending on how hungry you are. The resident cats are a pleasant distraction.

OLD BAGAN: The Moon $
Vegetarian   Road Map C3
North of Ananda Temple
Guacamole poppadoms and tamarind leaf curry are the standout dishes on The Moon's imaginative, though strictly vegetarian, menu. The café's roadside premises, north of the Ananda Temple, are spotless, the food freshly prepared, and the service friendly, if a little slow.

OLD BAGAN: Yar Pyi $
Vegetarian   Road Map C3
North of Ananda Temple
An innovative home-cooked menu is offered at this family-run vegetarian café. Try the eggplant or pumpkin curries, smoked tea-leaf salad, and lassi. Great value.

OLD BAGAN: Sarabha II $$
Pan-Asian   Road Map C3
Tharabar Gate
Everyone staying at the nearby Tharabar Gate Hotel eats here – it is twice as good and half the price. Tasty curries, salads, and soups, and plenty of Chinese and Thai options are served up in the pretty, open-sided dining hall.

OLD BAGAN: Star Beam $$
Burmese/French   Road Map C3
North of Ananda Temple
Tel *(0) 9402502614*
Dine on carefully prepared Myanmar specials, including delicious Rakhine-style seafood curry, and a range of popular Western dishes, from avocado salad to grilled fish fillet.

POPA TAUNG KALAT: Popa Mountain Resort $$$
International   Road Map C3
Mount Popa
Tel *(02) 69168*
Even if you are not staying at this hilltop resort, it is worth eating here for the view of the Popa Taung Kalat monastery on its volcanic outcrop. Diners also get to use the gorgeous infinity pool.

Mandalay Region

MANDALAY CITY: Aye Myit Tar $
Burmese   Road Map C3
530, 81st St
Tel *(02) 23167*
A great place to sample Burmese cooking at its best, in a totally authentic, hygienic environment.

Deep-fried nibbles served at a Burmese street stall

Spotlessly clean (plates arrive shrinkwrapped), the little café is packed with local families in the evenings. Prices are a bit higher than in the canteen-style places, but the food is all freshly cooked, and delicious.

MANDALAY CITY: Lashio Lay $
Shan　　　　　　Road Map C3
65, 23rd St (83/84)
Delicious Shan specialties cooked fresh each day for a mostly local clientele. Point out your main choice at the counter and they will serve it with all the usual trimmings. Cold beer is available.

MANDALAY CITY: Marie Min $
Indian Vegetarian　Road Map C3
27th St (74/75)
Deservedly popular backpacker hangout serving healthy, delicious Indian vegetarian dishes. The pumpkin curry and samosas are particularly good, as is the strawberry lassi for dessert.

MANDALAY CITY: Minthihar $
Teahouse　　　　Road Map C3
Corner of 72nd St and 28th St
Everyone comes to this famous traditional teahouse for the mutton puffs rustled up by waiters in matching burgundy shirts.

MANDALAY CITY: Nylon Ice Cream Bar $
Ice cream　　　　Road Map C3
83rd St (25/26)
Wonderfully old-fashioned, quintessentially Burmese ice cream parlor – one of the few places in the world where you can order durian flavor ice cream. A pleasant spot in the evenings.

MANDALAY CITY: Pakokku Daw Lay May $
Burmese　　　　Road Map C3
73rd St (27/28)
Scrupulously hygienic Burmese restaurant, with gleaming utensils, surfaces, and kitchen. The curries come at breakneck speed with a dozen side dishes.

MANDALAY CITY: Rainforest $
Thai　　　　　　Road Map C3
27th St (74/75)
Tel *(02) 36234*
This terrific little budget Thai place is popular mainly with backpackers for its tasty Panang curry, fish bamboo, and salads. Come early for a balcony seat.

MANDALAY CITY: Super 81 $
Southeast Asian　Road Map C3
582, 81st St (38/39)
Perfectly placed for a meal before a Moustache Brothers show, this ranks among the city's best value

Parathas being prepared at the famed Usman's Chapatis in Mandalay

restaurants. Try the soft-shell crab, delicious bean curd clay pot, or chicken with basil.

MANDALAY CITY: Usman's Chapatis $
Indian　　　　　Road Map C3
SW corner of 28th St & 82nd St
Grab a low chair at this legendary street food stall, specializing in Burmese-style Indian food. It offers a wide range of tasty curries that can be eaten with rice or mopped up with hot chapatis and parathas.

MANDALAY CITY: BBB $$
International　　　Road Map C3
292, 76th St (26/27), Chan Aye Thar Zan Township
Tel *(02) 25623*
An excellent option for those who've had their fill of curry and noodles, BBB offers club sandwiches, burgers, grills, pizza, and plenty of vegetarian options in a restaurant with a Swiss-chalet feel and ersatz American decor.

MANDALAY CITY: City Café $$
International　　　Road Map C3
66th St (East Moat Rd)
Vintage Burmese signs and plum-colored leather booths lend a retro edge to this hip diner opposite the palace in the heart of Mandalay city. Most foreign visitors come for the lobster, fish, or steak and chips – and the glacial air-conditioning.

MANDALAY CITY: Green Elephant $$
Pan-Asian　　　　Road Map C3
3H, Block 801, 27th St (64/65), Aung Daw Mu Quarter
Tel *(02) 61237*
Housed in a colonial building with a pleasant garden space, the Mandalay branch of this popular chain restaurant does a roaring trade with tour groups. All the curries are freshly prepared and full of flavor.

MANDALAY CITY: Ko's Kitchen $$
Thai　　　　　　Road Map C3
282, corner of 19th St & 80th St
Tel *(02) 69576*
Authentic, tasty northern Thai food served in a sparkling clean, air-conditioned dining hall just west of the Mandalay Palace complex. Try their scrumptious fried catfish salad with cashew nuts, or the spicy green chicken curry with rice.

MANDALAY CITY: Simplicity $$
Bakery Café　　　Road Map C3
35th St (91/92)
Located slightly away from the city's downtown core, this organic bakery café offers traditional Shan noodles, homemade dumplings, and other treats in addition to breads and scrumptious Chinese-style pastries.

MANDALAY CITY: The Golden Duck $$
Chinese　　　　　Road Map C3
192, corner of 80th St & 16th St
Tel *(0) 92058338, (02) 22935*
There is no better place in Mandalay to eat duck than this multistory Chinese joint in the city center. The meat is ordered by the half or whole, with a side helping of vegetables.

DK Choice

MANDALAY CITY: Koffee Korner $$$
International　　　Road Map C3
70th St (27/28)
Floodlit palm trees, funky Turkish lamps, and a large fish tank make this the most off-beat diner in town. The menu is as international as the clientele: Hungarian goulash, pizza, prawn thermidor, pasta pesto, and monster club sandwiches. Although Koffee Korner is far from the cheapest option in Mandalay, it is consistently good. Tiger Beer is available by the bottle.

MANDALAY CITY: Spice Garden $$$
Pan-Asian　　　　Road Map C3
Hotel by the Red Canal
417, corner of 63rd St & 22nd St
Tel *(02) 68543*
Fine Indian and Pan-Asian cooking is served up by the poolside of Mandalay city's nicest hotel, the boutique Hotel by the Red Canal. Their good value set menus comprise soup, salads, tempura, curry with sticky coconut rice, fruit, semolina cake, and tea-leaf salad with peanuts.

The charming courtyard of Monywa's Pleasant Island restaurant

MONYWA: Pleasant Island $$
Chinese/Thai   Road Map C3
Yone Kyi Or, Kan Thar Yar Lake,
Bogyoke Rd
Popular mainly because of its
position opposite the Win Unity
Resort, this tourist-friendly
restaurant sits on its own little
island. Serves pork, beef, chicken,
and fish in Burmese sauces.

PYIN U LWIN: Feel Café (Golf
Course) $$
Burmese/Thai   Road Map D3
Nandar Rd, near the Golf Club
Feel has two outlets in Pyin U
Lwin, and this one by the golf
course is the best, with bigger
portions, better food, and faster
service. Their smoky BBQ chicken
is the crowd puller.

PYIN U LWIN: Golden Triangle $$
Continental   Road Map D3
Mandalay–Lashio Rd
Settle into a wicker chair on the
pillared veranda of this lovely
bakery for a coffee and cinnamon
bun, or a more substantial pizza
or burger.

PYIN U LWIN: The Club
Terrace $$
Shan/Continental   Road Map D3
25, Club Road, Quarter No. 5
Tel *(085) 23311*
Wonderful Shan cuisine served
in an elegant colonial mansion,
with a delightful garden terrace
for drinks. The food, whether
local dishes, Thai, or European, is
excellent, the service friendly,
and the atmosphere relaxing.

PYIN U LWIN: Woodland $$
Continental   Road Map D3
53, Circular Rd
This large garden restaurant
is the most animated place in
Pyin U Lwin, hosting live music
most evenings. They have an
extensive menu: try the pizza
or soft-shell crab. Cocktails are
available. Guests have access
to free Wi-Fi.

Eastern Myanmar

HSIPAW: Mrs Popcorn's Garden $
International   Road Map D3
Myauk Myo
Relaxed backpackers' restaurant
on the outskirts of town serving
simple food made by the kindly,
eponymous owner herself,
including fried rice, juices, shakes,
fruit salad, and ginger lemon tea.

HSIPAW: Pontoon Coffee $
International   Road Map D3
Near Pontoon Bridge
Perfect chocolate-chip muffins
and espresso coffee, served by
welcoming Australian expat
Maureen, who has settled on
the leafy outskirts of Hsipaw. The
café is in a beautiful teak house
with a tranquil garden to the rear.
They also rustle up toasted sand-
wiches with real cheese and
homemade brown bread

DK Choice

INLE LAKE: Inthar Heritage $$
Intha   Road Map D4
Inpawkhon village
Tel *(0) 95251232*
The most congenial stop for
lunch on the lake. Recipes from
Intha grandmothers are lovingly
prepared using home-grown,
organic produce, and served in
a warm, wood-lined dining hall
with wonderful views over the
rice fields. Everything is exquisitely presented, and the prices
are reasonable. Recommended
for cat lovers, who will enjoy
watching the gorgeous resident
Burmese cats.

KALAW: Paye Pyae $
Shan   Road Map D4
Union Highway, next to Thirigayha
Restaurant
This simple, unpretentious little
café in Kalaw is packed all day
with locals eating its tasty Shan

noodle clay pot meals containing
an exotic array of vegetables
and mushrooms.

KENGTUNG: Azure $
Chinese   Road Map E3
Naung Tung Lakeside
Reasonably priced Chinese
restaurant facing the lake,
with tables under a shady tree.
Chicken in cashew nut sauce
is their most popular dish, and
draft beer is available.

NYAUNGSHWE: Everest Nepali
Food Center $
Nepalese/Indian   Road Map D4
Kuaung Tau Anau St
Tel *(0) 9428322745*
Light, fragrant, and mostly
vegetarian curries, dals, and
chapatis served up in a cozy,
cool dining room down a quiet
backstreet. Great flavors and
charming service. Chilled bottled
beers are available.

NYAUNGSHWE: Lin Htett $
Burmese   Road Map D4
Southwest corner of Mingalar
Market, Yone Gyi Rd
Traditional Burmese place in the
town center where you can order
a range of meat and fish curries,
served with all the trimmings,
for only a few dollars.

NYAUNGSHWE: Live Dim Sum
House $
Chinese/Shan   Road Map D4
Yone Gyi Rd, near November Hotel
Tel *(0) 9428136964*
Delicious dim sum and Shan tofu
clay pot meals, prepared in an
open kitchen (hence "live") and
served in a clean, well-presented
restaurant by enthusiastic staff.

NYAUNGSHWE: Min Min $
International   Road Map D4
Yone Gyi Rd, Kan Thar Quarter
The friendliest of welcomes is
guaranteed at Min Min, a lively
little backpacker haunt where
you can enjoy tasty, mild local
curries, pancakes, pasta pesto,
and cheap cocktails.

A variety of dim sum on offer at
Nyaungshwe's Live Dim Sum House

NYAUNGSHWE: Sin Yaw $
Pan-Asian   **Road Map** D4
Yone Gyi Rd, Kan Thar Quarter
Tel *(0) 940351883*
This great value place offers
flavor-packed local dishes such
as crispy fried lake fish, spiced
Shan pork, and white seaweed
salad, served in a cheerful diner
by a friendly family.

**NYAUNGSHWE: Thanakha
Garden** $
Burmese/Burgers   **Road Map** D4
*43, Thar Zi Quarter, near the Paradise
Hotel and Mingalar Market*
Tel *(0) 9428371552*
Well-presented restaurant run
with pride by a warm local family.
Prawn and vegetable tempura
and Inle fish curry are the
standout dishes. Come early if
you want a terrace table.

NYAUNGSHWE: Beyond Taste $$
Burmese/Western   **Road Map** D4
*10, Phaung Daw Pyan St,
Nant Pan Quarter*
Tel *(0) 9428358111*
A restaurant that consistently
generates superlative reviews,
and with good reason. It serves
local curries and Western food
(great pizza), plus cocktails. The
service is five-star.

NYAUNGSHWE: Green Chilli $$
Burmese/Thai   **Road Map** D4
Hospital Rd, Mingalar Quarter
Tel *(081) 209132*
Varied and deliciously spicy
curries are served in a beautiful
Shan-style house with local art
on the walls. The portions are
generous, the house wine good,
and the service attentive.

**NYAUNGSHWE: Viewpoint
Lodge** $$$
Shan fusion   **Road Map** D4
Near Canal Bridge
Tel *(081) 209062*
The classiest place to eat in town.
Go for the extravagant, tapas-
style "Shan Discovery" menu,
which comes in its own tabletop
long-tailed boat. There are plenty
of vegetarian options à la carte:
try the sublime tofu and potato
curry. The restaurant offers
snappy service and a lovely
setting, with views over rice
fields. A bit pricey, but worth it.

PINDAYA: Green Tea $$
Burmese/Shan   **Road Map** D3
Shwe Umin Pagoda St
One of the loveliest places to eat
in the region, both for its breezy
waterfront location – which
overlooks Pone Ta Lote Lake to
the stupas of Pindaya village –
and its fabulous, appealingly

presented Burmese and Shan
cuisine. Be sure to ask for a table
on the veranda.

TAUNGGYI: Sein Myanmar $
Shan   **Road Map** D3
Bogyoke Aung San Rd
This is a busy Shan place, famous
above all for its delicious *htamin
jin* – a regional specialty that
consists of balls of fermented
rice kneaded with Inle Lake fish,
tomato paste, and potatoes. The
perfect stop for travelers heading
back to Inle Lake after visiting the
stupa complex at Kakku.

**TAUNGGYI: Sunset Wine
Garden** $$$
International   **Road Map** D3
Aythaya Vineyard, Htone Bo
Tel *(081) 208653, (01) 651141*
Set amid rolling vineyards on
the outskirts of the city, this
smart restaurant serves dishes to
complement its wines, including
fish in banana leaves and mutton
balls with bean sprouts.

Northern Myanmar

BHAMO: Shamie $
Indian   **Road Map** D2
Tiyet Rd
Filling, flavorsome Indo-Muslim
biryanis, kebabs, and meaty
curries, as well as filled parathas
and chai for breakfast. A handy
choice if you're staying at the
nearby Friendship Hotel.

KATHA: Shwe Sisa $
Chinese Barbecue   **Road Map** C2
Strand Rd
This beer station enjoys a prime
spot on the riverside, and does
grilled chicken and pork ribs to
accompany your drinks. It is also
one of the few places in town
that screens live soccer.

MYITKYINA: Kiss Me $
Burmese   **Road Map** D2
Zaw John Rd
Fine river views and an extensive
menu of mostly Burmese
specialties, including a tasty tea-
leaf salad, are on offer at this
restaurant, a taxi ride north of
the center of town, next to the
Su Taung Pyi Pagoda complex.

MYITKYINA: River View $
Burmese   **Road Map** D2
Zaw John Rd
The dim sum served at this
waterfront restaurant gets less
enthusiastic reviews than the
sunset vistas, which are sublime.
A good spot for a leisurely
evening drink of cold beer.

The unpretentious interiors of the Mi Cho
café, serving Indian food in Mawlamyine

MYITKYINA: Bamboo Field $$
Burmese   **Road Map** D2
313, Su Taung Pyi Rd (Union St)
Myitkyina's most upscale
restaurant hosts weekend dance
shows and karaoke. The menu
is as diverse as the clientele – a
mix of visiting businessmen and
foreign aid workers.

Southeastern
Myanmar

HPA-AN: San Ma Tau Myanmar $
Burmese   **Road Map** D5
290, Bogyoke St
Clean, friendly restaurant whose
smorgasbord of fragrant curries
and stir-fries draws crowds from
across the town. You'll find it hard
to spend more than a few dollars.

HPA-AN: White $
Burmese   **Road Map** D5
Thitsa St
Eat your fill of Shan noodle dishes
and spicy mashed potato with
tangy gravies, plus great *mohinga*
and a variety of Myanmar snacks
at this bustling Burmese all-day
breakfast place.

**MAWLAMYINE (MOULMEIN):
Mi Cho** $
Indian   **Road Map** D5
North Bogyoke Rd
Great Indo-Muslim food in a tiny,
cramped café. Get there early for
the famous biryani. They also
cook delicious dal and rice, and
chicken curry with mango pickle.

**MAWLAMYINE (MOULMEIN):
Ykko** $$
Pan-Asian   **Road Map** D5
*Corner of Kannar St & Htarwai
Bridge St*
Tel *(0) 9041591212*
With a riverside setting, Ykko is
a spruce, modern chain with
reliable Wi-Fi and blissful air-
conditioning offering a choice of
a hundred different Asian dishes,
iced coffees, and ice cream.

For more information on types of restaurants *see pages 206–7*

SHOPPING IN MYANMAR

Myanmar's traditional arts and crafts have experienced a sharp revival during the recent tourism boom. Lacquerware, carved wood, metalware, marionettes, brocade embroidery, and colorful cloth paintings fill stalls and shops around the country's main attractions, creating vibrant photo opportunities and a mouthwatering prospect for lovers of authentic Southeast Asian crafts. In the big cities, meanwhile, multistory malls are where the affluent middle classes shop for modern, imported consumer goods. For fresh produce, covered and street markets are still very much a staple throughout Myanmar, and provide an enthralling spectacle for foreign visitors more accustomed to supermarkets. The one common denominator, regardless of the size and kind of shop, is the politeness and good-natured demeanor of the vendors. Although haggling is very much the norm, it is unfailingly conducted in a relaxed spirit, often over a glass of tea and plate of nibbles.

Shoppers at Yangon's Bogyoke Aung San Zei, commonly known as Scott's Market

Opening Hours

Most city shops are open from 9am to 8 or 9pm. Yangon and Mandalay malls open by 10am and close around 10pm. It is worth keeping in mind that staff frequently begin closing well before the appointed hour if trade is slack. Traditional *zeis*, or markets, generally operate from sunrise to sunset. Some *zeis* also host busy night markets in the surrounding streets, which run until midnight, or later. Virtually all shops open seven days a week, except during the annual New Year festival of Thingyan (April), when they close for four or five days.

Bargaining

Apart from stores in shopping malls, high-end tourist shops, and food and drink outlets, where prices are by and large non-negotiable, the first sum quoted is almost always far higher than the final one the seller will accept. To reduce the amount, the buyer has to be ready to haggle. Effective negotiation requires three things: patience, persistence, and a sense of humor. Maintain a pleasant attitude throughout – remember that this is a social encounter as much as a commercial transaction. Don't rush the process – driving down a price may take ten minutes or longer. And if all else fails, try walking away, which tends to prompt a drastic reduction.

How to Pay

Only a handful of the high-end boutiques and emporia in Myanmar accept credit or debit cards; the others accept payment only in cash, with mint condition, or nearly new, unfolded US dollar bills (*see pp232–3*). For big ticket items, such as objets d'art or pieces of quality lacquerware, paying with high value bills will bring the price down a little as the rate of exchange offered will be more favorable. Change is always given in Myanmar's currency, the kyat. Kyat can be used to purchase low-priced or everyday items, such as cotton clothing and simple souvenirs. Receipts tend to be issued only in higher-end handicraft shops and modern malls, but they are available on request almost everywhere.

Rights and Refunds

As a rule, sales are final. Although modern shops in malls may have a returns policy, on the whole, once the money has changed hands, there's no going back. Guarantees tend only to apply to imported electrical goods, and cover replacements not refunds.

Open-air riverside market at Bhamo in Northern Myanmar

Shwedagon Pagoda's *zaungdan* shops with religious paraphernalia, textiles, and crafts

Packaging and Posting

When shopping in tourist souvenir emporia, visitors will commonly be offered export packaging. Goods will be wrapped very well for safe transport on a plane, with layers of newspaper and padding in the case of more expensive or fragile items. This service is always included in the price. With larger, valuable purchases, such as furniture or rugs, some kind of international shipping service may also be offered.

Crafts, Antiques, and Souvenir Emporia

The widest choice of traditional and antique Burmese items is offered in large emporia located at major tourist centers and in the big cities. Wonderful storehouses of hand-crafted woodwork, palm-leaf etchings, handwoven textiles, paintings, stone figurines, and Buddhas of bell-metal, bronze, and brass, these emporia tend to stock both antiques and recently made items – although it can be difficult to tell the two apart, as newer objects are often distressed or artfully worn. Lacquerware (*yun-de*), in the form of round boxes, pedestal dishes (*kalat*), stemmed rice bowls with spired lids (*hsun ok*), tea trays, stackable tiffin carriers (*hsun gyaink*), trunks, screens, and polygonal tables, domi-nates the showrooms, along with walls of colorfully attired string puppets and *kalagas*,

panels of velvet elaborately embroidered with gold and silver thread, showing Hindu or Buddhist mythological scenes.

In Yangon, one of the oldest established and best-stocked stores is **Nandawun**, on Baho Road, which also has a branch in the National Museum (*see p72*). In a similar vein is **Elephant House**, run by the owners of the popular Green Elephant chain of restaurants, and **Augustine's Souvenir Shop** in Kamayut Township, one of Myanmar's foremost antique specialists. In Mandalay, **Soe Moe Memento World** on 36th Street near the palace is a great one-stop souvenir shop, as is **Shwe War Thein Handicrafts**, near the Tharabar Gate in Old Bagan, where visitors may watch teams of artisans at work. Most of the five-star hotels also have quality Burmese handicraft boutiques, among them the famous Strand Hotel on Strand Road in Yangon, home to the glittering **J's Irrawaddy Dream**.

Many stores offer traditional Delta parasols for sale, but for the widest selection it is best to visit the workshops in Pathein (*see p104*) or, failing that, the delightful **Shwe Pathein** in Yangon, where handmade parasols are displayed in a wood-lined showroom.

Intricately decorated string puppets (*yok thei*), depicting characters from Burmese mythology and folk history, make popular souvenirs. They

may be seen on sale at emporia, shops, and stalls across the country, and come in a range of different sizes and levels of detail. Most expensive of all are the large antique marionettes embellished with sequins and brocade. A huge selection is available at the shop attached to the **Mandalay Marionettes** theater in Mandalay.

Shopping Malls

Multistory shopping malls are springing up in all of Myanmar's major towns and cities, but particularly in Yangon and Mandalay. Air-conditioned and impeccably clean, with multiplex cinemas and Western-style food and drink outlets, they can be great places to recuperate from the heat of the streets, although the shops, which sell mostly imported consumer goods and modern fashion clothing, tend to appeal less to foreign visitors than the souvenir emporia. In Yangon, **FMI** on Bogyoke Aung San Road is the largest mall located downtown. **Blazon Shopping Center** offers brand-name stores. Farther north, the **Taw Win Center** (*see p221*) and **Dagon Center** are both more recent additions. Visitors to Mandalay are spoilt for choice when it comes to malls. The downtown **Mann Myanmar Plaza** and **Diamond Plaza** are the two largest in the country. **78 Mall** is also worth a browse.

Carved wooden statues at a handicrafts workshop in Mandalay

Markets

Burmese *zeis*, or markets, come in a variety of different forms, but the main ones, in big towns and cities, are nearly all covered, and divided into separate sections for fresh produce, clothes, hardware and so on. Bordering on the scale of a mega mall, but with a distinctly old-fashioned Burmese feel, **Bogyoke Aung San Zei** (open 10am–5pm Tue–Sun) in down-town Yangon is Myanmar's largest covered market, with around 2,000 retailers packed on two floors of a huge, pink, colonial-era building. Cheaper than the emporia and tourist shops, its stores sell a full range of traditional Burmese arts, crafts, and antiques, in addition to regular local goods. The equivalent in Mandalay is the sprawling **Zegyo Market** *(see p143)*, ranged over four stories.

Each town also has municipal markets where everyday goods and fresh produce are sold from dawn onward. In Yangon, **Theingyi Zei** near Mahabandula Road is the largest, with an extensive covered section that spills into the surrounding streets. **Mani-Sithu Market** in Nyaung U (Bagan) offers a range of fresh vegetables and fruit, as well as clothing and collectibles.

In Shan State it is worth making time for one of the "five-day markets," held in specified towns every fifth day according to a rotating calendar. Local travel agents and guides will know the full schedule. In Inle Lake, the two main ones are at **Nyaungshwe** *(see p169)*, next to the main street, where a scaled-down version functions daily, and at **Inthein** *(see p166)*. Both attract large numbers of minority people from the surrounding hills, and are prime sources of authentic souvenirs, such as cheroots, handwoven head-scarves, Shan jackets, Intha paja-mas, and other traditional attire.

Some streets around large *zei* also double as night markets. In Yangon, barbecue bars spring up after dark on **19th Street** in the heart of Chinatown (also known as Tayote Tan). Popularly called Beer Bar Street – or

Inle Lake flower seller with bunches of pink lotus, Eastern Myanmar

occasionally Myanmar Lan Kwai Fong – it attracts diners from across the city with grilled meat skewers, steaming bowls of dumplings, and exotic Chinese delicacies, including toasted grasshoppers. In Mandalay, a similar night market operates in the roads around Zegyo Market.

Pagodas

Zaungdan, the covered, stepped approaches to large pagodas, are usually lined with brightly lit, beautifully arranged market stalls specializing in religious paraphernalia such as incense, candles, floral offerings, and ritual utensils. These little shops are also good places to pick up Buddha figurines in wood, stone, and metal; sequin-encrusted ensembles worn by young boys at their *shin pyu* ceremonies; and various musical instruments, especially temple bells, drums, and wind chimes.

The largest such bazaars radiate from the **Shwedagon Pagoda** *(see pp74–7)* in Yangon, whose eastern entrance, spanned by sumptuously carved and decorated roof beams, is arguably the most attractive. In Mandalay, the **Mahamuni Temple's** *(see p142)* four entrances are also lined with stalls selling crafts, textiles, and clothing, as well as religious offerings. Two other noteworthy temple bazaars, both specifically aimed at foreign tourists, are those held on market day in the village of Inthein *(see p166)*, on Inle Lake, and at the **Ananda Temple** *(see pp124–5)* in Bagan.

Gemstones and Jewelry

Myanmar is the source of the world's finest jade and rubies, as well as many other precious and semiprecious gemstones, although buying them is probably best left to experts – jade is notoriously difficult to value accurately. That said, most of the jewelry shops in Yangon's Bogyoke Aung San Zei are reputable, as are the pieces of inlaid silver on sale at upscale hotel boutiques and emporia. Nearly all of the jade mined in Myanmar passes through the fascinating **Jade Market** in Mandalay *(see p142)*, where pieces both large and small are bought, sold, and polished.

Tiny carvings made from a variety of colored jade, Bogyoke Aung San Zei

Clothing and Textiles

Traditional Burmese *longyis* and *htameins* are sold at shops and market stalls around Myanmar, along with more contemporary fashions. For luxury versions in silk, worn for special occasions such as weddings, visit the large malls in Mandalay and Yangon, or Bogyoke Aung San Zei. Some of the finest Myanmar silk is woven in workshops on Inle Lake, where thread from the stems of lotus blooms is spun and transformed into shimmering garments, both pure and mixed with standard silk and cotton. The workshop most famous for lotus silk weaving is **Ko Than Hlaing Silk and Lotus Weaving**, in Inpawkhon village, where it is possible to watch the manufacturing process in action, and whose showroom is lined with *longyis*, blouses, shirts, and scarves in a variety of colors. The five-day markets held in towns and villages are also good places to find local clothes, especially the Thai fisherman-style pajamas traditionally worn by the Intha, and vivid yellow and red scarves favored by local Pa-O women. In Mandalay, **Sut Ngai** is a famous source of traditional Kachin costume, including the button- and silver-adorned black velvet jackets, and the handwoven sequined hats worn at festivals.

Books and Art

Yangon is by far the best place in Myanmar to stock up on English-language books. **Bagan Book House** in the downtown area is a city institution that stocks an unrivaled selection of specialist guides and other titles on the country, as well as a great range of paperback fiction. **Myanmar Book Center** and **Monument Books** are two other excellent bookstores that cater mainly to students and expatriates, and have branches

Monument Books in Yangon, catering mainly to students and expatriates

in both Yangon and Mandalay. For an excellent selection of contemporary Burmese sculpture, painting, and photography, visit Yangon's **Pansodan Art Gallery**, **River Gallery**, or **Gallery Sixty Five**. Pansodan also has old advertisements, posters, and photographs.

DIRECTORY

Crafts, Antiques, and Souvenir Emporia

Augustine's Souvenir Shop
23, Thiri Mingalar Rd (Attia Rd), Kamayut Township, Yangon. **Tel** (01) 705969.
W augustinesouvenir. com

Elephant House
Shopping Arcade, Inya Lake Hotel, 37, Kaba Aye Pagoda Road, Yangon.
Tel (0) 973231674, (01) 400262. W elephant-house.com

J's Irrawaddy Dream
City Map E5.
Strand Hotel, 92, Strand Rd, Yangon.
Tel (01) 243377, ext 1903.

Mandalay Marionettes
Road Map C3. 66th St (26/27), Mandalay.
Tel (02) 34446. W mandalaymarionettes. com

Nandawun
City Map B3. Baho Rd/ Ahlone Rd, Yangon.
Tel (01) 221271. W myanmarhandicrafts. com

Shwe Pathein
City Map D5. 276, Strand Rd, Pabedan, Yangon. W myanmarhandmade. com

Shwe War Thein Handicrafts
Road Map C3. Tharabar Gate, Old Bagan.
Tel (061) 67032.

Soe Moe Memento World
Road Map C3. 36th St (77/78), Mandalay.
W freewebs.com/ smoe/soemoe.htm

Shopping Malls

78 Mall
Road Map C3. 38th St (78/80), Mandalay.

Blazon Shopping Center
City Map C1. U Wisara Rd/Chindwin Rd, Yangon.

Dagon Center
City Map B1. Pyay Rd/ Bagaya Rd, Yangon.

Diamond Plaza
Road Map C3. 34th St (77/78), Mandalay.

FMI
City Map D4.
380, Bogyoke Aung San Rd, Yangon.

Mann Myanmar Plaza
Road Map C3. 28th St (84/85), Mandalay.

Markets

19th Street
City Map C4. 19th St, Chinatown, Yangon.

Bogyoke Aung San Zei
City Map D4. Bogyoke Aung San Rd, Yangon.

Mani-Sithu Market
Road Map C3. Junction of Lanmadaw Rds 1 & 2, Nyaung U, Bagan.

Theingyi Zei
City Map C4. From 26th St to Shwedagon Pagoda Rd, between Anawrahta Rd and Mahabandula Rd, Yangon.

Clothing and Textiles

Ko Than Hlaing Silk and Lotus Weaving
Road Map D4.
Inpawkhon, Inle Lake.
Tel (0) 95211891. W silkandlotusweaving. blogspot.co.uk

Sut Ngai
Road Map C3. 237, 33rd St (82/83), Mandalay.
Tel (0) 92051707.

Books and Art

Bagan Book House
City Map E5. 100, 37th St, between Merchant Rd and Mahabandula Rd, Yangon. **Tel** (01) 377227.

Gallery Sixty Five
City Map D4. 65, Yaw Min Gyi St, Yangon.
W gallerysixtyfive. webstarts.com

Monument Books
City Map C1. Yangon: 150, Dhammazedi Rd.
Road Map C3. Mandalay: 87/2, 77th St (26/27).
W monument-books. com

Myanmar Book Center
City Map B3. Yangon: Baho Rd/Ahlone Rd.
Tel (01) 212409.
Road Map C3. Mandalay: Diamond Plaza Mall, 34th St (77/78).
W myanmarbook.com

Pansodan Art Gallery
City Map E4.
268, Pansodan St, Yangon.
W pansodan.com

River Gallery
City Map E5. Strand Hotel, 92, Strand Rd, Yangon. W rivergallery myanmar.com

ENTERTAINMENT IN MYANMAR

Decades of military rule have had a stifling effect on Myanmar's entertainment industry. Visitors tend to spend evenings in hotels and restaurants, although the big cities also have a handful of venues that showcase traditional music, dance, and puppetry. The performers are mostly graduates of Mandalay's National School of Performing Arts, a crucible of talent for classical Burmese forms that now survive largely due to government support and income from tourism. The country's once thriving movie industry has fallen on hard times, and today its films tend to be low-budget romantic comedies on DVD; cinemas survive on Hollywood and Bollywood block-busters, and Cantonese Kung Fu flicks. The club scene, although limited to a small num-ber of upscale hotels, is developing fast with the rise of the Internet and a new generation of well-heeled youngsters in the big cities.

Performer in traditional costume at the Mintha Theater in Mandalay

Classical Burmese Music and Dance

Most of Myanmar's five-star hotels, and a few dedicated theaters in the big cities, host regular recitals of Burmese music and dance *(see pp36–7)*.

Enlivened by striking traditional attire, the performances are as much of a feast for the eyes as the ears. They vividly underline how exotic and otherworldly Burma's classical culture must have appeared to foreign trav-elers in the 19th century, when the elegant forms currently staged were developed, refined, and codified in the court of the Konbaung Dynasty.

As in centuries past, Mandalay city is the place where visitors can most reliably expect to experience traditional music and dance presented in an authentic form. The **Mintha Theater**, near the palace com-plex, hosts a special tourist show from 8:30 to 9:30pm each evening, featuring top dancers in fabulous costumes accom-panied by a five-piece classical orchestra. In Yangon, the equiv-alent venue is the impressive **Karaweik Palace**, floating on Kandawgyi Lake *(see p79)*, where traditional songs and dances are presented against a sump-tuous backdrop.

Pwe and A-nyeint

Apart from *nat* festivals, it is almost impossible to find traditional *pwe*, but perfor-mances of its folk theater form, *a-nyeint (see p36–7)*, are staged daily by Mandalay's world-famous **Moustache Brothers**. Their notoriety derives from the fact that they spent years in detention for parodying the military government, and that their fate was publicized by Amnesty International. Ever since, crowds of foreign visitors have filled the makeshift theater in their home in downtown Mandalay to experience the show – a mix of slapstick, song, clowning, and satire, delivered in often incomprehensible English. Although Par Par Lay, the group leader, died in 2013, Lu Maw and Lu Zaw continue to perform. The rest of the com-pany is made up of the wives and daughters-in-law of the trio, as well as members of the wider family. Many visitors complain that the show has become overcommercialized and has little entertainment value, but it is nevertheless a cultural institution in the city.

Marionettes

While most culture shows held at hotels and venues in the country usually include a short taste of traditional puppetry,

Colorfully dressed Kachin folk dancers at the Karaweik Palace, Yangon

A local cinema in Yangon displaying film posters

only **Mandalay Marionettes**, in a tiny theater near the palace complex, stage complete performances, with several different puppets and live music. Shows last an hour and could include a short introductory talk and buffet supper, as well as musical interludes on the Burmese harp, and a memorable candle dance.

Traditional Burmese marionettes used in *yok thei pwe* puppet theater productions

Cinemas

Very few English-language movies make it past Myanmar's government censors, though this may change in the coming years. In the meantime, foreign visitors hankering for the silver screen must content themselves with a choice of Indian, American, Cantonese, and South Korean movies. Since the onset of military rule in the 1960s, the country's own film industry has been in sharp decline. Only around 70 of the 244 grand cinema halls that used to exist in Myanmar survive. However, foreign investment has fueled the growth in

Yangon and Mandalay of new multiscreen cineplexes with state-of-the-art digital 3D projectors and surround sound. In Yangon, two of the most conveniently located include the one in the **Taw Win Center** on Pyay Road, near the National Museum, and in the **Junction Maw Tin** on Anawrahta Road.

Clubs and Bars

Yangon is the only place in the country with anything close to what foreign tourists would recognize as a nightlife. A handful of small, exclusive clubs and bars attached to the city's five-star hotels – patronized by a mix of youngsters from elite Myanmar families, aid workers, expatriates, and business travelers – host DJ gigs most weekends, and dancing until around midnight. The most consistently lively are the **Music Club** at the Park Royal, **DJ Bar** near the Inya Lake Hotel, and **GTR** on Kaba Aye Pagoda Road, the latter being the only one where the female clientele aren't almost entirely sex workers. **BME2**, near the Summit Parkview Hotel, is similar to GTR, but tends to attract a slightly older crowd, and stays open the latest (usually until 3am). For local atmosphere, try **19th Street** *(see p219)* in Chinatown, which metamorphoses into the brightly lit Beer Bar Street (also called Myanmar Lan Kwai Fong) night market, where an alfresco meal of grilled meat and cold beers can be eaten at rows of Formica tables.

DIRECTORY

Classical Burmese Music and Dance

Karaweik Palace
City Map E2.
Kandawgyi Nature Park,
Kandawgyi Lake, Bahan Tsp,
Yangon. **Tel** (01) 295744.
w karaweikpalace.com

Mintha Theater
Road Map C3.
27th St (65/66), Mandalay.
Tel (0) 96803607.
w minthatheater.com

Pwe and A-nyeint

Moustache Brothers
Road Map C3.
39th St (80/81), Mandalay.
Tel (0) 943034220.

Marionettes

Mandalay Marionettes
Road Map C3.
66th St (26/27), Mandalay.
Tel (02) 34446.
w mandalaymarionettes.com

Cinemas

Junction Maw Tin
City Map C4. Junction Complex,
Anawrahta Rd, Yangon.
Tel (01) 218161.
w junctioncentregroup.com/
junction-mawtin.html

Taw Win Center
City Map C3.
45, Pyay Rd, Yangon.
Tel (01) 8600111, ext. 3333.
w tawwincentre.com/cinema

Clubs and Bars

BME2
City Map C3. 350, Ahlone Rd
(next to the Summit Parkview
Hotel), Yangon.

DJ Bar
U Htun Nyein St,
Near Inya Lake Hotel,
37, Kaba Aye Pagoda Rd, Yangon.
Tel (0) 95116767.

GTR
Near Inya Lake Hotel, Yangon.
Tel (0) 973090680.
w facebook.com/GTRClub

Music Club
City Map D4. Park Royal Yangon,
33, Alan Pya Pagoda Street,
Yangon. **Tel** (01) 250388.
w parkroyalhotels.com

SPORTS AND OUTDOOR ACTIVITIES

The national pastime of *chinlone (see pp40–41)* aside, participation in sport has been at low levels during the decades of military rule in Myanmar. With access to satellite TV, however, the country has seen a dramatic surge in the number of people watching and playing soccer. Among the elite, golf has also grown in popularity: Yangon has many international-standard courses, and there are numerous others farther afield. Swimming and cycling are likely to be the outdoor pursuits most often enjoyed by foreign visitors, although with enough of a budget, scuba diving in the Andaman Sea is another possibility.

Soccer

The Burmese are mad about soccer. This passionate, country-wide following for the sport is a relatively new phenomenon. Only about a decade ago, there were just a handful of semi-professional sides. Now, between 12 and 14 fully pro-fessional teams play in the Myanmar National League, inaugurated in 2009, whose three top sides are Mandalay's Yadanabon FC, Yangon United FC, and Kanbawza FC of Taunggyi. Fixtures are adver-tised on the teams' websites, and tickets (inexpensive by international standards) may be purchased at the gates.

If anything, support for European leagues, particularly the English Premiership, is even more enthusiastic than for domestic competitions, and foreign matches are routinely screened in bars. Manchester United enjoys the widest fan base across Myanmar.

Golf

A legacy of Burma's colonial heritage (and Scottish connec-tions), golf enjoys a strong following among the country's upper classes, explaining why Yangon boasts one of the most impressive courses in Southeast Asia. Designed by Gary Player, the **Pun Hlaing Golf Club**, 8 miles (13 km) west of down-town across the river, is set amid a manicured tropical landscape, and kept in tournament condi-tion year round. The same is true of the **Royal Mingalardon**, another prestigious course nearby. Yangon is also home to the **City Golf Resort**. For a more

historic feel, visit the grand **Yangon Golf Club**, founded in 1909 and Myanmar's oldest functioning golf club. Another vintage course is the one at **Pyin U Lwin**, the former British summer capital of Upper Burma. The **Yay Dagon Taung Golf Resort** in Mandalay, a half-hour drive from the town center, is the region's finest, with the **Shwe Man Taung Golf Resort** at the foot of Mandalay Hill a close second. A quality 18-hole course has been built at **Bagan**, and there is a 9-hole course at **Thandwe/Ngapali.**

Trekking

Kalaw is Myanmar's prime trekking destination *(see p173)*, thanks to its proximity to Inle Lake and several minority villages. **Ever Smile** and **A1 Information and Trekking Service** are among many Kalaw operators who organize day hikes and overnight stays. Less frequented alternatives, from where it is also possible to trek into ethnic minority areas, include Hsipaw, farther north, and Kengtung, to the east. In Hsipaw, local guesthouses such as **Lily The Home** or guides such as **Than Htike** can make all the necessary arrangements; in Kengtung the **Princess Hotel** can organize guides and treks.

In the far north, treks into the spectacular terrain around Hkakabo Razi, the country's highest mountain (19,294 ft/ 5,881 m), begin at Putao in Kachin State, where **Putao Trekking House** is the recom-mended operator. In the far west of Myanmar, routes up the highest peak in Chin State, Nat

Ma Taung, also known as Mount Victoria (10,016 ft/3,053 m), start on the massif's eastern side.

Cycling

Bicycles are widely available for rent at Inle Lake; at Bagan, where cycling offers a healthy alternative to the horse carts; and at Ngapali for leisurely tours of the fields and groves behind the beach. Most of the cycles are Chinese made, gearless, and usually in dubious states of repair. Test drive a few and check that the brakes work and that the steering column is sound. However, some com-panies have started renting out mountain bikes, which are more expensive but also sturdier and more comfortable.

In Yangon, **Bike World Explores Myanmar** is a Burmese -Australian outfit who run pop-ular weekly guided city rides (6:30am on Sundays), as well as custom tours to most parts of the country. They run mountain-biking expeditions up Mount Victoria from Nyaung U and can arrange permits for the ascent.

The countryside around Inle Lake in Shan State, ideal for trekking and cycling

Swimming

Many mid-range and all five-star hotels in Myanmar have swimming pools, although few open their doors to non-residents. One exception is the **Sedona** in Yangon, which has a huge, curviform pool with an island bar that is busy with expatriate families after school hours, but peaceful during the day.

While swimming in the country's rivers is not recommended, the waters of the Andaman Sea are blissfully warm, and safe, in Myanmar's top three resorts: **Chaungtha** (see p105), **Ngwe Saung** (see p105), and **Ngapali** (see p106). The latter has the clearest water.

Diving and Snorkeling

One of the world's last great tropical marine wildernesses, the Myeik Archipelago in the far south is among Southeast Asia's least explored diving destinations. The government maintains strict control over access to this ecologically fragile area,

Strolling next to the warm and clear waters off Ngapali beach

which offers no accredited diving schools or accommodations. Anyone wishing to dive here must join an expensive live-aboard diving tour out of Phuket or Ranong in Thailand. To keep costs down, clients may arrange for the boat to pick them up in Kawthaung, Myanmar's southernmost town, two or three days into the tour, and drop them off in the same place. Recommended Thailand-based diving companies include **Nautica Diving** and **AIDC Dive**. Permits to enter the Myeik Marine Reserve must be arranged in advance through

the Myanmar Travels and Tours office in Yangon (see p229).

Good diving is also available in the relatively unexplored waters off Ngapali (see p106), with most hotels offering trips to coral reefs, islets, wrecks, and caves. Alternatively, contact the diving specialists **Ngapali Water Sports** at their office in the village, or via their website. A cheaper option would be to jump on a local fishing boat for a snorkeling tour in the crystal-clear waters just to the north of the resort; these leave every morning and afternoon from various sites on the beachfront.

DIRECTORY

Golf

Bagan Golf Course
Road Map C3. Anawrahta Rd, Nyaung U. **Tel** (0) 9402630885.
bagangolfresort.net

City Golf Resort
Thiri Mingalar Rd, Insein Township, Yangon.
Tel (01) 641763.
citygolfresort.com

Pun Hlaing Golf Club
Pun Hlaing Golf Estate Ave, Yangon. **Tel** (01) 684021.
punhlainggolfestate.com

Pyin U Lwin Golf Club
Road Map D3.
Golf Club Rd, Pyin U Lwin.
Tel (085) 22382.

Royal Mingalardon Golf Club
1, Mingalardon Garden City, Off NH 3, Yangon.
Tel (0) 9449222222.
royalmingalardongolf.com

Shwe Man Taung Golf Resort
Road Map C3.
On the west side of Mandalay Hill, Mandalay.
Tel (02) 60570.

Thandwe/Ngapali
Road Map C4.
Off Ngapali beach, near Thandwe.

Yangon Golf Club
Kha Yae Pin St, Yangon.
Tel (01) 635563.
yangongolfclub.com

Yay Dagon Taung Golf Resort
Road Map C3. Near Yay Tay Gun Hill, Mandalay.
Tel (02) 88731.

Trekking

A1 Information and Trekking Service
Road Map D4.
Merchant St, Kalaw.
Tel (0) 949585199.
a1trekking.blogspot.co.uk

Ever Smile
Road Map D4. Mrs Toe Toe, Yuzana St, Kalaw.
eversmiletrekking.com

Lily The Home
Road Map D3. 108, Aung Tha Pyae Road, Hsipaw.
Tel (082) 80077, 80408.

Princess Hotel
Road Map E3. 21, Zay Dan Kalay Rd, Kengtung.
Tel (084) 21319.

Putao Trekking House
Road Map D1. Putao.
putaotrekkinghouse.com

Than Htike
Road Map D3. Hsipaw.
Tel (0) 936186646.

Cycling

Bike World Explores Myanmar (BWEM)
10F, Khabaung Rd (Martin Avenue), 6 Miles Pyay Road, Yangon.
cyclingmyanmar.com

Swimming

Sedona Hotel
1, Kaba Aye Pagoda Road, Yankin Township, Yangon.
Tel (01) 666900.
sedonahotels.com.sg

Diving and Snorkeling

Andaman International Dive Center (AIDC)
97/21, Phet Kasem Rd, Moo 1, Ranong, 85000 Thailand.
Tel (+66) (77) 834824.
aidcdive.com

Nautica Diving
via Dive Asia,
24, Karon Rd, Phuket, 83100 Thailand.
Tel (+66) (76) 330598.
diveasia.com
nautica-diving.com

Ngapali Water Sport
Road Map C4. Ngapali.
Tel (0) 949577070.
ngapaliwatersport.com

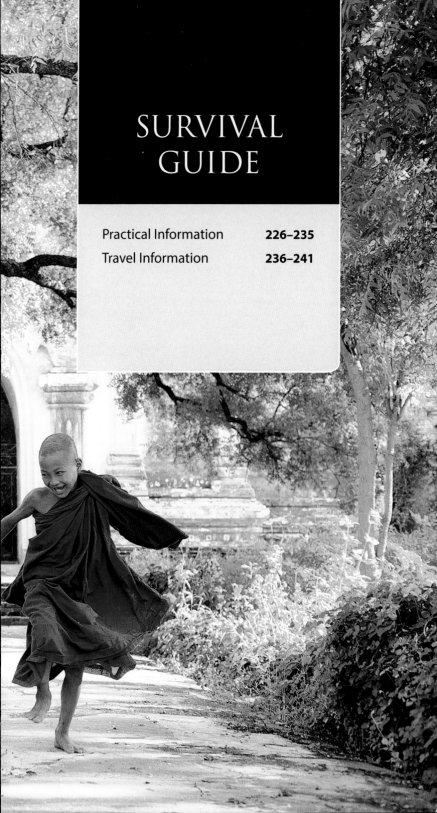

SURVIVAL GUIDE

PRACTICAL INFORMATION

Since the tourism boycott was relaxed in 2010 and ended two years later, record numbers of travelers have visited Myanmar, whose infrastructure, however, has struggled to keep pace. Accommodations have been in short supply at all levels, although dozens of new hotels are under construction to help meet the spiraling demand. There has also been a boom in domestic air travel, a consequence of the generally poor state of the roads. That said, it is possible to get almost anywhere by public transport. Some regions remain off-limits to foreigners due to the ongoing insurgencies, but these are mostly peripheral areas, away from the tourist hubs. Given the complexities of travel, it is wise, at least for those not traveling on pre-arranged tours, to seek help from a Yangon-based travel agent.

When to Go

The tourist season starts in early October, once the monsoon rains have cleared, and peaks between December and February, when temperatures even in the central dry zone around Bagan and Mandalay are bearable during the day. From March onward, the heat builds steadily, regularly rising above 40° C (104° F) in Yangon and the Delta and to 45° C (113° F) in the Upper Ayeyarwady area, although Inle Lake remains pleasant. The southwest monsoon erupts in May, disrupting travel across the country for around five months, especially in the far south and southeast. While temperatures are lower at this time, humidity levels are considerably higher.

Advance Booking

The relatively short duration of the tourist season, from October to March, puts great pressure on hotels and other essential services in the main visitor destinations. This is especially true during peak season from December to mid-February, when it can be difficult to find any kind of accommodations in places like Bagan and Inle Lake. It is best to make hotel reservations for this period at least a couple of months in advance, and confirm your booking a few days before arrival. It is also a good idea to book any internal flights as far ahead as possible, as seats on more popular routes may be in short supply. A reliable travel agent *(see p229)* will be of invaluable help when trying to make advance bookings.

Visas and Passports

Tourist visas are required by visitors from all countries. The Myanmar government has been slow to embrace the Internet, so applications have to be made in person at a Myanmar embassy. The forms, downloadable from Myanmar embassy websites, are simple and should be accompanied by a couple of passport photographs, a copy of flight bookings, and the requisite fee. A letter from an employer may be needed. Travelers on pre-arranged tours will also require a letter by fax from their ground agent in Myanmar (also known as the "land operator") confirming travel arrangements, but this is generally taken care of by the main tour operator.

Standard tourist visas are valid for three months from the date of issue and last 28 days, extendable by two or four weeks. Short overstays of less than a fortnight on the 28-day visa are not regarded as a serious offence, although anyone who stays on after their tourist visa expires has to pay a fee for every day they overstay, payable to emigration officials at the airport on departure. Only

Burmese villagers near the town of Monywa carrying local produce to market

◄ Young novices playing outside a monastery in the ancient city of Bagan passports that are valid for a minimum of six months after the intended date of arrival will be granted visas. Visitors should be aware that Myanmar does not recognize dual nationalities.

Customs Information

Customs regulations are straightforward in Myanmar. Visitors are allowed to bring two liters of alcoholic beverage and 400 cigarettes with them. Any foreign currency exceeding $2,000, along with valuable pieces of jewelry or gold, must be declared. Upon arrival, a Passenger's Declaration Form (PDF) should be completed, a copy of which will be handed to you. When leaving Myanmar, gemstones (including jade), jewelry, and silverware bought in the country may only be exported on production of a cash memo compiled by an authorized retailer. A full list of customs regulations appears on the **Myanmar Customs** website.

What to Take

Travelers are advised to take with them everything they may require on their trip, especially medicines, toiletries, electronic gadgets, batteries, and chargers, all of which are either of inferior quality or in short supply in Myanmar. A flashlight or head torch will be useful when walking along unlit roads or uneven sidewalks at night. Luxury hotels go to some lengths to ensure guest rooms are free of mosquitos, but a mosquito net could be useful if staying in inexpensive hotels or in rural areas. Pale colored, lightweight cotton clothing is best for Myanmar's intense tropical heat, as is a broad-brimmed hat. A robust and light water bottle will come in useful, and a packet of purification tablets, for those rare times when it may not be possible to find safe bottled water, is recommended. Travelers who wish to avoid generating unnecessary plastic waste might also consider purchasing a compact pump-action water filter.

Responsible Travel

During the tourism boycott led by the National League for Democracy (NLD), "responsible travel" in Myanmar meant avoiding the country altogether. That changed in 2010 when the ban was relaxed, but only a small percentage of the millions of foreign visitors since have followed NLD requests to travel independently rather than with a tour operator, and to stay in small, family-run guesthouses rather than large hotels owned by supporters of the former military government. One reason for this has been government reluctance to issue permits to potential B&B and homestay owners, which has limited the availability of ethical alternatives. However, plenty of local accommodations do exist, and they have significantly less environmental impact than luxury hotels. Spending money with local people also ensures more of it ends up benefiting the host community rather than companies whose interests may extend into illegal logging, mining, narcotics production, and other culturally or environmentally damaging concerns.

Such issues are particularly relevant in Inle Lake, where the surge in visitors has not resulted in an improvement in the living standards of the locals. Few ordinary Burmese dare articulate opposition to development initiatives by powerful interests, but the proliferation of luxury lake resorts, and consequent inflation in the price of staples, has been far from welcome.

Tourists on a locally hired canoe on a lake near Saddar Cave, Southeastern Myanmar

Universally recognized sign advertising a doctor's clinic in Myanmar

Vaccination

Proof of vaccination against yellow fever is required for anyone arriving from countries in the infected zone (most of Africa and South America), or for anyone who has visited these regions less than six days prior to arrival. The World Health Organization recommends that travelers are also immunized against diphtheria and tetanus; measles, mumps, and rubella (MMR); varicella (chickenpox); hepatitis A and B; and typhoid. While almost eradicated from Mandalay and Yangon, malaria is a problem in the rest of the country. Some strains recently identified in Myanmar are known to be resistant to Larium (Mefloquine), so Malarone or Doxycycline are recommended as prophylaxis.

DIRECTORY

Embassies

Australia
City Map E5. 88, Strand Road, Yangon. **Tel** (01) 251810.
Ⓦ burma.embassy.gov.au

United Kingdom
City Map E5. 80, Strand Road, Yangon. **Tel** (01) 370865.
Ⓦ ukinburma.fco.gov.uk

United States
110, University Avenue Road, Kamayut Township, Yangon.
Tel (01) 536509.
Ⓦ burma.usembassy.gov

Customs Information

Myanmar Customs
Ⓦ myanmarcustoms.gov.mm

Tourists looking at a site map at one of Myanmar's visitor attractions

Visitor Information

The Myanmar government is in the process of developing a tourism infrastructure, and as yet there are no official tourist information offices other than the state-run travel agent, **Myanmar Travels and Tours** (MTT) in Yangon. MTT's office on Mahabandula Garden Street serves as the main information point for the city, handing out free maps for destinations across the country. Their agents can also help arrange permits to visit restricted regions, such as Hkakabo Razi in the far north and the Myeik (Mergui) Archipelago. For assistance with planning an itinerary or for arranging accommodations and transport, privately run agencies such as those listed in the directory offer a more efficient and reliable service.

Opening Hours

Shops in Myanmar open from 9:30am to 6 or 7pm Monday to Saturday, sometimes closing on Saturday afternoons. Markets start just before dawn and tend to close by 11am or noon. Banks work 10am to 3pm Monday to Friday, and government offices (including post offices) from 10am to 4:40pm. Opening times, however, are generally more flexible in tourist centers such as Nyaungshwe (Inle Lake) and Bagan, where businesses trade for as long as there are customers to service. This includes corner shops, Internet cafés, and bars, although travel agents tend to wind up by 7pm.

Admission Charges

Admission charges are levied at most major sites, including monuments, museums, and botanical gardens. In Bagan, the government issues tickets that have to be paid for in US dollars on arrival. Mandalay's combination ticket covers all the principal tourist locations and can be bought in kyat. Some important pagodas, including Yangon's Shwedagon and Botataung, charge foreign visitors for entry. Photographers should note that many places of worship demand an additional fee for the use of cameras.

Disabled Travelers

Facilities for the disabled are rare, although major pagodas and sites such as Mandalay Hill have elevators that bypass the stairways. Car access is generally good for most destinations, but wheelchair users will have to arrange a vehicle with sufficient trunk space. At Bagan and some other archeological sites, horse carts are on hand to aid access to the monuments. Throughout the country, sidewalks are uneven and present a major challenge, especially in the big cities with heavy traffic.

High-end hotels, by contrast, usually have luggage ramps and elevators. Mid-scale and budget places tend to be spread over several floors and may not always have functioning elevators. As yet, dedicated disabled toilets are nonexistent.

The websites of **Disability World, Mobility International USA, Society for Accessible Travel and Hospitality, Accessible Journeys**, and **Disability Rights UK** offer a range of useful resources for international travel.

Traveling with Children

Children are adored and welcomed almost everywhere in this family-oriented country. Parents traveling with offspring of all ages are a common sight at pagodas and other attractions. However, diapers, formula powder, baby food, wipes, and other childcare products are a rarity outside big city malls. Waste disposal facilities are also uncommon, so consider switching to reusables. All restaurants are welcoming to youngsters, although most do not offer any special menus, and much of the food may be too spicy for kids. Yogurt and ice cream, however, are widely available. Given the state of city sidewalks, strollers (pushchairs) are more trouble than they're worth, so bring a good carrier or backpack.

Families with children enjoying an evening on the beach in Myanmar

Language

With its tonal variations, Burmese can be a challenging language to learn. However, in tourist areas, most vendors, taxi drivers, and boatmen will speak and understand some English, albeit fractured and accented. By contrast, the English spoken in hotels, airline offices, and banks tends to be more fluent. When traveling in rural areas, especially the ethnic minority ones, it makes sense to employ an English-speaking guide.

Etiquette

The Burmese are exceptionally polite and considerate, and expect foreigners to behave in a similar way. Should you need to express frustration or complain about something, do so calmly and without raising your voice. As in any part of the world, losing your temper is likely to be counterproductive. When meeting people of the same sex, it is customary to shake hands. However, between people of different sexes it is not, except in a business context, where international norms apply. Men's names are prefixed by the honorific "U," women's by "Daw." Touching people's heads is considered highly disrespectful; avoid it even with children. Never point at or touch objects with your feet or sit with your legs outstretched, particularly when visiting pagodas. Bear in mind, too, that Myanmar is a highly conservative country and that local people may be offended by public displays of affection such as hugs or kisses.

Religious sites require sober dress. Keep arms and legs covered at all times (no shorts or crop tops), and be sure to leave footwear at the entrance to any pagoda; racks are usually provided for storage.

Finally, exercise great caution when discussing current affairs or politics. Although in recent times the regime has become nominally more democratic and transparent, and the press freer, criticism of the government in public can lead to trouble with the authorities for local people.

Photographing the sunset from atop a pagoda, Bagan Archeological Zone

Photography

The fabulously photogenic pagodas and landscapes of Myanmar can be freely photographed. People are generally happy to pose, but always seek permission first. It is never acceptable to take photographs of women bathing in the open. Photographing meditating monks is considered disrespectful. Some ethnic minorities dislike tourists taking pictures of pregnant women, and soldiers and police may also refuse to be snapped while on duty. Finally, never photograph a military installation or vehicle.

Time and Calendar

Myanmar Standard Time (MST) is six and a half hours ahead of GMT, ten and a half hours ahead of New York, 13.5 hours ahead of Los Angeles, an hour ahead of India, and an hour behind Thailand. Myanmar runs according to the standard seven-day week, but the Buddhist week has eight days, with Wednesday split into two halves. The traditional Burmese calendar also differs from the Gregorian one, being based on lunar months: Tabodwe (January/February); Tabaung (February/March); Tagu (March/April); Kason (April/May); Nayon (May/June); Waso (June/July); Wagaung (July/August); Tawthalin (August/September); Thadingyut (September/October); Tazaungmon (October/November); Nadaw (November/December); and Pyatho (December/January).

Electricity

Myanmar runs on 230 volts/50 Hz and uses two-pin plugs, for which a universal adapter is required when bringing devices from abroad. Electricity supplies are frequently interrupted, even in the big cities, and most hotels and business premises have diesel generator backup.

DIRECTORY

Visitor Information

Ayarwaddy Legend Travels & Tours
City Map E5. 104, 37th St (Lower Block), Kyauktada Township, Yangon. **Tel** (01) 252007.
W ayarwaddylegend.com

Good News Travels
City Map E5.
Room 1101, 12th Floor, Olympic Tower Building, 225/227, Bo Aung Kyaw St, Yangon. **Tel** (01) 375050. W myanmargoodnewstravel.com

Indochina Services Travel
City Map B1. 11, Maha Myaing Street, Yangon. **Tel** (01) 504502.
W indochina-services.com

Myanmar Travels and Tours
City Map E5. 118, Mahabandula Garden Street, Yangon.
Tel (01) 371286. W myanmartravelsandtours.com

Tour Mandalay
City Map D1.
2/3, 3rd Floor, Pearl Condominium, Block A, Kaba Aye Pagoda Road, Yangon.
Tel (01) 540475.
W tourmandalay.travel

Disabled Travelers

Accessible Journeys
W disabilitytravel.com

Disability Rights UK
W disabilityrightsuk.org

Disability World
W disabilityworld.com

Mobility International USA
W miusa.org

Society for Accessible Travel & Hospitality
W sath.org

Personal Security and Health

The combination of a highly authoritarian government and an exceptionally law-abiding population ensures that Myanmar is one of the world's safest destinations. Violent crime is rare and visitors can travel without undue fear of assault or robbery, even at night. That said, petty crime is on the rise in the big cities, especially around busy train and bus stations. Food in restaurants is generally safe to eat, although it's better to drink only bottled or purified water. Healthcare, however, lags behind that of Myanmar's neighbors. Seriously ill travelers have to be airlifted to Singapore or Bangkok, so it is essential to have insurance with adequate medical evacuation cover.

General Precautions

The main security risk for foreign travelers is petty theft, such as pickpocketing or bag snatching. Thieves know that foreigners have to pay for many things in US dollars and are likely to be carrying cash in their bags. It is therefore wise to keep money and valuables in a belt hidden inside your clothing when walking around crowded places. Secure your camera and purse when walking or riding on a bike, as motorcycle-mounted thieves have been known to grab items at intersections. Most high-end hotels have electronic safes in their rooms, or a large safe at the reception where passports, cash, tickets, and other valuables may be stored. Another basic tip is to take photocopies or scans of your passport, travel insurance, departure card, and other important documents, which will aid replacement in the event of theft or loss.

Police

Myanmar's police, distinguished by their grey uniforms, combat helmets, and yellow, blue, and red shoulder patches, have a high profile by the standards of Southeast Asia. They are rarely of help to foreign travelers, though, except in the event of a robbery, when they may issue a report for insurance purposes. Their demeanor on the whole tends to be forbidding; they do not like to be photographed and few officers speak English. However, Yangon has recently set up a tourist police division with English-speaking officers specifically to assist visitors.

Yangon traffic policeman with tricolored arm patches

Medical Facilities

The government's expenditure on healthcare as a percentage of GDP is among the lowest in the world, and during the years of the NLD-led boycott, international donor organizations gave less to Myanmar per capita than to any other nation. As a consequence, healthcare standards are low, even in big cities. Wealthy locals or tourists requiring medical attention tend to seek it abroad. Local hospitals are crowded and poorly provisioned, medicines in short supply, and staff inadequately trained. The widespread reuse of unsterilized equipment and insufficient blood screening are other reasons to avoid them.

The country's best medical facility is Yangon's French-run **Myanmar International SOS Clinic**, which offers full outpatient facilities, a dependable pharmacy, and a team of fully qualified international doctors. More limited services are also available at the international-standard **Pun Hlaing Hospital** in the north of the city.

Pharmacies

Basic drugs, such as painkillers and indigestion tablets, are available over the counter at local pharmacies, but foreign pharmaceuticals should not be purchased as they may be counterfeit or adulterated. Travelers are advised to bring sufficient medical supplies for the duration of their trip.

Travel Insurance

It is always a good idea to buy travel insurance before leaving home, but particularly so for a trip to Myanmar. Medical facilities being what they are, the policy should cover the potentially high price of emergency medical evacuation, plus theft, lost luggage, and costs run up by delays and cancellations.

Food- and Water-Borne Diseases

The most common ailment that afflicts travelers to Myanmar is an upset stomach. Caused by unfamiliarity with otherwise harmless local bacteria in food, mild diarrhea is best left untreated; it will pass of its own accord after 24–36 hours. Drink plenty of fluids, supplemented

Yangon General Hospital, established in 1899 in a Victorian-style building

with rehydration salts (available locally) if necessary, and refrain from eating until the attack has passed. If it lasts for more than 48 hours, a more serious infection such as dysentery or giardiasis may be the cause, requiring a stool test and antibiotics.

Many stomach problems can, however, be avoided by taking some common-sense precautions: peel fruit before eating it; wash hands before meals; avoid food that has not been properly cooked, or which has obviously been reheated; stick to bottled water, or take along your own water purifier (which cuts down on plastic bottle waste); think twice before eating in an empty restaurant; and steer clear of meat or fish, unless you can be sure it is fresh and has been adequately cooked.

Narcotics

As one of the world's prime sources of methamphetamine and heroin, Myanmar suffers high levels of drug addiction. The country is the world's second largest producer of opium. The worst affected areas are the hills of the Golden Triangle border regions, where opium is grown (see p177) and crystal meth manufactured, and in Myitkyina, in Kachin State in Upper Burma, where the drug trade has financed the long-standing armed conflict with the state. Attempts to crack down on the trade are hampered by the complex political situation – the narcotics industry is controlled by ethnic minority syndicates with which the government needs to be on good terms to ensure the progress of its reforms.

Heat

Myanmar's heat and humidity can be intense, and to avoid sunstroke while on explorations of archeological sites, such as Bagan and Mrauk U, travelers should wear suitable sun hats, carry a Burmese paper parasol, or try *thanaka*, a

Burmese child wearing *thanaka* paste, a traditional natural sunscreen

natural plant-derived sunscreen used by the Burmese. Drink sufficient water as dehydration can cause headaches, dizziness, and more serious conditions such as kidney stones.

HIV-AIDS

Due largely to the prevalence of intravenous drug use in the country, as well as the illegality of prostitution, Myanmar suffers the third highest rate of HIV-AIDS in Asia, and the disease is on the increase. At least one third of the sex workers in the country are thought to be infected, and antiretroviral drugs are in short supply.

Women Travelers

Myanmar is, on the whole, a relaxing destination for women visitors, whether traveling alone or with friends. Harassment is rare – men will look away rather than be seen to be staring, and are courteous to the point of chivalric on public transport. The chance to interact with other women is likely to be one of the most satisfying aspects of the trip. Many women travelers choose to fit in by adopting *htameins* – a great icebreaker when meeting local women, elegant, and well suited to the climate. Women should be aware, though, that some pagodas prohibit them from climbing up to the upper terraces, entering the sanctum, or touching the deity.

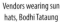

Vendors wearing sun hats, Bodhi Tataung

Gay and Lesbian Travelers

Gay and lesbian sex is illegal in Myanmar, and although the law is seldom, if ever, enforced, attitudes remain highly conservative. There are very few openly LGBTQ public figures, and no gay bars, clubs, or pride marches, although cruising does go on in the trendier nightclubs of Yangon. Young people suspected of homosexuality tend to be sent to a monastery or nunnery in an attempt to straighten their sexual orientation. However, one indication that public opinion is slowly softening, at least in the pro-Western, affluent suburbs of Yangon, has been the creation of the group **Colors Rainbow**, which has organized gay pride forums and produced a cable TV show for the local LGBTQ community.

Public Toilets

Public toilets are few and far between. Travelers tend to rely on washrooms in restaurants, which will be well scrubbed and aired if in an upscale establishment, but very basic, with squat-style toilets in local cafés and tea shops. Carry a good supply of toilet paper (routinely supplied by hotels), or adopt the local custom of using water.

DIRECTORY

Medical Facilities

Myanmar International SOS Clinic
Inya Lake Hotel,
37, Kaba Aye Pagoda Road,
Yangon. **Tel** (01) 657922.
W internationalsos.com

Pun Hlaing Hospital
Pun Hlaing Golf Estate Avenue
(near the golf course), Hlaing
Thayar Township, Yangon.
Tel (01) 684323.
W punhlainghospital.com

Gay and Lesbian Travelers

Colors Rainbow
W colorsrainbow.com

Banking and Currency

Although Myanmar's banking system is fast catching up with the rest of the world, for the time being its undeveloped state means that most transactions by foreign visitors have to be made in US dollars. The kyat is accepted for small payments, but for larger ones (such as hotels bills), only mint, or near-mint, US dollar bills will do. Credit and debit cards are rarely accepted, and traveler's checks and VisaMoney are not taken anywhere. Currency exchange no longer has to be carried out on the black market, but even the banks require dollars – which means visitors have to carry enough US currency into the country to see them through their entire trip.

Security guards at the doors of a branch of KBZ Bank

US Dollars

It is essential that any dollar bills brought to Myanmar are in pristine condition. The Burmese will reject one if it has even a tiny fold, pen mark, blotch, or tear. When buying US currency prior to departure, check each bill front and back. Some travelers even resort to smoothing out potentially offensive wrinkles with a hot iron. Protect the bills from dirt and moisture inside a plastic bag if they are stored in a money belt.

An ATM (cash machine) operated by one of Myanmar's banks

Kyat

Myanmar's unit of currency is the kyat, pronounced "chaat" and abbreviated to "K" (or "MMK"). Although US dollars remain the currency of choice it is useful to keep some kyat handy for smaller expenses – taxi fares, admission, camera tickets for pagodas, and restaurants and street stalls. Bear in mind that the kyat cannot be converted outside Myanmar, and is not accepted in the transit areas of international airports.

Banks and Exchange

Until recently, the Myanmar government set absurdly unfavorable exchange rates for all banks and bureaux de change, so imported dollars had to be changed on the black market – in backstreet offices, travel agencies, shops, or hotels. Since 2013, however, local banks have been permitted to offer rates higher than those on the street, rendering the black market redundant. Modern and efficient, private banks such as **CB Bank** and **KBZ Bank** are the quickest and easiest places to change currency. Some banks have also started offering Western Union and MoneyGram money transfer services at selected branches. When checking your encashment make sure that a certificate or receipt has been issued, as it may later be demanded by customs officials.

Banking Hours

Banking hours are generally 10am–3pm Monday to Friday. Outside these times, currency can be changed at hotels, markets (such as Bogyoke Aung San Zei in Yangon), and large souvenir emporia, although the rates they offer may be lower than those of the banks. Note that better rates of exchange are given for higher denomination bills, so bring more hundreds than fifties and twenties.

ATM Services

Myanmar still has comparatively few cash machines, or ATMs, and those that are open do not always dispense cash advances against foreign credit or debit cards. When they do, a large transaction fee (typically of around K5,000 or 4 percent) is levied, and the money is dispensed in kyat. Large branches

DIRECTORY

Banks

CB Bank, Yangon
City Map D5. 334–336, corner of Strand Rd and 23rd St, Latha Township, Yangon. **Tel** (01) 372646. 🔳 cbbankmm.com

CB Bank, Mandalay
Road Map C3. E1–3, 78th St (27/28), Chanayethazan Township, Mandalay. **Tel** (02) 69901. 🔳 cbbankmm.com

KBZ Bank, Yangon
City Map D5. 331, Strand Rd, Yangon. **Tel** (01) 218500 🔳 kbzbank.com

KBZ Bank, Mandalay
Road Map C3. 230, 80th St (31/32), Chanayethazan Township, Mandalay. **Tel** (02) 30145. 🔳 kbzbank.com

of both the CB and KBZ banks have ATMs in most of the main tourist destinations; they accept foreign-registered MasterCard, Visa, and Cirrus cards.

Credit and Debit Cards

Although an increasing number of airlines, restaurants, shops, and hotels accept cards, the overwhelming majority don't and visitors should never count on being able to use one. Places that do take cards usually charge a very large transaction fee for the privilege.

Traveler's Checks

Traveler's checks, and equivalent digital travel money, are useless in Myanmar, even if issued by major international agencies such as Thomas Cook, Visa, or American Express.

A donation box, commonly seen at pagodas and temples across Myanmar

10,000 kyat

5,000 kyat

1,000 kyat

Banknotes

Myanmar banknotes are circulated in denominations of 50 pya, K1, K5, K10, K20, K50, K100, K200, K500, K1,000, K5,000, and K10,000. However, the smaller denominations are rarely used and are being phased out. Bills with tears or repairs tend to be refused, but may be exchanged at banks.

500 kyat

200 kyat

100 kyat

Coins

Although coins are legal tender, it is extremely rare to find them actually in use. One kyat is divided into 100 pya. Officially Myanmar uses the following coins: 10 pya, 50 pya, K1, K5, K10, K50, and K100.

Communications and Media

Myanmar's communication network is as archaic as its transport system, although both look set to change rapidly over the coming years as the country opens its doors to foreign investors. For the time being, however, cell phone use remains minimal, and the Internet slow, expensive, and partially censored. Press censorship has eased considerably since 2011, but choice is still severely limited, and criticism of the regime and its policies muted. The state-run postal system also falls well below international standards – it can be unreliable, and for sending souvenirs home, private couriers are still the safest option.

A street stall advertising a public telephone service in Yangon

Intha-style stilt structure housing the Ywama Post Office on Inle Lake

Post and Courier Services

There is no shortage of post offices in Myanmar, and while staff are smiling and helpful, postal services can be a bit undependable. Because there has never been a standardized way of transliterating Burmese into English, postal addresses in Myanmar are notoriously hit-and-miss – except in the city of Mandalay, whose grid plan system makes addresses easy to find. Foreign travelers typically report a success rate of 50 percent or less for postcards. For sending souvenirs home, the only sensible option is to use a private courier such as **DHL** or **Express Mail Service International (EMS)**.

Telephone Calls

International calls can be made from most hotels and local sidewalk telephone centers, but are extremely expensive (several US dollars per minute). Calls to trunk or local landline numbers are considerably cheaper, but still quite costly compared to other countries. Although Voice over Internet Protocol (VoIP) calls were banned for years – allegedly to protect revenue from international calls earned by the state-owned telecom company – it is now possible to cut costs by making web-based VoIP calls using applications such as Skype and GTalk.

Cell Phones

The cell telephone revolution has yet to happen in Myanmar. Licenses for foreign telecom companies to expand the existing networks were only auctioned in 2013. At present, less than ten percent of the country's population uses a cell phone – the overwhelming majority in the two major cities of Yangon and Mandalay. Local

SIM cards are currently not available to foreign tourists, but you can hire a phone with a card at Yangon and Mandalay airports. Global roaming has started to work, but only for selected Asian networks, not US or European ones. For booking accommodations and other routine calls while in the country, it works out far cheaper to use local landlines.

Internet Facilities

Less than 1 percent of Myanmar's population currently has access to the Internet, and nearly all of those 500,000 people live in the big cities. Installation costs and subscription charges are high, which is why the majority of users rely on Internet cafés. Most of these are cramped and crowded, with old computers and keyboards, although some of the better ones do have air-conditioning and modern equipment. Most hotels offer Wi-Fi to guests. However, connection speeds across the country tend to be slow – in fact, among the slowest in the world. Out in the provinces meaningful browsing is frequently impossible.

Access to websites that are deemed to be critical of the government is still routinely blocked, and although Twitter, CNN, and the BBC are no longer officially banned, social media usage is generally low due to the cost and speed of Internet connections. Email remains the way most travelers keep in touch during their trip.

A newspaper vendor sorting out his deliveries in Yangon

Newspapers and Magazines

A watershed moment in Myanmar's modern history took place in the spring of 2013, when four independent, privately owned newspapers hit the stands in Yangon – the first of more than a dozen similar publications to be published across the country in that year. Before this landmark relaxation of the formerly tight state control of Myanmar's press, the only papers available were held in check by threats of censorship, imprisonment, and torture for any journalist critical of the military regime. English-language editions are published by two newspapers. *The New Light of Myanmar* is essentially a propaganda tool for the government, favoring articles about the achievements of the military. The *Myanmar Times* is also close to the government, despite being partly foreign-owned. For a more impartial perspective on the nation's

current affairs, *Irrawaddy* is a quality magazine produced by Burmese exiles living in Thailand. The *Democratic Voice of Burma* (DVB), as its name suggests, is more overtly aligned with the pro-democracy movement. Based in Norway, DVB is a banned organization and publishes only online on a website hosted on Norwegian servers. It also makes TV and radio broadcasts.

Television and Radio

As with the rest of the media in Myanmar, television and radio are tightly controlled by the state. The main channels are TV Myanmar and Myawaddy TV, which show a mix of soaps, entertainment, and news in Burmese. Satellite networks such as MRTV-4 also bundle local stations with foreign ones, many of them in English. CNN, BBC World, and National Geographic can be viewed on most hotel television sets.

Young novices enjoying a television show in an Inle Lake monastery

DIRECTORY

Post and Courier Services

DHL
City Map B4. 58, Wa Dan St, Lanmadaw Township, Yangon. **Tel** (01) 215516/7/8. W **dhl.com**

Express Mail Service International (EMS)
City Map B1. 361, Pyay Rd, Yangon. **Tel** (01) 515151.
W **ems.com.mm**

Newspapers and Magazines

The New Light of Myanmar
W **moi.gov.mm/npe/nlm**

Myanmar Times
W **mmtimes.com**

Irrawaddy
W **irrawaddy.org**

Democratic Voice of Burma
W **dvb.no**

Useful Dialing Codes

- To call Myanmar from abroad, dial the international access code of the country you are in, followed by Myanmar's country code, 95, the city code, and finally the phone number.
- To make a domestic long-distance call in Myanmar, dial 0 followed by the city code and phone number.
- City codes: Yangon 1; Mandalay 2; Bagan 61; Bago 52; Hsipaw 82; Kalaw, Nyaungshwe, Taunggyi 81; Kawthaung 59; Kengtung 84; Mawlamyine 57; Meiktila 64; Myitkyina 74; Pathein 42; Pyay 53; Pyin U Lwin 85; Sagaing 72; Taungoo 54; Thandwe and Sittwe 43.
- Cell phone numbers usually have 8 to 12 digits, including the cell phone prefix 9, while landline numbers have 5 to 7 digits without the city codes.
- To make an international call from Myanmar, dial 00 followed by the country code, city code, and phone number.
- Country codes: UK 44; USA and Canada 1; Australia 61; New Zealand 64; France 33.

TRAVEL INFORMATION

Overland travel from neighboring states to Myanmar is tightly controlled, and the vast majority of international arrivals in the country are by air, at Yangon's Mingaladon Airport. From there, foreign tourists tend to take a domestic flight to one of several regional hubs. Hampered by poor infrastructure, travel by road and rail tends to be slower and more uncomfortable, although plenty of backpackers brave grueling overnight journeys to reach Inle Lake, Mandalay, and Bagan. Hired cars with drivers provide a less arduous alternative. A more leisurely, and quintessentially Burmese, form of long-distance transport are the river boats plying the Ayeyarwady, whether old government ferries or luxury cruisers. Whichever method of travel you opt for, however, bear in mind that pressure for tickets is particularly intense from December to February (the height of the winter tourist season) and that bookings should be made as far in advance as possible, either in person or with the help of a dependable local travel agent *(see p229)*.

Mandalay International Airport, with traditionally designed *pyatthat* roofs

Arriving by Air

Nearly every foreign visitor to Myanmar arrives by air at Yangon, although Mandalay International Airport also hosts flights from Kunming in China and Bangkok and Chiang Mai in Thailand. The majority of Yangon flights originate in Singapore or Bangkok, but there are direct flights from Kolkata with **Air India**, Tokyo with **All Nippon**, Seoul with **Asiana**, Hong Kong with **Dragonair**, Hanoi with **Vietnam Airlines**, and Doha with **Qatar Airways**. Larger carriers such as **Malaysia Airlines**, **Singapore Airlines/ Silk Air**, and **Thai Airways** generally rely on smaller subsidiaries to fly the connecting leg from their hub to Myanmar. The Malaysia-based low-cost airline **Air Asia** also flies daily from Bangkok. This is the cheapest way to get to the country, but may mean a long layover in Thailand. There are no direct flights from the US, the UK, or Europe, only from the Gulf and Southeast Asia.

Air Fares

The cost of flying to Myanmar varies with the season, the airline, and the travel agent. The busiest, most expensive period is from December to January and during the Thingyan festival in April, when lots of Burmese workers travel home to their families. Discounted tickets are usually available during the monsoon (May to September). Usually, the most cost-effective route is to buy a late-availability charter flight to Bangkok from Europe or the US, then fly into Myanmar on a low-cost airline.

Arrival

Mingaladon International Airport lies on Yangon's outskirts, about 12 miles (20 km) north of downtown. Arrival, immigration, and customs formalities are conducted at a brisk pace by the standards of most of Asia, and the airport facilities are well maintained. Be sure to keep the duplicate customs slip handed back to you as it will be needed when leaving Myanmar. Note that luggage is often scanned prior to exiting the airport.

In the arrivals hall is a foreign exchange facility where visitors can exchange dollars and euros for kyat at reasonable rates. There is also a dependable ATM (cash machine) here.

Departures sign in Burmese and English at Thandwe Airport near Ngapali

Getting from Mingaladon Airport to Yangon

Visitors on prearranged tours are usually whisked away in air-conditioned buses or mini-buses, while independent travelers rely on local Toyota taxis – drivers wait outside the arrivals concourse. Although they are generally honest, it makes sense to check the correct fare in advance with your hotel manager or guesthouse owner when you book your accommodations as none of the taxis are metered. Note that the night rate is 30 percent higher than the day fare. As yet, there are no dedicated shuttle buses in operation. The trip from the airport to downtown Yangon can take as little as 45 minutes on clear roads at night, or a couple of hours during rush hour in the daytime.

City taxi available at Yangon Mingaladon International Airport

Cost-conscious travelers on tight budgets may wish to save a few dollars by catching a municipal bus, which costs less than US$1. To do this, turn right once out of the terminal and walk for 10 minutes until you reach Pyay Road. Bus no. 51 runs every 20 minutes from a stop there to downtown Yangon as far as Sule Pagoda from 7am to 10pm.

Overland Travel

It is sometimes possible to enter Myanmar overland at the Ruili–Muse entry point on the Chinese border in Yunnan. The necessary visas and paperwork may be arranged in Kunming. However, Burmese border officials have been known to refuse entry to foreigners, or restrict onward travel to Lashio, or insist that travelers leave the country via the same point afterward.

Five border crossings with Thailand are now open to foreigners: Mae Sai–Tachileik; Ranong–Kawthaung; Mae Sot–Myawaddy; Ban Phu Nam Ron–Htee Khee; Three Pagodas Pass. The latter issues only a one-day permit for a visa run. At Tachileik special permits used to be required, but now only a valid visa is needed. However, onward travel overland is allowed only as far as Kengtung, but visitors are permitted to fly out from there. The crossings at Kawthaung, Myawaddy, and Htee Khee are completely open. No special permits are needed and visitors can travel onward without any restrictions, other than the usual controls applicable to all tourists. Note, though, that overland travel from Kawthaung to Myeik is not possible; you must take a ferry.

Myanmar visas are not issued at any of these border points and need to be arranged in advance, unless you only want the one-day permit for a visa run (Thai visas are available at all these crossings). There are no permitted points of entry by land or sea from India, Laos, or Bangladesh.

DIRECTORY

Arriving by Air

Air Asia
City Map D4. 37, Level 1, Room 111, La Pyae Wun Plaza, Alan Pya Pagoda St, Dagon Township, Yangon. **Tel** (01) 251885, 251886.
w airasia.com

Air India
City Map D4. 127, Sule Pagoda Road, Pabedan Township, Yangon. **Tel** (01) 253601, 253597, 253598, 650574.
w airindia.com

All Nippon Airways
City Map D4. 0201 Sakura Tower, 3rd Floor, 339 Bogyoke Aung San Road, Kyauktada Township, Yangon. **Tel** (01) 255412.
w ana.co.jp

Asiana
City Map D4. Room 804, 9th Floor, La Pyae Wun Plaza, Alan Pya Pagoda St, Yangon. **Tel** (01) 371382. w flyasiana.com

Dragonair
City Map D4. 1107 Sakura Tower, 12th Floor, 339 Bogyoke Aung San Road, Kyauktada Township, Yangon. **Tel** (01) 255320.
w dragonair.com

Malaysia Airlines
City Map D4. 1st Floor, Central Hotel, 335–357 Bogyoke Aung San Road, Pabedan Tsp, Yangon. **Tel** (01) 24100720 ext 121/122.
w malaysiaairlines.com

Qatar Airways
City Map D5. Rooms 22, 23, 24, 3rd Floor, Centrepoint Towers, No. 65, corner of Sule Pagoda Rd & Merchant Rd, Yangon. **Tel** (01) 379845. w qatarairways.com

Singapore Airlines/Silk Air
City Map D4. 0202 Sakura Tower, 3rd Floor, 339 Bogyoke Aung San Road, Kyauktada Township, Yangon. **Tel** (01) 255289.
w silkair.com

Thai Airways
City Map D4. 1101 Sakura Tower, 12th Floor, 339 Bogyoke Aung San Road, Kyauktada Township, Yangon. **Tel** (01) 255499.
w thaiairways.com

Vietnam Airlines
City Map D4. 1702 Sakura Tower, 339 Bogyoke Aung San Road, Yangon. **Tel** (01) 255066.
w vietnamairlines.com

The spot where the borders of Myanmar, Laos, and Thailand meet, Golden Triangle region

Getting Around

With the exception of the new Yangon–Mandalay Expressway, road travel is slow and bumpy. Vehicles tend to be dilapidated and journeys long and uncomfortable. Rail travel is only a little more appealing, due to the lack of modern rolling stock and a very limited network. To cover long distances, travelers have to be prepared to either rough it, or else catch internal flights between the key sights and cities. Myanmar's domestic air services have expanded rapidly over the past few years, and with a degree of flexibility it is usually possible to get a seat when you need it. The same applies to traveling the Ayeyarwady by boat – an option for visitors with more time. But for those wishing to see much along the way, it is hard to beat renting a car and driver, which allows you the freedom to stop where you want and make the odd detour.

A locomotive of Myanmar Railways, which operates thousands of miles of track

Domestic Airlines

Myanmar's domestic air capacity has grown rapidly to cope with the sudden surge in demand since 2010. There are now several private carriers in addition to the state-run **Myanma Airways**, including **Asian Wings Airways**, **Yangon Airways**, **Air Bagan**, **Air KBZ**, **Golden Myanmar Airlines**, and **Air Mandalay**. Foreign visitors have tended to avoid Myanma Airways due to its poor safety record and all-round unreliability, but some of the new private firms have fared little better. Of the seven serious incidents logged in the country since 2007, private operators were involved in three, including the December 2012 crash at Heho Airport (Inle Lake), in which two passengers were killed and 11 injured after an Air Bagan Fokker 100 landed in a field in thick fog. The good news is that the old Fokkers are

being phased out and replaced with modern aircraft. Even so, for the time being, it is probably wise to avoid flying with Air Bagan and Myanma Airways, who still use them. The others have newer fleets maintained to international standards.

Theoretically, online booking is available through the websites of all the domestic airlines, although the process is far from seamless. Tickets are more easily purchased in advance at the airlines' offices in Yangon. Bear in mind, though, that by leaving reservations until only a day or two before your intended departure means that the seats may have sold out in busy periods. In Yangon, agents will make the booking on your behalf for the same price as the published fare, or sometimes a little less. Booking through a tour operator in your home country is the more expensive but most secure option.

Trains

The British laid nearly 3,000 miles (4,800 km) of railroad in Burma and nearly all of it is still in use. Unfortunately, a lack of government investment over the past few decades has left the network and most of its rolling stock in a very rundown state. Fares are also much more expensive than on buses (up to 400 percent higher), and foreigners pay five times as much as the locals for the same ticket.

Despite the higher fares, some routes are popular with visitors, particularly the 388-mile (622-km) overnight haul from Yangon to Mandalay, which takes 15–16 hours. Other journeys worth considering are the five-hour trip to Kyaiktiyo for the Golden Rock Pagoda, which benefits from a state-of-the-art, comfortable new express train inaugurated in 2013; the rattling ride over the Gokteik Viaduct from Mandalay or Pyin U Lwin to Hsipaw and Lashio; the even more juddery ride along a branch line from Mandalay to Shwenyaung (near Inle Lake); and the night train from Yangon to Bagan. Whichever route you travel on, however, expect long delays, especially on branch lines and in the far north.

Express services are far quicker and more comfortable than local ones, and offer the choice between upper class, which has upholstered, reclining seats, and ordinary class, which

Small propeller aircraft at Thandwe Airport, the closest domestic airport to Ngapali

has upright ones. Some trains also have sleeper carriages with berths. Foreigners' fares are available for all these classes. The **Seat 61** train travel website has several useful resources on journeys in Myanmar.

Demand for tickets is high at all times of the year, but especially during the winter tourist season, when you should aim to book at least a couple of days in advance, or longer for a sleeper. The best place to do this in Yangon is at the **MTT office** on Mahabandula Garden Street *(see p229)*, which has access to special tourist quotas. Or you can join the queues at the **Myanmar Railways Booking Office** (6–10am and 1–4pm daily). Reservations open three days prior to departure.

Buses

Buses are considerably faster, more comfortable, and cheaper than trains, although somewhat less characterful. Most long-distance services, such as the Yangon–Mandalay route, leave in the evening and travel over-night, stopping every hour or two at cafés along the route, so don't expect much sleep. The more luxurious coaches have air-conditioning but it is rarely needed as temperatures tend to plummet in the small hours; take along a fleece or blanket for comfort. Tickets are sold from counters at the bus stations or through local travel agents, and should be bought two or three days in advance for popular routes such as Bagan–Inle Lake or Yangon–Mandalay.

Note that even if you only want to travel part of the way, you still have to pay the full fare.

Motorcycle and Car Rental

Most hotels, guesthouses, and travel agents in Yangon and the country's principal visitor destinations can arrange a car and driver for day trips or longer tours. Although far from being the cheapest way to travel, this is certainly the most flexible and least uncomfortable. Dedicated, air-conditioned tourist cars are the most expensive. They are hired out for 12 hours per day, and the fee will include gas, tolls, and the driver's expenses. You can also find cheaper "private drivers" with older, non-air-conditioned cars, who will typically charge 30 percent less. Self-drive is extremely rare, costly, and difficult to arrange, which is probably just as well given the driving conditions in Myanmar. Motorcycles, a handy way of getting around, are available for rent in many visitor destinations, including Mandalay, where **Mr Jerry** has Chinese-made 125cc bikes in various states of repair.

Ferries

At any given time, thousands of Burmese, and around half the country's freight, will be travel-ing on Myanmar's rivers, the majority of them in dilapidated government ferries run by the Inland Water Transport (IWT). Tickets may be purchased in advance from any IWT jetty.

While this is the slowest way to travel in Myanmar – it takes four days to reach Mandalay from Yangon by river, a route covered in two hours by plane – it affords memorable glimpses of local life. The most popular route among foreign visitors is the one between Mandalay and Bagan, which is also covered by a fleet of small private boats.

DIRECTORY

Domestic Airlines

Air Bagan
City Map C1. 56, Shwe Taung Gyar St, Bahan, Yangon. **Tel** (01) 513322. **W** airbagan.com

Air KBZ
City Map D5. 33–49, corner of Bank St & Mahabandula Garden St, Yangon. **Tel** (01) 372977. **W** airkbz.com

Air Mandalay
City Map C1. 34, Shwe Taung Gone Ave (Golden Hill Ave), Yangon. **W** airmandalay.com

Asian Wings Airways
City Map C1. 34 (A1), Shwe Taung Gyar Street, Bahan, Yangon. **Tel** (01) 515261. **W** asianwingsairways.com

Golden Myanmar Airlines
1st Flr, Sayar San Plaza, University Avenue Road, Yangon. **Tel** (01) 8604035. **W** gmairlines.com

Myanma Airways
City Map E5. 104, Kannar Road (Strand Road), Yangon. **W** myanmaairways.aero

Yangon Airways
City Map E3. 166, Level 5, MMB Tower, Upper Pansodan Street, Yangon. **Tel** (01) 652533. **W** yangonair.com

Trains

Myanmar Railways Booking Office
City Map E4. Bogyoke Aung San Road, opposite Sakura Tower, Yangon.

Seat 61
W seat61.com/Burma.htm

Motorcycle and Car Rental

Mr Jerry
Road Map C3. 83rd St (25/26), nr Mandalay City Hotel, Mandalay.

Riverboat cruising down the Ayeyarwady near Mingun, Mandalay Region

Local Transport

Public transport in Myanmar is, like most of the country's infrastructure, poorly resourced and in need of upgrading. Buses are overcrowded, airless, hot, and falling apart, and the only suburban train line – in Yangon – supports a slow skeleton service. As a consequence, both locals and visitors tend to be reliant on taxis, which are ubiquitous and relatively inexpensive, and come in a variety of shapes and sizes, from shiny new Japanese imported cars to rickety trishaws. To cover short distances, horse carts can be a useful alternative, especially for exploring archeological sites. For market runs, however, pick-up trucks, which cram dozens of people on wooden boards placed over the rear flatbed, are the favorite local option. In the cities, plenty of private companies also run sightseeing tours and short excursions to local and regional places of interest and these frequently offer good value.

agree a fare and ride with the windows open. Taxis are plentiful, except in the evenings, when there may be a somewhat longer wait. Drivers will also be reluctant to take on longer trips to the suburbs at this time, preferring to remain downtown. If you are staying in a guesthouse or hotel, it might be best to ask the manager or owner to arrange a taxi on your behalf; they'll fix the fare and ensure the driver knows where you want to go.

In Mandalay and some other towns, motorcycle taxis are a popular alternative to cars – they are cheaper and faster at congested times.

Buses and Minibuses

Fleets of buses grind through the streets of all the main towns and cities in Myanmar, although few foreigners ever use them. Packed solid with passengers, they are horrendously uncomfortable and poorly maintained. The absence of numbers in English, and route maps, also make the systems hard to navigate.

The same applies to the smaller minibuses that work the routes mainly to and from markets, stopping for passengers whenever they are hailed from the roadside. Taxis are a more convenient option than minibuses and buses as fares are low and they are easy to come by (except during the evening rush hour).

Motorcycle Taxis and Taxis

Sign advertising taxis and bicycles for rent

The past few years have seen a gradual phasing out of the old taxis that used to serve the cities of Myanmar and a proliferation of more reliable, spacious new Japanese Toyotas. The best of the new taxis are metered and air-conditioned, but most are not. After flagging one down,

Suburban Railroad

Only Yangon has a suburban rail line. Because trains travel at an average of only 10 mph (17 kph), and don't loop through the commercial district, the suburban rail is not of much use to the city's commuters, most of whom make the journey to work by road. Passing through the loop does, however, offer a novel sightseeing opportunity for visiting foreigners. Trains run from 3:45am to 10:15pm, starting and ending at Yangon Train Station on Bogyoke Aung San Road, and take three hours to complete the 28-mile (46-km) circuit, with 39 stops en route.

A Myanmar Railways train passing a lush field in the countryside

The quirky trishaw, a mode of transport popular in Myanmar

Trishaws and Horse Carts

In smaller towns where bus services are limited, trishaws or *sei-kar* (a corruption of the English word "sidecar") are the most convenient option. Invented in Mandalay in the 1930s, these quirky little vehicles are popular in Myanmar. They are essentially bicycles with a passenger seat attached to the side that can accommodate two people, one facing forward, the other to the rear. Compact, easy to ride, and environmentally friendly, they are perfect for navigating narrow side streets and lanes. Fares are also very low.

Horse carts or *myint hlei* still operate widely in the rural areas of Myanmar, particularly on market days. Visitors will come across them in large numbers at archeological sites such as Bagan, Inwa (Ava), and Mrauk U, where they provide a gentle way to get around the sandy lanes leading to the monuments. At these tourist sites, the horse cart drivers generally speak a little English and act as guides. They usually charge per day of sightseeing. The fee rises if booked through a hotel or travel agent.

Pick-up Trucks

Pick-up trucks or *lein ka* (from "line car") often run alongside buses in cities, covering similar routes to the outlying suburbs from market districts, and also operate between towns and villages. Passengers ride in the usually covered flatbed section

to the rear, sitting on planks of wood, makeshift seats attached to the sides, or simply squashed in on top of sacks of provisions. Young men and boys also ride on the roof if there's no room inside. Foreigners tend to avoid traveling this way unless desperate as the lack of legroom can be excruciating after a few miles. However, in some places, *lein ka* are unavoidable. One example is the Golden Rock Pagoda at Kyaiktiyo, which can only be reached in a crowded pick-up. Fares are comparable with local buses. For an extra 50 percent fee, it is sometimes possible to secure a more comfortable seat in the cab up front.

Tours

Several companies in Yangon and Mandalay offer half- and full-day trips to sights in and around the cities, usually in air-conditioned minibuses or cars. As a rule, you will be picked up and dropped off at your hotel.

The price may or may not include meals. Shop around as costs vary dramatically. Tried-and-tested operators include **Asian Trails**, who offer city tours of Yangon as well as trips to Bago and other towns, and **Diethelm Travel**, who offer cycling trips around Inwa's ruins and walking tours of Yangon's old colonial enclave. In addition to city sightseeing tours, **Shan Yoma Travel and Tours** and **Green Myanmar Travels and Tours** also offer guided trips around Bagan and Inle Lake.

A tour group shelters under umbrellas at the massive stupa at Mingun

General Index

Acknowledgments

Dorling Kindersley would like to thank the following people whose help and assistance contributed to the preparation of this book.

Author

Born and raised in Wales and the Middle East, David Abram began travel writing after answering an advertisement for writers for a new guide to India. The subsequent Rough Guide was called "the Bible for any visitor" by *Condé Nast Traveler* and is still in print. He returned to Asia in 2010 to overhaul the Insight Guides Myanmar book, and now divides his time between updating trips, writing travel features, photographic assignments, and tour company consultancy. David lives in Somerset, UK, with his partner and two children. davidabram.co.uk; Twitter @DavidRAbram.

Fact Checker John Oates
Proofreader Debra Wolter
Indexer Ankita Awasthi Tröger
Phrase Book Andiamo! Language Services Ltd
Editorial Consultant Anna Streiffert
Editorial Assistance Fay Franklin, Scarlett O'Hara
Additional Illustrations Sunita Gahir
Additional Photography Philip Blenkinsop, Ian O'Leary

Picture Credits

a = above; b = below/bottom; c = center; f = far; l = left; r = right; t = top

The publishers would like to thank the following individuals, companies, and picture libraries for their permission to reproduce their photographs:

4Corners: Richard Taylor 173br.
David Abram: 40cr, 175cra.
Alamy Images: 19th era 57bl; AF archive 40tr; age fotostock/Erich Häfele 191cr; age fotostock/Ignacio Palacios 104t; Rex Allen 176tl; Pablo Andreolotti 213tc; Steve Bly 195br; epa european press photo agency b.v. 232cla; F1online digitale Bildagentur GmbH 132tr; GM Photo Images 123cr; Chris Hellier 37cra; hemis.fr/ Franck Guiziou 39br, 43cr; Imagestate Media Partners Limited/ Impact Photos/Alain Evrard 59bl; Maurice Joseph 43tl, 44cr; JTB Media Creation, Inc. 37br; Frans Lemmens 96bl; Yadid Levy 33br, 166cl; Scott Mallon 41tr; National Geographic Image Collection/Alex Treadway 182b; Pictorial Press Ltd 57br; Graham Prentice 29br; Robert Harding Picture Library/James Strachan 128tr; V&A Images 36tr; Wim Wiskerke 190br; Xinhua 40cl.

Amara Group Myanmar: amaragroupmyanmar.com 28cl.
AWL Images: Michele Falzone 121cr; Katie Garrod 21br, 51bc, 178; Christian Kober 42–3; Nigel Pavitt 39bl, 44bl, 101b; Jane Sweeney 177tl.
The Bridgeman Art Library: Luca Tettoni 8–9.
Corbis: epa/Law Eh Soe 161t, 161crb; Flame/Angelo Cavalli 5t; Hulton-Deutsch Collection 51cb; Ocean 182t.
CPA Media: 38tr, 38c, 38cr, 41b, 49crb, 49bc, 50bc, 52cb, 52br, 53tr, 53bc, 53br, 54tr, 55clb, 55br, 56tl, 56bl, 57crb, 58c, 77bc, 92cb, 98tr, 99crb, 115tc, 145tl, 185br.
Dreamstime: Steve Allen 100, 124cla, 129bl, 170–71, 196–7; Chirawan 31bl; Fischer0182 25cl; Abdul Sami Haqqani 58br; Hamsterman 38bl; Song Heming 25bc; Jackmalipan 12t; Jasmina 124cb; Kjersti Joergensen 23tr; Anthony Aneese Totah Jr 24clb; Kkg1 25cr; Georgios Kollidas 58bl; Martin Lehmann 60–61; Hugo Maes 168bl; Mathes 25tr; Danilo Mongiello 42cla; Jerzy Opoka 33bl; Ornthariga 54bc; Panuruangjan 24cl; Rgbe 25cb; Witchu Sermsawadsri 1; Valery Shanin 240b; Szefei 224–5, 235bl; Timurk 32tr; Tiverylucky 30–31; Wing Ho Tsang 237c; Voraorn 2–3; Wilczon 25crb; Zzvet 4br, 36cr, 36–7c, 37cl, 220cl, 220bl.
FLPA: Biosphoto/Michel Gunther 24bc; Imagebroker 25bl, 237bl; Imagebroker/Egmont Strigl 25cla; Photo Researchers 24crb.
Getty Images: Flickr/John Seaton Callahan 187b; Hulton Archive/Print Collector 36br; Keystone 58bc; National Geographic/Steve Winter 27cla; Oxford Scientific/Gerard Soury 24bl; Universal Images Group 24cra.
Green Hill Valley Elephant Camp: 172tr.
Himalaya Trekking and Culture Travels and Tours Co. Ltd./S'Nyein Lwin: snyeinlwin@gmail.com 62tr, 185tl.
iStock: garth11 107br; Craig Lovell 177br.
Aung Myo Chit: nkgmaymyo@gmail.com 183br.
NASA: Earth Observatory 27br.
Nature Picture Library: Inaki Relanzon 37tc.
Paukan Cruises: 28tr, 28–9c.
Photoshot: U Aung 43br; Mel Longhurst 136cl, 167cr, 234cla; Picture Alliance/P. Wegner 24c; Ezequiel Scagnetti 59br, 105bl; Xinhua/U Aung 46b, 47cra.
Robert Harding Picture Library: Jean-Pierre de Mann 36cl, 176b; Richard Maschmeyer 127bc; Luca Tettoni 37bl, 129tl; Alison Wright 59tr.
Front Endpaper: All images © Dorling Kindersley except AWL Images: Katie Garrod Rtl; Dreamstime: Steve Allen Lclb.
Jacket Images: Front and spine top: Robert Harding Picture Library: Alison Wright.

All other images © Dorling Kindersley
For further information see: www.dkimages.com

Phrase Book

Burmese is the official language of Myanmar, and the first language of 32 million people, with a further 10 million speaking it as their second language. Although Myanmar has about 135 minor ethnic groups, each with their own language, Burmese is used throughout the country. It is a part of the Tibeto-Burman subgroup of the Sino-Tibetan family of languages. Spoken Burmese is a tonal, pitch-register, and syllable-timed language, meaning that phonemic contrasts can be made on the basis of the tone of a vowel. Pitch, phonation, intensity, duration, and vowel quality are included in these contrasts. Burmese is an analytic, mainly monosyllabic language with a subject-object-verb word order, unlike English, which has a subject-verb-object order. Pronouns vary according to the gender and status of the audience. The written form uses the Burmese script, which was derived either from the Mon or the Pyu script, both of which stemmed from the ancient Brahmi script of the Indian Sub-continent. The Burmese alphabet consists of 33 letters and 12 vowels. It is written from left to right and does not require spaces between words; single syllables are joined together to make sentences which, as a whole, carry meaning. However, modern writing generally contains spaces to improve readability. Most Burmese loanwords are in the form of nouns and adopted from Pali (the liturgical language of Theravada Buddhism), Mon, and English, and, to a lesser degree, from Sanskrit, Hindi, and Chinese.

Guidelines for Pronunciation

When speaking Burmese the tone used is significant as the wrong tone can not only change the meaning of the sentence but make it sound impolite or discourteous.

The three basic tones are:

Rising tone (long)	*Marr*, which means "fault"
Low tone (normal)	*Mar*, which means "hard"
High tone (sharp)	*Ma*, which means "from"

Basic Burmese words are pronounced in a similar way to English words. For example, *May*, which means "mother," is pronounced the same way that an English speaker would say "May" when referring to the fifth month of the year.

Burmese has 33 consonants, and some of them have the same phonetic sounds. Consonants are both aspirated and unaspirated, but as a uniform system of transliteration does not exist, they are romanized variably. The chart below shows the pronunciation of some frequently used consonants.

Guide Symbol	English Example
B	**b**oss, **b**all
Ch	**ch**art, tea**ch**
D	**d**og
F	**ph**one
G	**g**o, be**g**in
H	**h**and, **h**ouse
J	loun**ge**
K	s**k**y, chi**ck**en
Kha	as in the name **Kha**n
Ky	**j**eep, or like the Chinese **ky**in
L	**l**ane
M	**m**an
N	**n**ation
Ng	si**ng**ing, thi**ng**
Ny	o**ni**on, mi**ni**on, or like the Malay **nya**-**nyi**
P	**sp**ot, **p**urple
Ph	**p**ot
S	si**ng**, **s**ee
Shw	**sh**ed
Hs	**s**ound
T	**st**op
Th	**t**ongue
W	**w**ind, **w**alk
Y	**y**es
Z	**z**oo

Spoken Burmese emphasizes different consonants than English. For example, in English, the final consonant of the following words would be pronounced:

Bac**k**
Ca**t**
Ru**de**

In Burmese, however, final consonants in many syllables become glottal stops or are nasalized, and are therefore rarely emphasized or pronounced. For example:

K as in Kyai**k**tiyo, which is pronounced *Chaih-Tee-Ou*
Ne as in Mawlamyi**ne**, which is pronounced *Mau-La-Myain*
Ng as in Sagai**ng**, which is pronounced *Za-Gainh*
R as in Myanma**r**, which is pronounced *Myan-Ma*
T as in Tha**t**byinnyu, which is pronounced *Thah-Byin-Nyu*

In an Emergency

Help!	*Ku-Nyi-Par*
Fire!	*Mee*
Where is the nearest hospital?	*A-**Nee**-Sone-Say-Yone-Bae-Mar-Lal?*
Call an ambulance!	*Lu-Nar-Tin-Car-Ko-Khaw-Par*
Call the police!	*Ye-Ko-Khaw-Par*
Call a doctor!	*Sa-**Yar**-Win-Ko-Khaw-Par*

Communication Essentials

Hello	***Min**-Ga-Lar-Par*
Goodbye	*Note-Sat-Par-Tal*
Yes	*Hote-Par-Tal*
No	*Ma-**Hote**-Par*
Please	*Kyay-Zuu-**Pyu**-Pe*
Thank you	*Kyay-Zuu-Tin-Par-Tal*
I don't understand	*Kya-**Note**-Narr-Ma-**Lal**-Par*
I don't know	*Kya-**Note**-Ma-**Thi**-Par*
Sorry	*Taung-Pan-Par-Tal*
Excuse me	*Kya-**Note**-Ko-Khwint-Pyu-Par*
What?	*Bar-Lal?*
Why?	*Bar-**Kyaut**-Lal?*
Where?	*Bal-Mar-Lal?*
When?	*Bal-A-**Chain**-Lal?*
How?	*Bal-Lo-Lal?*

Useful Phrases

How are you?	*Tin-Nay-Kaung-Par-Ta-**Lar**?*
Very well, thank …you	*Kaung-Par-Tal, Tint-Ko-Kyay-Zuu-Tin-Par-Tal*
Not very well	*Tate-**Ma**-**Kaung**-Par*
What is this?	*Dar-Ka-Bar-Lal?*
How do I get to…?	*…Ko-Kya-**Note**-Ba-Lo-Twar-Ya-Ma-Lal?*
Where is the…	*…Ka-Bal-Mar-Shi-Lal?*
Where is the restroom/toilet?	***Tant**-Sin-Khann-Lar?*
Do you speak English?	*Tin-Englate-Lo-Pyaw-Par-Ta-**Lar**?*
I can't speak Burmese	*Kya-**Note**-Myanmar-Lo-Ma-**Pyaw**-Tat-Par*

Useful Words

woman/women	*A-**Myo**-Ta-**Mee** / A-**Myo**-Ta-**Mee**-Myar*
man/men	*A-**Myo**-Tar / A-**Myo**-Tar-Myar*
child/children	*Ka-**Lay** / Ka-**Lay**-Myar*
family	*Mi-Tar-Su*
hot	*Puu-Tal*
cold	*Aye-Tal*
good	*Kaung-Tal*
bad	*Soe-Tal*
open	*Phwint-Par*
closed	*Pate-Htar-Tal*
left	*Bal-**Phat***
right	*Nyar-**Phat***
straight ahead	*Tae-Tae-Twer-Par*
near	*Nee-Tal*
far	*Way-Tal*
entrance	*Win-Paut*
exit	*Htwet-Paut*
toilet	*Tant-Sin-Khann*

Money

I want to change US$100 into Burmese currency	*Kya-**Note**-Dola-Tit-**Yar**-Ko-Myanmar-Kyat-Ngwe-To Pyaung-Lal-Lo-Par-Tal*
I'd like to cash these traveler's checks	*D-Kha-**Yee**-Twer-Check-Lat-Mat Myar-Ko-Kya-**Note**-Ngwe-Tar-Ya Lo-Par-Tal*

exchange rate	Ngwe-Lal-Lal-Nome
bank	Ban
money/cash	Pite-San
credit card	Credit Card

Keeping in Touch

I'd like to make a telephone call	Kya-**Note**-Telephone-Sat-Lo-Par-Tal
I'd like to make an international phone call	Kya-**Note**-Naing-Gan-Charr-To Telephone-Sat-Lo-Par-Tal
mobile phone	Mobile Phone
telephone enquiries	Telephone-Nint-Pat-Tat-Ywe-Sone-Sann-May-Myann-Chinn
public phone box	**Amyarr**-Tone-Phone-Yone
area code	Day-**Ta**-Nan-Pat
post office	Sar-**Dite**
letter	Sar
registered letter	Mat-Pone-Tin-Hter-Taw-Sar
address	Late-Sar
street	Lann
town	Myo
village	Ywar
Internet café	Internet-Sine
email	Email

Shopping

Where can I buy…?	…Ko-Bal-Mar-Wel-Naing-Par-Ta-**Lal**?
How much does this cost?	Di-A-**Yar**-Ka-Zay-Bae-Laut-Lal?
May I try this on?	Kya-**Note**-Dar -Ko-Sann-Kyi-Naing-Par-Ta-Lar?
I would like…	Kya-**Note**… Chin-Par-Tal
Do you have…?	Tint-Twin… Shi-Par-Ta-**Lar**?
Do you take credit cards?	Tin-Credit-Card-Myar-Lat-Khan-Par-Ta-**Lar**?
What time do you open/close?	Tin-Bal-A-**Chain**-Twin-Phwint / Pate-Par-Ta-**Lal**?
How much?	Bal-Lout-Lal?
expensive	Zay-Kyi-Tal
cheap	Zay-Cho-Tal
to bargain	Zay-Sit-Yan
size	A-**Yawe**-A-**Sarr**
color	A-**Yaung**
black	A-**Net**-Yaung
white	A-**Phyu**-Yaung
red	A-**Ne**-Yaung
blue	A-**Pyar**-Yaung
green	A-**Sane**-Yaung
yellow	A-**War**-Yaung
bookstore	Sar-Oat-Saing
department store	Kone-Sone-Saing
market	Zei (Zayy)
pharmacy	Say-Saing
supermarket	Supermarket
souvenir shop	A-**Mat**-Ta-**Ya**-Pyit-See-Saing
souvenirs	A-**Mat**-Ta-**Ya**-Pyit-See-Myar
lacquer painting	Yoon-Pa-**Chi**
painting on silk	Poe-Htae-Pa-**Chi**
wooden statue	Pa-Pu-**Yote**-Htu
silk scarf	Poe-Pa-**War**

Sightseeing

bay	Pin-Lal-Aww
beach	Kann-Chay
cave	Umin
countryside	Kyay-Latt-Day-Ta
covered stairway	Zaungdan
festival	Pwal-Daw
forest	Tit-Taw
island	Kyunn
lake	Yay-Kan
monastery	Kyaung
mountain	Taung
museum	Pya-Tite
nature spirit	Nat
ordination hall	Thein
pagoda	Pha-**Yarr** / Zay-Di
pavilion	Tazaung
river	Myit
temple	Pha-**Yarr**-Kyaung
tourist office	Naing-Gan-Char-Kha-**Yee**-Tal-Yone
travel agent	Kha-**Yee**-Twar-Ko-**Sar-Lal**

Getting Around

When does the train for… leave?	…Ya-**Htar**-Bal-A-**Chain**-Twin-Htwet-Khwar-Ma-**Lal**?
A ticket to… please	Kyay-Zuu-Pyu-Ywe… To-Lat-Mat-Tit-**Saung**-Pay-Par

How long does it take to get to…?	… To-Yaut-Yan-Bal-Laut-Kyar-Ta-**Lal**?
I'd like to reserve a seat, please	Kyay-Zuu-Pyu-Ywe-Kya-**Note**-A-**Twet**-Htaing-Khone-Tit-**Nay**-Yar-Mar-Yu-Lo-Par-Tal
Which platform for the… train?	…Ya-**Htar**-A-**Twet**-Sinn-Kyan-Ka-Bal-Har-Lal?
Where is the bus stop/station?	Car-Mat-Tine / Car-Sate-Bal-Mar-Lal?
airport	Lay-Sate
arrivals	Site-Yaut-Mu-Myar
bus	Bus
bus station	Car-Kyi-win
bicycle	Sat-Bee
car	Car
car rental	Car-A-**Ngar**-Htar-Na
ferry	Kyo-Po-Yin
motorbike	Cycle
one-way ticket	Kha-Yee-Tit-**Kyaung**-Sar-Lat-Mat
plane	Lay-Yin
plane ticket	Lay-Yin-Lat-Mat
return ticket	A-**Pyan**-Lat-Mat
taxi	Taxi
ticket	Lat-Mat
train	Ya-**Htar**
train station	Bu-Tar-Yone

Accommodations

Do you have a vacant room?	Tin-Do-C-Twin-A-**Khan**-Loot-Shi-Par-Ta-**Lar**?
Room	A-**Khan**
Double/twin room	Na-**Yaut**-Khan
Single room	Tit-**Yaut**-Khan
I have a reservation	Kya-**Note**-Kyo-Tin-Mar-Hter-Par-Tal
hotel	Hotel
guesthouse	Tae-Kho-Khan
air-conditioning	Lay-Aye-Pay-Chin
bathroom	Yay-Choe-Khan
passport number	Naing-Gan-Kuu-Lat-Mat-Nan-Pat

Eating Out

A table for two, please	Kyay-Zuu-Pyu-Pe-Na-**Yaut**-A-**Twet**-Sa-**Pwal**-Pay-Par
May I see the menu?	Kya-**Note**-Menu-Ko-Kyi-Ywe-Ya-Par-Ta-**Lar**?
I am a vegetarian	Kya-**Note**-Di-Tat-Tat-Loot-Sarr-Tu-Pyit-Par-Tal
Do you have any special dishes today?	Tint-Twin-Ya-**Nay**-A-**Twet**-A-**Htoo**-Hinn-Lyar-Myar-Shi-Par-Ta-**Lar**?
Can I have the bill, please?	Kyay-Zuu-Pyu-Ywe-Kya-Tint-Ngwe-Shinn-Pa-Ya-Say
bitter	Khar-Tal
breakfast	Na-**Nat**-Sar
Burmese specialties	Myanmar-A-**Htoo**-Pyu-A-**Sarr**-A-**Sar**-Myar
chopsticks	Tu
fork	Kha-**Yinn**
knife	Darr
restaurant	Sarr-Taut-Saing
sour	Chin-Tal
spicy (hot)	Sat-Tal
spoon	Zoon
sweet	Cho-Tal
to drink	Taut-Yan
to eat	Sarr-Yan
Western food	A-**Naut**-Tine-A-**Sarr**-A-**Sar**

Menu Decoder

apple	Pann-Tee
baguette	Pyin-Tit-Paung-Mote-Lone
bamboo shoots	Myit
banana	Nga-**Pyaw**-Tee
bean sprouts	Pal-Pin-Paut
beer	Bee-Yar
beef	A-**Mal**-Tar
bottle	Pa-**Linn**
bread	Paung-Mote
butter	Htaw-Pat
chicken	Kyat-Tar
chilli	Nga-**Yote**-Tee
coconut	Own-Tee
coffee	Coffee
coriander	Nan-Nan-Pin
crab	Ga-**Nann**
dessert	A-**Cho**-Pwal
drinks	Taut-Sa-Yar-Myar
duck	Bal-Tar
egg	Oo
fish	Ngar

fish sauce	Ngar Ngan Pyar Yay
fruit	Tit-Tee
fruit juice	Tit-Tee-Phyaw-Yay
garlic	Kyat-Ton-Phyu
ginger	Ginn
glass	Phan-Khwat
ice	Yay-Khae
ice cream	Yay-Khae-Mote
lamb	Toe-Tar
lemon	Tan-**Pa**-**Yo**-Tee
lemongrass	Sa-**Par**-Lin
lime	Tan-**Pa**-**Yar**-Tee
lobster	Kyaut-Pa-**Zon**
mandarin orange	Lain-Maw-Tee
mango	Ta-**Yat**-Tee
meat	A-**Tar**
menu	Menu
milk	Nwar-No
mineral water	Taut-Yay-Tant
mushrooms	Mo
noodles	Khaut-Swal
noodle soup	Mohinga
onion	Kyat-Ton-Ne
papaya	Tin-Baw-Tee
paté	A-**Tarr**-Nit
peach	Mat-Mon-Tee
pepper	Nga-**Yote**-Kaung
pork	Wat-Tar
potato (sweet potato)	Arr-Luu (Ka-Soon-Oo)
prawn	Pa-Zon
rice	Hta-**Min**
salad	A-**Tote**
salt	Sarr
soft drinks	A-**Cho**-Yay-Myar
soup	Hinn-Yay
soy sauce	Pal-Ngan-Pyar-Yay
spring rolls	Kaw-Pyant-Myar
stir-fried	Mwe-Kyaw-Hter-Taw
sugar	Ta-**Kyarr**
tea	Lat-**Phat**-Yay
vegetables	Hinn-Tee-Hinn-Ywat-Myar
water	Yay
wine	Wine

Health

What's the matter with you?	Tin-Bar-Pyit-Ter-Lal?
I do not feel well	Kya-**Note**-Nay-Ma-Kaung-Par
It hurts here	Di-Nay-Yar-Mar-Nar-Tal
I have a fever	Kya-**Note**-Twin-A-**Phyar**-Shi-Tal
I am allergic to…	Kya-**Note**-Di… Nint-Ma-Tae-Par
accident (traffic)	Ma-**Taw**-Ta-**Sa**-Mhu (Yin)
allergy	Ma-**Tae**-Chinn
ambulance	Lu-Nar-Tin-Yin
antibiotics	Poe-Tat-Say-Myar
bandage	**Pat**-Tee
blood	Tway
blood pressure (high/low)	Tway-Paung-Chain (Myint-Di / Nal-Di)
cough	Chaung-Soe-Tal
diabetes	See-Cho / Tway-Cho
diarrhea	Wann-Shaw-Tal
dizzy	Muu-Tal
doctor	Sa-**Yar**-Win
ear	Narr
flu	Tote-Kway
food poisoning	A-**Sar**-A-**Sate**-Tint-Tal
headache	Khaung-Kite-Tal
heart	Na-Lone
hospital	Say-Yone
hygiene	Tant-Shinn-Mhu
illness	Phyarr-Nar-Chin
injection	Htoe-Say
malaria	Ngat-Phyar
medicine	Say
operate	Khwal-Sate-Tal
prescription	Say-Sar
sore throat	Lal-Pinn-Nar-Tal
temperature	A-**Pu**-Chain
toothache	Twar-Nar-Tal

Time, Days, and Seasons

minute	Mi-Nit
hour	Nar-Ye
day	Nay-Yat
week	A-**Pat**
month	La
year	Nit
Monday	Ta-**Ninn**-Lar-Nay

Tuesday	In-Gar-Nay
Wednesday	Bote-Da-Huu-Nay
Thursday	Kyar-Tar-Ta-**Tay**-Nay
Friday	Taut-Kyar-Nay
Saturday	Sa-**Nay**-Nay
Sunday	Ta-**Ninn**-Ga-**Nway**-Nay
season	Yar-Tee
spring	Nway-Oo-Yar-Tee
summer	Nway-Yar-Tee
fall	Saung-Oo-Yar-Tee
winter	Saung-Yar-Tee
dry season	Chaut-Tway-Yar-Tee
rainy season	Moe-Yar-Tee
rain (it is raining)	Moe (Moe-Ywar-Nay-Di)
wind	Lay
sunny	Nay-Tar-Di
weather	Yar-Tee-Oo-Tu
warm/cold	Nway-Tal / Aye-Tal
morning	Na-**Nat**
midday	Nay-Lal
afternoon	Nay-Khinn
evening	Nya-Nay-Khinn
night	Nya
What time is it?	Bal-A-**Chain**-Shi-P-Lal?

Numbers

1	Tit
2	Nit
3	Tone
4	Lay
5	Ngar
6	Chaut
7	Khun
8	Shit
9	Koe
10	Tit-**Sal**
11	Ta-**Sat**-Tit
12	Ta-**Sat**-Nit
13	Ta-**Sat**-Tone
14	Ta-**Sat**-Lay
15	Ta-**Sat**-Ngar
20	Na-**Sal**
21	Na-**Sal**-Tit
22	Na-**Sal**-Nit
23	Na-Sal-Tone
24	Na-**Sal**-Lay
25	Na-**Sal**-Ngar
30	Tone-Sal
40	Lay-Sal
50	Ngar-Sal
60	Chaut-Sal
70	Khun-Na-**Sal**
80	Shit-Sal
90	Koe-Sal
100	Ta-**Yar**
200	Na-**Yar**
1,000	Ta-**Htaung**
10,000	Ta-**Taung**
100,000	Ta-**Tane**
1,000,000	Ta-**Tan** / Sal-**Tane**

Road Map of Myanmar (Burma)